BARRY CREYTON

Beyond Togetherness
A LIFE

First published in 2026

ORiGiN™ Imprint
An imprint of ORiGiN™ Theatrical
47-49 Murray Street
Pyrmont NSW 2009
Australia
Phone (61 2) 8514 5201
Email enquiries@originmusic.com.au
Web originimprint.com

A catalogue record for this book is available from the National Library of Australia

ISBN 978-1-7636909-0-5

Printed in Australia by Lightning Source
Cover photo by Lisa Thompson
Cover design by Michael Mortlock
Typesetting and layout by Amber Quin

PRAISE FOR BEYOND TOGETHERNESS

"This is a story told with enormous wit, heart, and intelligence. That Barry Creyton's contributions to Australian television and theatre are legendary is not opinion. It is fact. And his exploits across many decades and several continents are fascinating.

In Beyond Togetherness: A Life, he shares many memorable incidents, but he also defines an entire era, relishing the structure and history of everything in the entertainment world that came before him, while innovating and becoming a central part of bringing about great change–certainly to Australian television–but also to international stages. Best of all, Creyton's boundless curiosity about what might be around the corner is expansive and modern–he seizes life by the balls and we get to ride on the back of his motorcycle, thrilled to be part of his adventures.

Samuel Garza Bernstein
Bestselling author, screenwriter, and playwright

"My first recognition of Barry Creyton was as the urbane and dashing panellist on Blankety Blanks. Wit and charm spilled from his being. It's apparent from this memoir that this has been his default setting all through his life. I've been waiting since Blankety Blanks for Barry to complete this memoir–he's written everything else–screenplays, radio plays, theatrical triumphs, novels, recipes... and at last... the memoir! This is an essential record that contributes much to the preservation of our artistic heritage, from one of our greats."

Peter Eyers
Producer/writer

"I have known Barry Creyton for sixty years and could therefore be seen as biased. I am not. I approached Beyond Togetherness as an ardent fan of memoirs, particularly those set in the world of entertainment, but also as a harsh critic of those that do not please me, such as the dull and laboured, the deceitful, the self-serving, or the just plain boring.

Beyond Togetherness has none of these failings. It ranks up there with the best of them. In fact, in terms of eloquence, elegance and wit in detailing Creyton's multi-faceted career and his admittedly rocky personal life, it surpasses many biographies that I have read.

As a lyricist, I learned to make every word count when writing a song for Barry Creyton, because the audience will actually hear every single one of those words. And now, in Beyond Togetherness he has demonstrated once again that in frankly telling the story of his life, his talent for impeccable delivery is not just vocal but as a story-teller in putting words on paper."

David Sale

Television screenwriter, playwright, producer, director, actor and journalist.

"Barry Creyton steps us through his wonderful life with his customary eloquence and brutal honesty - sparing no detail, taking no prisoners. This is a book about a lifetime spent doing what you love, but what shines through most is that he was born to do this - and born to tell us about it."

Simon Burke AO

"Barry was born with one wry eyebrow already raised at the world; a sophisticate from the outset. Today, a celebrated playwright, actor, novelist, and director - his perceptive, dry wit has never left him. It permeates this revealing autobiography, along with a dash of theatrical wisdom and more names dropped than you'd find on the electoral roll.

Barry was an integral part of the Philip St revues and television's Mavis Bramston Show. Without them, Sydney's long-running Wharf Revue could not have existed. I am proud to be part of that comedy lineage, and blessed to call Barry and Vaughan my dear friends."

Phil Scott
Actor, comedian, composer, pianist

"What a life - the Sydney years which I remember well with the Mike Walsh Show sketches, your bike accident and of course Nunsense - what a good time we had with those nuns especially in Dublin. And your crowning glory Double Act - an international hit!"

Sue Farelly
Producer

DEDICATION

In memory of the late Babette Stephens AM MBE. In my green teen years, she took me under her very grand wing, mentored me, stretched my acting muscles, and gave me more good advice about Theatre than anyone before or since. She also became a lifelong friend. I owe her an incalculable debt.

FOREWORD BY NOELINE BROWN

I HAVE BEEN TRYING to convince Barry Creyton to write his memoir for years and at long last he has done so. Barry's story is a fascinating one. He was born in Brisbane, at a time when the city was not the vibrant place it is today, and a life in show business was not thought possible—and Barry's mother was not one to encourage his dreams.

Barry and I have been friends since 1962, when we met at rehearsals for what was called an 'intimate revue' at the Phillip Theatre. I thought he was one of the most handsome men I had ever met, and the most polished. He was dressed very sharply in a slim-fitting dark suit with winkle picker shoes and a thin black tie. I was surprised to discover he was only twenty-two, a year younger than I was and that Barry's polish masked a wicked sense of humour, and an enormous ability for hard work. In fact, he was exhausting to be around.

Apart from acting in many theatre productions (with me in many of them, I am proud to say), he was creating other shows. He wrote melodramas for the Music Hall in Sydney, where he was also the brilliant resident villain and then was catapulted into fame as a star of the 'Mavis Bramston Show' on TV where he performed sketches and wrote many of the musical numbers. I don't think he ever slept. During his spare time, he also composed the score of a wonderful never-performed musical called 'Mrs 'Obbs', which I hope we might see one day.

Barry was extremely thin as a young person and was often invited to my parents' house for a meal. He had a huge appetite in those days and would always have second helpings, or maybe even a third. The first time my father met him he said to me later 'That Creyton could eat the arse off a corpse'.

Barry became a household name on TV in Australia and even went on to host his own show. He was a big star well before he turned thirty. Of course, we knew because of his talent he was probably going to leave us for overseas and he did, first working in the UK successfully as an actor and later moving to the States where he would eventually spend 30 years working as a writer and theatre director. Fortunately, while he was in Los Angeles, he wrote several plays for the two of us to perform in – the Lunts as he used to call us. Or at least, that's what I think he said. (For those who don't remember, Alfred and Lynn Lunt were a famous theatrical duo.) Many people thought Barry and I were a double act, too. I remember us being followed by some women after a matinee, and one of them said to her friends, 'Of course they work well together, they lived together for years'. We did not ever live together and that's probably one of the reasons we are still such firm friends.

Barry had some important mentors in the early days of his acting career but is mostly a self-made man, influenced by the works of the greats, including Noel Coward. This book is not only Barry's story, but a record of the times in Australia when it was a more narrow-minded place and where the arts were not often appreciated. It is also an honest account of the difficulties faced by the actor-director.

Barry's memoir is full of wonderful anecdotes involving many stellar performers, whose names you will know, but it is more than that. It is a warm and honest account of the life of a tremendously talented and generous person who has close friends all over the world. I am thrilled to be one of them.

I am also glad to tell you, without disclosing anything, his book has a happy ending.

Noeline Brown, May 2023

PREFACE

IT'S MEANT TO comfort us when well-meaning people say that age is just a number. Being advised that one's friends are ageing at the same rate is meant to soothe us, but I've reached an age where I'm afraid to invite contemporaries to lunch in case they don't make it through dessert.

What better time to write a memoir?

Some names have been changed to protect the innocent. Others have been stated clearly to expose the motherfuckers.

ONE

I WAS BORN IN Brisbane, on the 29th of December, 1939. The Brisbane of my childhood and teens was not the vibrant city it is today—it was a sprawling industrial city with an alarmingly brown river. The south of the river, now devoted to leisure parks and the entertainment centre was, in my day, lined with unattractive commercial buildings and warehouses

I knew at an early age that my paternal grandfather and grandmother were actors at the turn of the 20th century, but my mother despised them and limited my childhood visits to them, for no other reason than that I was fond of them. I treasured their anecdotes, their vast collection of old show tunes on 78s, and their boundless enthusiasm in encouraging me to follow my dream, whatever that might be.

Their forward-looking kindness was the direct antithesis of my mother's stern denial of any personal aspirations I had as a child, and the professional dreams I had as a teenager.

But more of my mother later.

~

My paternal grandfather was the son of celebrated Shakespearean actor William Hoskins. Hoskins was a leading member of the Samuel Phelps company at Sadler's Wells, London, in the mid-19th century, and tutor to a young Henry Irving, securing Irving's first acting job for him. Hoskins emigrated to New Zealand in 1856 to take up management of a theatre. The teenage Irving intended to accompany him, but family duties detained him in England where, as Sir Henry Irving, he became the greatest exponent of Shakespeare in 19th Century British theatre. Irving never forgot Hoskins and paid him warm tribute in his autobiography.

As actor-manager, Hoskins played in Sydney, Melbourne, New Zealand and toured America. His performances were legend in their time, and when he died in New Zealand in 1886, his obituary stated "as a student and critical reader of Shakespeare, he had no superiors in any part of the world".

Hoskins' son, Thomas George Hoskins, was born in New Zealand and was trained as an actor by his father.

Wanting to escape from the considerable shadow of his father's fame, Thomas changed his stage name to Paul Creyton, and the name was ultimately adopted throughout the family. Paul Creyton left New Zealand for Australia in 1897 and performed in Sydney and Melbourne before establishing his own theatre company in Queensland. Here, he produced, directed and acted in the melodramas of the day, and according to the reviews I've seen, was pretty good! My grandmother, Ada, was twenty years younger than he, and played in many of his productions before delivering three co-productions with Paul: Arthur, Pauline and my father, Douglas—none of whom inherited the theatre gene. But as a measure of respect for his father, Paul gave my father the middle name of Hoskin.

In the early teens of the 20th century, Paul Creyton abandoned theatre in favor of politics and became an outspoken and greatly respected trade unionist. He lived to a hearty and always jovial ninety-nine.

Of the infrequent visits to Paul's and Ada's home in the seaside town of Sandgate, I have happy memories of being granted total control of their windup gramophone and their vast collection of recordings, some opera, some symphonic, but my favorites were the considerable stash of show songs. There were selections from the operettas of their day, "Rose Marie", "No No Nanette", "The Cat and the Fiddle", "The Desert Song", and even better, singles from movies such as "Broadway Melody of 1929", "Golddiggers of 1933", and George M. Cohan recordings including "Yankee Doodle Dandy," and "Give My Regards to Broadway."

My interest in theatre began with a walk around the seaside town with my grandfather. I was ten, he a hale ninety-six. I had to race to keep up with him as he described various points of interest along the way. When we reached the town hall, he led me inside. The hall had been set up for a concert or some theatrical event. We stood at the rear of the auditorium and surveyed the rows of empty seats.

My grandfather supplied a commentary on the venue which, even at ten, I found fascinating. We walked down the center aisle and up onto the bare stage. He pointed out the lighting grid, the wings, explained the purpose of the fly tower, we explored the dressing rooms—all of which aspects he knew well from his early life. He described the spectacles, illusions, comedies and tragedies that could take place on this bare platform, all inhabited by real live people—actors—not shadows on a screen. To this day, whenever I walk onto a stage in an empty theatre, I feel the same thrill of anticipation as on that day in 1950.

My grandmother furthered my interest in plays and players on the occasional visits my mother would allow. I was obsessed with reading, but there was little opportunity at home as neither of my parents read books—the occasional magazine perhaps. But apart from school texts, I had to beg for books. After my grandfather's death, when I was thirteen, on those treasured visits, my grandmother would take old playscripts down from a shelf, and we two would sit on the front porch of her house in the sun and read aloud from them. Among many others, I had the pleasure of playing the hero to her heroine in a melodrama, *The Snowball*, *Pygmalion*'s Higgins to her Eliza, and we read a few scenes from the celebrated melodrama, *East Lynne*—she playing the heroine, a role she'd played in her teens, and I the villain, which my grandfather had played opposite her. A decade later, I would establish my name in Sydney theatre playing that very villain in the opening production at the Neutral Bay Music Hall. But during those pre-teen years, if I ever expressed wonder at the early lives of my grandparents, my mother would dismiss them disdainfully as insignificant.

A couple of my grandmother's anecdotes are worth recording. My grandfather Paul produced and directed for his own theatre company. His chosen hero for East Lynne, a member of the repertory company, was a drinker. As Lady Isabel expires on her deathbed, her husband kneels by her side in floods of tears. The leading man fuddled his lines so often in this scene, that Ada was obliged to lay the script on her chest for him to read out of sight of the audience. One night Ada inadvertently pulled the bed cover over the script. The leading man briefly searched his brain for the lines, failed to remember them, and to fill the embarrassing silence, dredged up lines from a play he knew well—which happened to be a farcical comedy. Lady Isabel died to gales of laughter.

In another melodrama set on the high seas, Paul designed a

magnificent set in which the bow of a ship was set amongst rolling waves, the roll produced by a stage hand cranking them from offstage. The bibulous actor missed his cue to emerge on the ship's prow as its captain, and found himself on the wrong side of the stage. He made his entrance by trudging over the roiling sea and climbing onto the ship from behind.

After the performance, Paul raged onto the stage and yelled, "Who the hell do you think you are, Jesus Christ?"

The actor's tenure was soon terminated.

~

My father, Douglas Hoskin Creyton, had no interest in theatre whatsoever. He was an amiable man who painted cars for a living. No protections such as masks were used in his day and the result of the constant inhalation of spray paint fumes in his early adult life resulted in his death from lung cancer in 1970.

On his return from a working day, he was assailed nightly by my mother's invective. He became a drinker and it occurred to my brother and me much later in life that his excessive drinking was the result of my mother's constant, nagging rebukes. As kids, my brother and I heard only our mother's impassioned cries of being badly done by, married to a drunk, her life a misery. Only long after his death did we realize the villain of the piece was our mother, and he the victim.

Doug's idea of theatre was the resident burlesque show at Brisbane's Theatre Royal—a glorious Victorian theatre with a horseshoe balcony, now sadly demolished. It was here, a historian informed me long after my parents' death, that my grandfather had played in melodramas at the turn of the twentieth century. This was never revealed to me by either parent.

As a small child, I was dragged to the Royal to see *George Wallace*

Jr. and the Nudie Cuties—Change Weekly Revue! Until that day my grandfather walked me through the deserted town hall, I was convinced that live theatre consisted exclusively of tits and feathers.

~

My mother, Beryl May Spence, was one of three sisters of a Victorian upbringing, long on rules, regulations and morals, short on actual education and common sense. Due to her constantly bitter assertions, her ludicrously strict edicts, dictated without reason as far as we could see, home was not a place of warmth, affection or encouragement. Rack my brain as I might, I can't actually remember an utterance of, "I love you," from my mother throughout my entire childhood. In fact, as children, my brother and I endured her continual prediction that we would not live to old age. It's easy to deduce that this pronouncement was a consequence of the Victorian attitude inflicted on her by her nineteenth century parents. One has only to see so many popular paintings of the period depicting dying children. There was something in the Victorian ethos which bolstered the view that life was short, fraught with disease, and generally not intended to be enjoyable.

Just as a historian contacted me with the history of my celebrated great grandfather just fifteen years ago, my brother was only recently informed of the extraordinary story of our mother's grandmother who, in a fit of insanity, poisoned five of her six children and herself—this shocking revelation long after our mother was dead.

Marion Friar travelled to the Queensland town of Maryborough in 1878. She was 18 years old. She probably made the worst decision in her young life by marrying William Spence. Spence, a drinker, had serious anger issues, and his physical abuse resulted in Marion's frequent fits of depression.

On the 9th of June 1894, she corralled the children and told them she was giving them medicine. The "medicine" was actually carbolic acid. John, the eldest (14), saw what was happening and ran for help. The other children, Annie (11), Matilda (8), Mary (5) and Jeanie (4) died in agony as did their mother. The youngest child, William (2) coughed up most of the poison and survived, but remained severely disfigured due to the acid.

The newspaper reports of the scene make for harrowing reading: five children in the screaming throes of death, and a surgeon cutting open an already deceased Marion in a futile attempt to save her unborn baby.

It doesn't take a Freud or a Jung to deduce that this event, a scandal which made sensational headlines, colored my mother's life and perhaps her psyche.

TWO

MY BROTHER TREVOR is five years my junior, and we became close only in adulthood. We remain so to this day, not merely due to the tie of flesh-and-blood, but as good friends. Yet as children, we scarcely knew each other. Five years is a hard gap to bridge in childhood. When I was thirteen and wading through the mysteries of puberty, Trevor was a rambunctious eight. At a point where we could have come to know each other better, when I was eighteen, my tolerance of my mother's psychoses reached a limit I could no longer bear, and I left home. So, eight more years passed before Trevor and I would get to know each other.

~

At nine years old, I was rushed to hospital for an emergency appendectomy. I remember distinctly the phone call my mother made to my father after the diagnosis. "Your son has appendicitis!" She announced this in an accusatory tone—as if it were somehow his fault. And I was acutely aware of the designation, "*your* son." It was clear, even to a nine year old, that this was not a marriage made in heaven.

I was hospitalized at once, and placed in a ward with just one other patient, a Mr. Grace, who was kind and spoke to me as he would to an adult, an approach greatly appreciated by nine year olds. Today, an appendectomy is almost an outpatient procedure. In 1949, it required two weeks in hospital. I bear the scar still; unlike the inch of scar left these days, mine was six ugly inches across my lower abdomen. The two weeks in hospital, the easy conversation with nurses and Mr. Grace were, frankly, a joy. So much so, that when my parents came to drive me home, I cried floods of tears. I would have given them another appendix if I'd been allowed to remain in the pleasant surroundings of a hospital ward with intelligent conversation.

So much for hearth and home.

~

We were not dirt poor, but we were certainly poor. The three-bedroom house in which Trevor and I grew up was a rental. Trevor and I shared a bedroom until at thirteen, I demanded a room of my own, and junk was cleared from the spare room to give me privacy.

The one bathroom had a wood heater, which allowed about nine inches of water in the bathtub. This we used once or twice a week to augment the daily body scrubbings with washers. The kitchen was equipped with a wood stove and one lonely gas ring. We had an ice box which, in the 'forties, was supplied with a heavy block of ice on a weekly basis, delivered by the "iceman." And the toilet was of the traditional Australian outdoor type, complete with redback spiders. Indoor plumbing didn't enter our lives until 1952. The icebox was abandoned in favor of a refrigerator at around the same time.

The landlord never maintained the house as he should, and when he decided to bequeath it to a relative in 1954, we were obliged to move to a much smaller house in a distant suburb. I had to share a bedroom with my brother and again, privacy was an alien concept.

By this time, my mother had reached a peak of berating my father. This led to his lingering over drinks with the workmates to delay his return home in the evening where a barrage of invective awaited. Often, he'd smile affably throughout, and when my mother paused for breath, he'd try to tell us of some amusing incident that had occurred at work. These were rambling accounts meant only to bring a sense of normalcy to the evening. But my brother and I saw only the unhappiness of both parents, one expressing it openly, the other trying to make the best of things.

This led to my loathing of twilight, for it was always at this time that the arguments were at their peak. If I went outside the house to escape the enmity, I saw the rows of houses with living rooms, dining rooms, kitchens lit warmly, spilling that glowing warmth across front lawns. I assumed the families within were busy being happy behind those windows. My dislike of twilight remained with me for decades, and would grow into a phobia when I was thirty and found myself in a state of severe depression.

~

School in Brisbane in the late 1940s, and early 1950s was black and white. There were no subtle shades in education then, just the drumming of knowledge by rote, no allowance for special talent, and certainly none for imagination. My passion for reading was not rewarded by my parents who didn't read at all, and simply couldn't understand my need for it. Once in a while, generally at Christmas, I was given a much pleaded for Enid Blyton, or a Biggles yarn. Apart from those rare gifts, I had my school texts. They were given at the end of the school year, and over the six weeks summer holiday, I read every one, cover to cover before school started up again. Consequently, the rest of the year spent listening to these texts being read to us tediously in class month after month was redundant, and I gave the impression of being a lazy student.

When I started earning trifling pocket money, I plundered the second hand bookshops for soft covers.

The question has often been asked, "When was the golden age of science fiction?" The answer is simple: When you're thirteen. And at that age, I discovered SciFi in a big way—hard core science fiction, I hasten to add. I had no interest in fantasy. The speculative oeuvre of Clarke, Heinlein, Silverberg, Knight, Asimov were a drug to me. My sole venture into anything resembling fantasy was Ray Bradbury's breathtaking anthology, *The Golden Apples of the Sun*—A collection I re-read once in a while with as much pleasure as on first discovery. The simple little story, "A Great Wide World Over There" still breaks my heart.

At around twelve, my interest in science and mechanics in general led me to build my own crystal set radios. An uncle provided copper wire, crystal, and headphones. The meticulous process of winding coils, setting tuning capacitors and diodes gave me as much pleasure as listening to the result of my labors. Much later in life, when I moved to Los Angeles, I took fiendish delight in building my own desktop computers, chip by chip.

~

My sanity savers as a pre-teen kid were the plays on the Lux Radio Theatre. Sunday nights, I'd lie on the living room floor, my head to the speaker of the console radio, riveted to them. The plays featured

Australian actors whose voices I came to know intimately, many of whom I'd get to work with in the 1960s. And sometimes they imported Hollywood stars: Miriam Hopkins in *Sorry, Wrong Number*, Vincent Price in Orwell's *1984*. Years later, I met and became friends with Vincent who remembered the event with affection, but less so the technical aspects of the production. After the live broadcast, he treated the entire cast and crew to supper at a smart restaurant. In the elevator as they left the studio, a technician panicked. "I'll have to go back. I forgot to lock up the equipment!"

Vincent said deadpan, in that languid baritone, "Anyone who'd steal equipment from 2UE would steal a douche can from a whore house."

School was a chore, but shy and skinny as I was, I found I could run faster than my peers, and that led to a brief fling with sports. I tired of it quickly in favor of spending time in the school library. Here, there were the joys of Jules Verne, H. G. Wells, Dickens, Lewis Carroll and histories, albeit slight, of Ancient Rome and Greece. Detailed histories of antiquity would become a passion in later life.

~

When I was eleven, I remember the geography teacher's provocative assertion: "Brisbane, like Rome, is built on seven hills."

Even at that tender age, I thought, *surely the similarity ends there.* Yet, on every shopping trip to the city accompanying my mother, I searched for evidence of Ancient Rome and saw only the columns fronting the city hall, the library, and the treasury building. I returned to my initial observation: the similarity did indeed end with seven otherwise unrelated hills.

I was never really bullied or picked on by the other boys. I was mostly left to myself, which was as I preferred. If any of the heartier boys decided to make a derogatory remark about me, I could counter with a wisecrack that would generally leave my assailant and his buddies laughing. Once, in class, when one of the tough guys whispered something to his buddy, the teacher reprimanded him for whispering in class and commanded him to repeat his comment out loud. With a little reluctance, he stood and announced, "Barry Creyton's shorts look like Bombay Bloomers." I was first to laugh. Humiliated, I might have been, but showing it would only have exacerbated the hilarity aimed at me; I realized at a young age, that laughing *with* was preferable to being laughed *at*.

On the subject of humiliation, another incident deserves recording. In the routine of junior school, I was devoted to a Miss Williams, one of my teachers when I was around twelve. She was probably in her mid-twenties and seemed a generous, good-natured woman who smiled a lot. She lived in my neighborhood, and occasionally, our paths would cross en route to Windsor State School. She always engaged me in conversation and I considered her an ally.

One lunch hour, I sat with a sandwich watching the girls from my class skipping rope. One of them called to me, "I'll bet you can't do this!"

Naturally, I proved I could, and as I basked in the triumph of skipping rope like a professional, Miss Williams came by and fixed me with a censorious glare. "Are you interfering with the girl's playtime?"

"No," I stammered.

"If you want to play with the girls, you can wear this for the rest of the day." She found a ribbon and tied it in my hair to the glee of the rope-skipping girls. I was mortified, and obliged to wear it for the rest of the afternoon. Needless to say, I took pains to avoid Miss Williams from that day on.

Shortly afterward, I happened upon a joke shop selling sneezing powder. "Amuse Your Friends!" the sign read. I forked out my entire fortune for a tiny can and took it to class—Miss Williams' class.

Surreptitiously, from my back row desk, I blew a cloud of it into the air. The sneezes started at the back and worked their way forward until Miss Williams too was convulsed with coughs and sneezes. A girl in my row snitched, and I was sent to the headmaster.

"Why are you here?" he demanded.

"I had sneezing powder in class."

He pondered this for a moment, smiled wistfully and said, "Extraordinary! Snuff in this day and age." He found his cane, and gave me a single rap on the hand which didn't hurt a bit.

Fast forward to 2018. I was at dinner in London with two powerful women, both writers and producers. Staunch feminists, they'd made a fortune writing a popular British TV series called *Footballers' Wives*. Conversation somehow got onto the subject of childhood grievances. I related the Miss Williams story and the humiliation and sense of betrayal I experienced.

One of my hosts clicked her tongue sympathetically. "A dreadful thing to do to a child," she said. "I'm sure it's colored your opinion of women throughout your life."

"Not at all!" I insisted. "I'm greatly supportive of women's rights." I paused, then added, "I don't think they should be allowed to drive cars, but apart from that…"

I was lucky to get out of the restaurant alive.

~

Actually, in support of women's rights, I boast that on the day Trump was inaugurated, my partner and I marched with 750,000 protesters in downtown Los Angeles. It didn't lessen the horrific effects he's had on the nation as a whole and women in particular in his four years in the White House. Now, thanks to the far-right zealots he appointed to the Supreme Court, women's health rights have been revoked, and other freedoms are being taken from all Americans, women in particular. If Trump, or someone like him is elected again, don't be surprised if American women are wearing burqas before long.

I had no definite political views in my youth, not even during the Bramston years. It seemed our writers were lacerating both sides equally and that was fair to my mind. After thirty-five years in the United States, my attitude has changed and I've become a rabid political animal and as long as my ageing knees will bear me, I'll join protests against the far right fanatics.

I add that in my household, we know Donald Trump affectionately as The Orange Turd.

THREE

AS A CHILD, I had a hunger for music, also something alien to my parents. At ten, I begged them to let me take piano lessons. Cursory debate decided we were too poor to afford a piano, so my father bought me a piano accordion. Many years later, on a show I was directing, musical director Michael Tyack learned of this and said, wistfully rather than unkindly, "Good taste is knowing how to play the piano accordion, and choosing not to." But at ten, it afforded me a 'prodigy' label.

I first took lessons from an Italian workmate of my father, Louis Petralia who, after a month, told my father that I was beyond what he could teach and certainly beyond the toy-like instrument I'd been given. Finance was found to buy me the largest accordion available, which, when strapped on, almost hid me from view. I went to the top teacher in town and by the time I was eleven, I was playing solos on a children's radio program. At twelve, I played on adult programs and was able to outline detailed arrangements for the piano accompaniment.

In my late teens, I went on to compose music for commercial jingles for radio and television, and shortly after, in my early twenties, numbers for the legendary revues in Sydney at the Phillip theatre, for Frank Strain's Downstairs Revue, and the Mavis Bramston Show, for which I composed a great deal of music including the theme, *Togetherness*.

~

Meanwhile, back in Brisbane in 1952, this twelve-year-old was urged into a well-meaning, if modestly talented concert party. It comprised the usual strangulated tenor, a glass-shattering soprano, a matronly contralto, a girl who sang popular songs and tapped, and me. We toured hospitals, retirement homes and on a few occasions, the Asylum.

At that time in Brisbane, the word "asylum" equated with the word "insane." But, the organizers assured us, even though deemed legally insane, the audience was composed of the better behaved inmates, all of whom were calm and appreciative. One of them I'll remember all my life.

After our first concert at the Goodna Asylum for the Insane, we were led from the stage to meet members of the audience. They all seemed quite lucid to me—but none more so than a man of about thirty, good-looking, obviously well educated, and extremely polite. We discussed music in general, my ambitions, and he shook my hand and wished me well. As we were bussed back to town that night, I asked why this man was incarcerated. In hushed tones, the leader of the troupe, Mrs. Smibert, informed me in a whisper that he was "a homosexual." I was perfectly aware of the word and its meaning.

I asked, "But is he insane?"

"Of course," Smibert said. "He was found..." long pause, "...in the company of another man." That, I discovered on further enquiry, was the *sole* reason he'd been committed to a lunatic asylum. The utter injustice shocked me to tears.

On my half dozen visits to the asylum, I insisted on talking with this man after the concert. He never gave the slightest hint of sadness at his situation, but seemed to accept it. We covered school, music, art, science, and while it was always on the tip of my tongue to wish him well, at twelve I couldn't find the words to express the incredible sympathy I felt for him. I merely shook his hand each time before I was led away to the bus.

I doubt a year of my life has passed since that I haven't thought about that man and the gross iniquity of an ignorant society that locked him away.

And that brings me to sex.

~

I was aware of my sexual orientation from a very early age. I was sufficiently savvy, even in my pre-teens, to accept my orientation, without ever questioning it as "a phase", or something that could be "cured." Thanks to the unfortunate inmate at the insane asylum, I also understood the stigma attached to its revelation, so kept my thoughts and feelings very much to myself. But if I was shy in social respects, I was certainly not so in pursuing sexual gratification.

Many child psychologists agree that upon discovering sexual desire, the minor will often instigate activity with an older partner. The downside is that the law, in its willful abnegation of psychology, blames the older participant by default.

Aware that severe penalties existed in the conservative social climate of the 'fifties, and particularly mindful of the kind and utterly sane man who'd been committed to an asylum, I was at immense pains to keep these relationships secret for the protection of my older partners.

A hyper-active libido is not unusual in a teenager, but in my case, it was extreme and indicative of addiction. And while it's an established fact that sexual orientation is innate, the expression of sexuality is often propelled by the events and surroundings of childhood. My childhood, so lacking in affection, can be seen pretty clearly as driving the need for closeness with others as I grew older.

I felt neither guilt nor shame in matters of sex. It was a driving force during my teen years, but I never misunderstood the act for more than it was. That came later, and by the time I was thirty, confusing sex with something deeper would result in the major mental health issue of my life, one from which I thought I might not recover.

~

From 1950 to 1953, we took a rental house in the seaside resort of Redcliff for our summer holidays. My father had a shorter break than we kids, so for two of our three weeks there, every morning at dawn, he'd take a bus back to the city to work. I'd walk him to the bus stop and after he left, I'd sit on the beach to watch the sun rise. It was a time for contemplation, respite from my mother's insufferable bitterness, and my brother's diametrically opposed interests of the time. Here, I read the following year's school texts, and any work of fiction I could lay my hands on. I also pored over the body-building magazines my meagre pocket money allowed.

At fourteen, in high school, I used my pocket money to join a gym in the city, but my mother insisted on accompanying me to my first day and succeeded in humiliating me before instructors and members alike. I dropped out after a week.

At least, I was in high school, and the necessity to travel across the city by public transport, gave me a certain independence and a certain freedom from the narrowed eyes of my mother.

~

I dived happily into three principal classes at Brisbane State High—Art, English and French. I submitted a small painting which got me into me the art class. Having discovered a little French literature, some French music of the 20th century, and French movies at the only cinema in Brisbane which showed foreign films, I longed to know more of the language. English classes gave me access to many of the books I'd been denied in my childhood, so that too was of principal importance.

I remember my Art and French teachers with affection. Alma Platen was a stylish woman in her thirties, greatly knowledgeable about all things art and art history. I was one of three boys in the class who had top marks, and received due praise. We three exploited Alma Platen's good humor with pranks, one day turning all the Picasso prints in the classroom upside down and waiting for her to notice. When she eventually did, she gave us a weary smile and a dry, "Very funny."

Nesta Brown was perhaps fifty, a pleasant, encouraging teacher who, discovering I had a passion for French, found me a French pen pal. We exchanged letters, mine in French, his in English.

At the end of my first year, when my gregarious sex life began to undermine my studies, my French suffered a decline. When exam results gave me a C in French, Miss Brown asked me to stay after class and lectured me in the kindest tones, urging me not to abandon my love of the language. Throughout my second year, I had a healthy succession of As in French with a solid A at my final Junior exam.

I also discovered an intense interest in chemistry and physics, but disliked the swaggering buffoon of a teacher, so those studies fell by the wayside. Maths? To this day, I find it difficult to add up a shopping list without employing fingers and toes. Yet, the other side of my brain understands binary math perfectly, and can build computers. Go figure.

I had one good friend in high school, Andris Stenders, and I vied with him for top marks in art. I boast that my pen and ink sketch won the junior prize and was featured in the year book. Andy went on to become a prominent architect and I'm happy these days to be in Facebook contact with his son, Kriv Stenders, the highly regarded Australian movie director.

I discovered the bookstores in Brisbane and thanks to the French's Acting Editions, began to read plays. I also became a theatregoer. Saturday mornings, I washed cars at a used car lot to make enough money to see matinees. Apart from the feathered cuties at the Theatre Royal, the only legitimate venue in Brisbane in the early 'fifties was His Majesty's Theatre where there was a constant stream of touring productions of musicals and plays under the J. C. Williamson banner. At a time when Australian talent was considered inferior, a British or American "star" was often imported to headline these production; these luminaries were usually plucked from the chorus, or the understudy ranks in their country of origin. This in no way diminished the shows' production values. And just as often a genuine name would be imported. I saw Sophie Stewart, Edwin Styles, Arthur Askey, the duo of Sybil Thorndike and her husband Lewis Casson in *The Chalk Garden*, the indelibly memorable Judith Anderson in *Medea*, and the great Googie Withers in *The Deep Blue Sea*. I'd already read the play, but to see it so beautifully realized by cast, designer and director was a revelation. I would later work with Googie and gained valuable lessons in stagecraft.

Of the musicals I saw in the early 'fifties, one of my first gave me insight into the value of the expedient ad lib. American Evie Hayes starred, exuberantly, in Irving Berlin's *Call Me Madam*. At the matinee I attended, there was a total power failure mid scene. Evie, as ambassador Sally Adams, was on a phone call to Harry Truman. The dialogue went:

"Harry? We're having a party!" Blackout—the theatre plunged into total darkness. Evie added in the pitch black, "It's a séance."

And at that theatre I saw my first opera, one which remains my favourite today due to its soaring score, transparent orchestrations, and tight dramatic construction—*Tosca,* sung by the great Australian soprano, Joan Hammond.

It would take a few more years before Australia would discover the value of the superior talent in its own back yard, and star Toni Lamond in *The Pajama Game,* and even later for Jill Perryman to become an unforgettable *Funny Girl,* and Nancye Hayes a perfect *Sweet Charity.*

~

Movies became an obsession and sometimes the pocket money took me to the Regent, the Wintergarden, Metro, St. James and the Tivoli, all now criminally demolished.

The technophile in me reveled in the short-lived mania for 3D and I delighted in having things hurled at me from the screen in *House of Wax*, *Bwana Devil*, and *Hondo.* Then came the revolution of CinemaScope. The Regent imported a specially built screen piece by piece from the United States, one of the largest and most precisely engineered screens for this medium in the world.

I kept a scrapbook of the screen innovations, of each ad for a movie in 3D, Scope or VistaVision, and articles about the invention of special lenses and projection equipment for the various formats. A school friend had a parent at a movie marketing office in Brisbane; knowing my passion for the movies, she gave me a collection of 10 x 8 production shots, and some movie star photos actually autographed, including Joseph Cotton, Jane Powell, Gene Tierney, Jane Russell. These were treasure to me. These photos, my cherished *Boys Illustrated Encyclopedia of 1949*, and a gift from my grandmother, a heavy, illustrated encyclopedia of technology from 1933, along with my voluminous scrapbooks were all destroyed by my mother while I was working in England in the 1970s. She considered them of no value and they cluttered a cupboard. As Kane did Rosebud, I lament their loss to this day.

~

I ended my junior year in high school with As in my favorite subjects, Art, French and English, and Bs in the rest. Restless, and not sure what I wanted to do with my life, as I turned sixteen, I decided to drop out of school entirely. My mother, saw it as the end of civilization. She determined I should find a job commensurate with my abilities and scholastic achievements—in her view, this pointed to an accountant (though I couldn't add), a commercial artist (because of my drawing talent), telephone technician (because of my fascination with technology); she all but frogmarched me to the Postmaster General's Department to enroll me in their technician program. I lasted two deeply unhappy weeks with the only memory of it a picture of new interns for the Brisbane morning paper. I was featured in the center of the photograph, which I considered small reward for a stultifying fortnight.

Next, came a clerical job at the Treasury Building. I did little more than occupy a desk in the typing pool where I stamped envelopes and rearranged files. Hardly the occupation of my dreams, but mind-numbing enough to allow me to read books of my choice carefully concealed under stacks of files. I spent several evenings a week after work in the nearby public library. Over the course of a year, I read the entire oeuvre of Robert Louis Stevenson, his *Strange Case of Dr Jeckyll and Mr Hyde* several times, fascinated by the prospect of a manifestation of one's evil subconscious. I devoured Edgar Allen Poe's stories, plays by Shaw, Coward and Rattigan, much science fiction, the whole of Freud's *Introduction to Psychoanalysis*, Wolberg's *Hypnoanalysis*, and *Hypnosis in Medicine*, many biographies of writers and actors, none of which would have been included in high school or university curricula, but all of which satisfied my boundless curiosity.

A couple of afternoons a week, I stayed back after work and, with a borrowed typing manual, taught myself to touch type on the giant Remingtons in the deserted office. It's a skill which has served me well throughout my entire life.

My closest friend at the time was a neighbor, Ron Smith, one of four orphaned boys living in foster care. He was a year older than I. We sat often at my kitchen table discussing various philosophies, the possibilities of psychokinesis, telepathy, reincarnation and hypnosis, and the esoteric wisdoms of the Rosicrucians. Research and deeper examination of our subjects soon eliminated most of our pet interests as rubbish—reincarnation as a fantasy, psychokinesis unlikely, telepathy a 'perhaps', and the Rosicrucians unworthy of deep study due to their contention that magic and science are correlated. That left hypnosis which interested me most of all.

I'd seen the flashy show hypnotist, The Great Franquin (Frank Quinn from New Zealand) at His Majesty's on two occasions and was intrigued by the phenomenon, if not by the somewhat degrading paces he put his subjects through for laughs. I'd read much about the success of analysis under hypnosis, and hypnotic anesthesia for surgery. This, I decided, was my purpose in life.

A former junior school friend of my age, sixteen, was the patient of a semi-retired hypnotherapist who was ex London Psychiatric Clinic. I understood my friend was battling his homosexuality, perhaps under family pressure, perhaps merely to conform to what he considered the norm. While today we have a clearer view of the destructive nature of so-called conversion therapy, these were less enlightened times, even for seasoned practitioners like the hypnotherapist. I gave my friend no opinion one way or another about his inner battle. It was his choice, and any advice I might give would seem to be colored by my own accepted orientation. He ultimately married and had children, how happily I don't know, we lost touch long ago. But for someone who, at sixteen, prized his recordings of Gertrude Lawrence in *The King and I*, it must have been an uphill battle.

I begged him to introduce me to his therapist. The man was genial, knowledgeable, and quite willing to talk me through the basics of hypnosis, the moral obligations of the hypnotist, of techniques, and he referred me to several texts I could find in the library. I read each one cover to cover and examined and discussed them in detail with the therapist.

I received my very first newspaper reviews at seventeen when I gave a demonstration of anesthesia under hypnosis for a group of Queensland university students. A news photograph shows a skinny chap, hovering over a subject in a deep trance. For someone with serious insecurities, this exercise overcame my shyness. I didn't realize it at the time, but it fell into the realm of performance. My confidence grew through several similar demonstrations.

I considered continuing with the brainless clerical job to support night school and perhaps university to study psychology seriously.

But then the acting bug bit.

FOUR

MY DESIRE TO be an actor had been in the back of my mind since childhood, since those afternoons reading plays with my grandmother. But where? It seemed an impossible aim in a city with no drama school, no legitimate theatrical venue beyond His Majesty's theatre which dealt only with polished productions from The South (which is how Brisbanites then referred to Sydney and Melbourne), far enough away as to be another dimension.

A chance meeting with a high school friend, Peter Morris, revealed there was a very healthy amateur theatre movement in Brisbane comprising three companies. Until catching up with Peter, I had no inkling of any of these. He was in a play for one of the companies and urged me to see it. I was surprised by the standard of production and acting. And I was hooked.

The three companies sported some exceptionally fine actors, all of whom would eventually shed the label "amateur" and be regarded as respected professionals when the State Theatre Company was formed in 1970.

In the 1950s, Brisbane Arts Theatre presented primarily farce, light comedy and the occasional popular drama, Twelfth Night Theatre produced principally classics, and Brisbane Repertory Theatre, perhaps the most commercially adept of the three, did fine productions of substantial contemporary plays. All played at the Albert Hall—basic, but spacious and well equipped to accommodate scenery and lighting. For me, it was a temple.

I saw a production of Rattigan's *The Sleeping Prince*, with Betty Ross as the lovable showgirl, and the formidable Babette Stephens as the dowager queen, the British farce *As Long as They're Happy* with a somewhat over-confident Bernard King, a quality he never managed to shed; Anouilh's *Ring Around The Moon* with a charming Earle Cross who became a good friend.

Peter encouraged me to audition for Brisbane Arts Theatre. Quivering with nerves, I read for a one act play being produced at a tiny hall in the mid-city. Somehow, perhaps because they needed a tall, skinny chap, I was accepted to play a small role in a Southern drama called *The Rope*. I became the target for the director's sharpest barbs, deservedly. I had no idea how to stand on a stage, how to be heard in the back row, and worse, I could not come to grips with the Southern accent. But it was a start.

I played a radio announcer (one speech, voice only) in *The Seven Year Itch* and wondered if this relegation to invisibility was a comment on my stage presence.

Next, I played one scene as the Young Collector in *A Streetcar Named Desire*. Blanche, movingly played by Betty Ross, flirts with the boy collecting money for the local newspaper and kisses him on the lips declaring that he looks like an Arabian prince. I'd work with Betty in radio productions a few years later, and many years on, she reminded me that she gave me my first stage kiss. I needed no reminder, it was a kiss I'll always remember as it was bestowed by someone I so admired.

I kept eyes and ears open, learnt the theatre lingo, found that I could be heard in the farthest reaches of the theatre, and gradually established a stage presence.

The company of Brisbane Arts Theatre leaned towards the bohemian. No surprise, given that the woman in charge was the eccentric Jean Trundle who enjoyed partying as much as she loved theatre. Of the many anecdotes concerning her and her husband Vic Hargreaves, my favorite remains the Easter Sunday morning when a neighbor witnessed a hearty band of Salvation Army collectors pounding on Jean's New Farm apartment door. Makeup skewed, still wearing the pillbox hat from last night's party, Jean wrenched the door open and said, "Yes?"

The leading Sally stepped forward and proclaimed joyfully, "Christ has risen!"

"Well I hadn't!" Jean shot back, and slammed the door.

I approached the Twelfth Night Theatre company who, at first, had no idea what to do with me. I played Organ Morgan with layers of age makeup in *Under Milkwood*, then, deciding I was juvenile material, they cast me as Cleonte in Moliere's *Le Bourgeois Genthilhomme*. The newspaper photo of me and my love interest, Lucille, both of us in elaborate period wigs, was pinned to the notice board at the office of my day job with the scribbled caption, "Which twin has the Toni?" But preparation for the Moliere role taught me much about period style.

For Brisbane Arts, I played the juve in *You Can't Take It With You*, and became achingly aware that juvenile roles are utterly thankless. So I was grateful to Joan Whalley, leading light at the Twelfth Night company, and a splendid actress, when she cast me as her paramour in Shaw's *The Millionairess*. I played the man she sets her sights on, a not-too-bright tennis player whom she marries only to have him spend her money on another woman.

I auditioned for ABC radio who produced many school-oriented short plays and serials, and a regular one hour dramatic play which often played nationally. I started getting roles and with them, an income, so at eighteen, I began to envisage a professional future in the business.

Shakespeare and I became passing acquaintances. I played *Sebastian* in The Tempest, and Bushy in *Richard II*. In this, Bushy bites the dust long before the end of the play, so I often went to the back of the theatre to watch the final moving scene where Richard's body is borne from a bare stage on a bier supported at shoulder height by four men—a solemn, stately procession which exited downstage between a scenery flat and the proscenium arch. It was a moment which always moved the audience to sympathetic silence.

On our final Saturday night performance, there'd been a children's matinee, and the *Richard* scenery had been moved to accommodate this, then moved back for the evening performance. Unfortunately, the downstage scenery flat had been positioned closer to the proscenium arch than before. When the stately funeral bier approached, it became apparent that it wouldn't fit through the gap. The bearers tilted the bier to make it through the exit—slightly, more, more still, until the dead Richard was forced to cling to the upper edge to stop from sliding off.

I laughed so helplessly, I didn't make the curtain call.

Now, at eighteen, good roles began to come my way. For the Twelfth Night company, I played Joseph Surface in a lavish production of *The School For Scandal.* It was designed by the renowned Australian artist, Margaret Olley. The director was meticulous in coaching the style of the period—the aristocratic entrance, the graceful, sweeping bow, the elegant hand gesture. My reviews were flattering and greatly encouraging.

I later played Charles Surface in a radio production of *School*. In this, due to the medium, no one got to see my exquisite gestures and bows.

The Twelfth Night company now trusted me to invent. They offered me the small part of The Waiter in Act Two of Goldoni's *Servant of Two Masters* with the suggestion that I might find some interesting way to interpret the character. I played him as an extremely old man with dementia and osteoporosis—and won my first ever award.

I continued to explore what is to me, one of the most important aspects of stagecraft, body language, and how this differs from Shakespeare, to Restoration, to the tennis player in *The Millionairess*, and the dusty, bewigged old man in *Servant*. I was not averse to changing body shape, facial features such as a little extra nose for Malvolio, but ultimately, I found that one's bearing said more about character than external appearance.

I think often of the friends I made and worked with in those learning years. Ron Finney and John Larkin were my closest acting buddies, both sadly gone now; Ron went on to teach, John became a renowned theatre critic and author. Rosalind Seagrave died recently, as did Earle Cross, both of whom I was in touch with frequently over the years. Berys Marsh remains a friend as do Eric Hauff and Bryon Williams. The late Kerry Francis and I did many radio plays together and he went on to become a leading radio actor at London's BBC. In those early days, there was never enough time to discuss everything that interested us—our theories, our idols, our ambitions. Ron Finney, John Larkin and I were obsessed with finding some little trick with which to make dialogue seem spontaneous. The answer was that there is no trick. One has to believe oneself as the character, convince oneself that this is the first time he's ever uttered the playwright's words, and spontaneity is the natural outcome.

We were unaware at that green time that our dilemma had been summed up in one phrase by George Burns: It's all about sincerity; if you can fake that, you've got it made.

~

Out of the blue, I had a telephone call from the formidable Babette Stephens, reigning monarch of the Brisbane Repertory Theatre. Her work as an actress was superior. I'd admired her extraordinary comedy timing in several plays and held her in great awe.

Hitherto, I'd hesitated to approach this company as their productions were of the highest standard and I was still fraught with insecurities.

Babette had seen my work and wanted me to play the officious Czech military Sergeant Javorsky in *The Great Sebastians*, which the Lunts had played on Broadway. Babette and Sydney actor, Mervyn Eadie played the phony telepaths who find themselves in the political mire of post-coup Czechoslovakia. For me, playing a baddie at last was a challenge. I chose to make the character militarily upright, charming on the surface, cold as ice at the core.

The success of this role led to Babette directing me as the evil Latvian Nazi in *Watch on the Rhine*. I had my hair dyed black and studied the accent with a Latvian immigrant. I came to a sticky end.

Then for Babette, I played Malvolio in Shakespeare's *Twelfth Night* with the greatest joy I'd had yet in my very short career.

By now I was aware of three entirely different methods of directing actors.

At Brisbane Arts, one was usually given moves, and character was assumed to be the actor's province. At Twelfth Night under Rhoda Felgate, line readings were more important—she would halt a run to read the line to the actor with the inflections *she* thought appropriate; under Joan Whalley, much more thought was given to motivation, to finding the core of the character. At Repertory, Babette Stephens as director embraced all of the above *except* dictating inflection. Character was discussed with the actor, and she directed with a view of the whole piece in mind, as it would be seen and interpreted by an audience. She also took no prisoners, I remember having a small hissy fit one day when unable to nail the right approach to a character. Babette's response was a beautifully underplayed, "Oh, pull yourself together." Sound direction.

My parents reluctantly came to see me in most of the productions, though my mother was never impressed and constantly badgered me to stop wasting my life and get a "real" job. Frankly, a job had never felt so blazingly real to me.

At nineteen, I was gaining a solid grasp of stagecraft, I was playing leads in radio, and did many commercial voice overs. And at last I had an income which allowed me to leave the suffocating claustrophobia of the clerical job.

Babette became my champion. She saw something in me worth nurturing and guiding. The accent was the start of it. She foresaw that the roles I would most likely play in maturity would be suave Brits, smooth talkers. Consequently she squeezed whatever was left of my Australian accent out of me and reconstructed my speech to match hers, the "received pronunciation" of the 1950's BBC. Babette's accent was that of a Lady Bracknell; her simplest utterance made the queen of England sound like a floozy. Yet she could shed this in a split second to tell the tag of an anecdote, or for comic effect. She corrected me if I mispronounced so much as a syllable. And she was right. I was usually cast as upper class British in Australia, even, amazingly, when I was in England in the 'seventies, I passed for Pom and played aristocrats, and quite a few characters who wore bowler hats and carried furled umbrellas.

As well as this contortion of accent, which was to serve me well for the rest of my career, I marveled at Babette's comedy timing as an actress. Never relinquishing character for a gratuitous reaction, she could get a laugh for doing nothing, equally as well as she could on a comic line. Comic timing, she informed me, is innate—she determined I had the gift and urged me to hone it. To this day, the sound of laughter as a result of a character foible, or on delivery of laugh line is as gratifying to me as the applause at the final curtain. Perhaps more so.

She also wrung the "Macready pause" out of my playing. William Macready, a nineteenth century British actor, was known for his very, *very* long pauses. Babette taught me that a legitimate pause is timing—a Macready pause is milking.

During those early years, Babette and her husband Tom became valued friends and remained so over three continents for the rest of their lives. So determined was she that I should become a known quantity in Brisbane theatre, that at her daughter Wendy's twenty-first birthday party, she engineered a press photo of Wendy on my arm, me clad in a rented dinner jacket. It impressed the crap out of my former office workmates.

I add that no matchmaking was intended. Babette was perfectly aware of my sexual orientation from the outset. It was never an issue, and certainly never an impediment to our long friendship. But the photo gave me a spotlight.

I made many friends during those formative theatre years. I'd always felt separate from my peers at school, and certainly at the tedious office job, but in the company of enthusiastic actors, designers and directors of all ages, I felt at ease—and at home—for the first time in my life.

FIVE

IN 1958, THE National Institute of Dramatic Art was established and auditions were held around the country. Several of us in Brisbane auditioned. Rather than use a well-trodden text, I adapted my pieces—one, a speech from the novel *Strangers When We Meet* by Evan Hunter, and a contrasting piece from Orwell's *1984*.

I remember walking on to the brightly lit stage of His Majesty's, peering into the darkened auditorium and giving my name to Clement McCallin who was conducting the auditions. He was a great actor whom I'd admired as Jason in the Judith Anderson *Medea*. I launched into my pieces and was thanked warmly after I'd done tearing myself to emotional shreds as Winston Smith in *1984*.

Months passed. Some of my contemporaries had letters of acceptance and left for Sydney to begin courses at NIDA.

I heard nothing.

I despaired for a while, then remembered Babette's immortal advice, "pull yourself together," so I applied myself to the tasks at hand with as much radio work as I could manage. I approached radio 4BH for work as an announcer to up the income. For them, I did unexceptional morning and evening music programs, but ambition reared its head and I recorded a pilot for a half hour program dedicated to theatre and movie news, newly released cast albums, and interviews. It was called, "Behind the Footlights." Television hadn't caught on yet in Brisbane, so radio still ruled the airwaves. My pilot was accepted and my weekly Sunday evening program became popular. One of the recordings I played received a particularly favorable response—it was Barry Humphries' first outing as Edna Everage, *Wildlife in Suburbia*. Years later, I was able to tell Barry of the reaction and how much I'd admired his early work.

One day, as I studied a script in our tiny house, my mother came to me clutching a letter. She revealed that it was an official notification of acceptance from NIDA, that my audition had been successful and they'd offered me a scholarship. The letter was almost a year old. My mother, determined that I should abandon frivolous theatrical pursuits, had kept the letter from me, and replied that I wasn't interested. To be fair, her admission was tempered with the somewhat sheepish hesitancy of one who suspected she'd gone too far.

She was right:

I left home.

By now, at nineteen, my income allowed me to share an apartment with ad writer Ian Austin whom I'd met while doing voice work for commercials. The flat was large and afforded the freedom to live as I chose, to work where I pleased, and invite actor friends for drinks, coffee, and the endless dissertations we enjoyed about all things theatrical. A frequent visitor was Babette in whose company we delighted, and whose anecdotes we treasured.

I spent two weeks in Sydney to attend a summer school of dramatic art at the Elizabethan Theatre Trust. But after just a few days of learning nothing more than I had in my few practical years in Brisbane theatre, I abandoned the course and spent the rest of the time living entirely for pleasure; and there was much of that to be had in Sydney at that time.

I made a beeline for *This is Cinerama* at the Plaza theatre and marveled at the technology, I delighted in the Australian musical, *Lola Montez*, but most exciting of all was *Around The Loop*, a revue at the Phillip Street Theatre featuring Gordon Chater, Wendy Blacklock and June Salter.

Up to this time, the only exposure I'd had to revue was the CinemaScope film of Leonard Sillman's lavish New York revue, *New Faces of 1952*; Phillip Street dealt with intimate revue: a small cast performing songs and sketches about contemporary figures and local events. Gordon's take on a popular barmaid at the Australia Hotel was a show stopper: "Gracious Greta, the Sweetheart of the Six O'clock Swill," remains embedded in my memory.

I longed to be involved in a show like this.

Back in Brisbane, I played the male lead in a national radio production for the ABC, Alan Seymour's thriller, *Swamp Creatures* and Babette cast me as the lead in the Repertory Theatre production of Noel Coward's *Nude With Violin*. If I'd been remotely religious, I would've thanked an omnipotent being for this role.

Sebastian, the soignée manservant of a deceased artist deals with a half dozen disparate characters who descend on him from around the world, all laying claim to the dead artist's fortune, having, they confess, painted all his masterpieces for him.

They had difficulty casting Fabrice, the non-speaking role of a toy-boy. He had to be good-looking and physically spectacular. I brought along one of my male models. Alan Walker was ideal—six feet two, blond, blue eyed and Babette was impressed not only by the physical beauty of the man, but eternally grateful to me—and asked no questions.

I should mention my other entrepreneurial gesture during this time: Brisbane Arts were having trouble casting the role of Turk in *Come Back Little Sheba*, the jock boyfriend of the ingenue who models for her painting in little clothing. I introduced them to my other male model friend, Bill Anderson, who fit the bill, as it were, perfectly. If you search the pages of Noeline Brown's book, *Living the 1960s*, you'll find a picture of him. …Page 130 for the curious.

Nude With Violin was a success and my reviews were glowing, one suggesting the promise I showed at this early age for roles I'd play when older. I was twenty, but with subtle makeup and streaks of grey in my hair, I played a believable forty.

So it went for the early part of 1960. A couple of my actor friends had traveled south to try their luck in a bigger pond. My good friend Berys Marsh had relocated to Melbourne. Correspondence with her encouraged me to make the move there.

Looking back now, it seems whenever I'd achieved the crest of some wave in my life, I sailed away on it rather than waiting for it to ebb.

SIX

1960. I HAD no agent, so I mailed tapes of some of my commercial voice work to Melbourne advertising agencies, and an excerpt from a radio drama I'd done for the ABC. Replies were promising.

I'd worked briefly on radio with the prominent actor Brian James and told him of my intention to try my luck in a more competitive field. He urged me to contact his nephew, journalist Gerald Mayhead who lived in a pleasant rooming house in an inner Melbourne suburb where there was a vacancy.

My parents came to the railroad station to see me off, my mother a grim harbinger of the doom that awaited me, my father bewildered by my wanting to leave my home town at all. My father's boss came too, he for whom I'd washed cars in my early teens to afford the cost of a matinee. He slipped me a five pound note with his good wishes.

The Melbourne rooming house was indeed pleasant, and the owner, Wyn Bryce, was not only an affable eccentric, but bore a startling resemblance to Bette Davis. She greeted me in the entrance hall of her house and there I stood, my unpacked bags by my feet while Wyn told me the story of her life. Only at the end when she revealed her innovative theory on how to escape a crashing plane—it involved a jar of Mum face cream—did she remember a message she'd received for me.

"Oh yes! You were due at ABC TV an hour ago."

I cabbed it to the studios and found I'd been cast as a spear carrier in a couple of scenes of *Macbeth*. Not a great start to a national career, but I had the joy of watching a consummate actor, Owen Weingott, play the lead role.

I settled in, got together with the friends I knew, and met their friends.

Melbourne was Australia's second largest city, yet gave the impression of being a village. The Melbourne theatre scene was like a club—everyone seemed to know everyone else. A popular coffee shop in Exhibition Street was always crammed with a hearty group of actors and writers, but a newcomer was treated with a degree of suspicion. It was like being tolerated politely at a party to which you hadn't actually been invited.

Pubs closed at six in those prehistoric days. Restaurant alcohol licenses also stopped at six. But here and there in Carlton, one could find an Italian restaurant which served wine in teacups. Had the place been raided, we'd have been obliged to pretend we were tea drinkers.

I did the rounds of the ad agencies and did a few commercial voice overs, then a few small parts in radio serials.

My first radio lead was offered to me at the ABC by Henry Cuthbertson, a meticulous director known for his cool, dry approach to the business of radio drama.

The play was Canadian. I was to play Barney, a farmer, and brushed up on my rural Canadian accent. My first speech was preceded by the direction: "Barney enters singing." I learnt the song, no chore given my background in music. At the first rehearsal, we did a complete run through of the play, and I approached the microphone on my first entrance, singing my heart out.

At the end, Cuthbertson came in from the booth and we all sat around for his notes. He turned the first page of his notepad, considered it for a moment, and said, "Mr. Creyton, can you whistle?"

So much for my singing.

I auditioned for a revue, a genre I'd seen only once at the Phillip Street Theatre in Sydney, and loved. The first question was, "Do you sing?"

I said, "Yes."

If it had been, "*Can* you sing?" I might've owned up with a "no."

It was called *Nothing Sacred*, and was staged at the converted Star Newsreel Theatrette and directed with good-humored care by Brian Crossley, ex D'Oyly Carte, so there were Gilbert and Sullivan parodies.

The writing was not of the standard I'd seen at Phillip Street, so it was a modest success only. I had the usual straight juvenile song about the joy of Sunday afternoons in Melbourne which I performed with the pretty ingenue. In the dance sequence, I was obliged to lift her gracefully and set her down just as gracefully. My dance skills are celebrated on three continents as an insult to Terpsichore, consequently the lift didn't always go as planned. If I was in the wrong position, the lift resulted in the ingenue's head vanishing into a large air conditioning duct above the stage—which it did often.

I was urged to see a production of the old Victorian melodrama, *East Lynne*, at a tiny theatre restaurant. It was played straight-faced, with all the stylized stance and gesture one might have seen in the original production in 1863. It was never mocked, but the very sincerity with which it was played was hilarious. It was a success for producer

George Miller—not the George Miller of *Mad Max* notoriety, I hasten to add. The upright hero was cheered, one wept for the badly-done-by heroine, and hissed the villain played with great panache and a devilish moustache by Jon Finlayson.

The piece was directed by British character actor Phillip Stainton. If you venture into the 1955 Ealing comedy, *The Lady Killers*, you'll see him as the tolerant police constable.

I was bowled over by the production. I didn't know then that this very play, once done seriously by my grandparents, would be a major turning point in my early career.

Radio serials supported me until the next audition for the small role of the Stage Manager in Clifford Odets' backstage drama, *Winter Journey* which was to star Googie Withers. Clement McCallin was playing opposite Googie as the alcoholic actor. At the first rehearsal, he shook my hand warmly and said how pleased he was that I'd persevered in spite of my mother's rejection of NIDA.

We played Melbourne, Adelaide, Brisbane and Sydney. There were many nights I stood in the wings watching Googie. I'd seen several of her movies, and was a dedicated fan, but to watch her in action was an object lesson in stagecraft. Asked in a TV interview if she cried real tears on stage, she replied, "The important thing is to move the *audience* to tears, and often one does that by holding back one's own." And that taught me a lot about the business I was now a part of.

"Good acting," as Sir Ralph Richardson once asserted, "is the ability to prevent a large group of people from coughing." In other words, acting on stage, no matter how immersed an actor is in his character, is manipulative. Particularly in comedy, the actor *must* be in control.

I turned twenty-one during the Melbourne season. My good friend in this production was actress Audine Leith. I'd told no one but her of my birthday, but she snitched. I was summoned to Googie's dressing room after the performance, convinced I'd committed some grave misdemeanor. Instead, John McCallum had joined her, along with the entire cast to toast me with champagne. Their gift was the great book, signed by all, *Actors on Acting*, a massive collection of essays by actors on their craft. I have it to this day, it having travelled with me to London for a decade, back to Sydney in the 80s, to New York, and it now resides in the library of my Los Angeles home.

The play toured to Adelaide, to Brisbane, where much was made of my presence in the starry cast, then to Sydney.

Here, a scene from *Winter Journey* was included in a benefit at Her Majesty's at which Vivien Leigh and John Merivale were present in a box. It was the scene where my character enters the alcoholic actor's dressing room while an intense argument takes place between Googie's character and the play-within-a-play's director, Brian James. In the course of the argument, Googie was obliged to slap Brian's face. Given the presence of Vivian in the house, Googie played the scene with increased intensity and slapped Brian James so solidly, he almost passed out.

I had every intention of returning to Melbourne when the play closed, but a few friends, some old, some new, gave me a farewell party and I was so touched, I decided to stay. It was a spur-of-the-moment decision, and perhaps one of the most significant I made in my life.

SEVEN

1961. I DID the rounds with my meagre resume, and the Vaude-Video agency chose to represent me. I did episodes of a few radio serials, and worked with some of my childhood idols, Neva Carr-Glynn, Sheila Sewell, Dinah Shearing, John Ewart, and played a couple of episodes of the children's radio show, *The Argonauts Club,* of which I'd been a member at the age of eleven!

My first major audition was for a lavish ABC-TV production of Shakespeare's *The Merchant of Venice*. My great grandfather had played Gratiano in this more than a century before. I was offered the role of Lorenzo, lover of Jessica who was played by a beautiful, seasoned TV actress, later to become a major star of British movies and TV, Annette Andre. We became friends during the production and remain so to this day.

Television, only four years old in Australia, was a new medium for me, but Alan Burke's meticulous direction gave me confidence. The cast was starry: Owen Weingott was a terrific Shylock and Tanya Haylesworth, hitherto known for reading the news, a powerful Portia, and Ron Graham an assertive Bassanio. These were the days before tape, so the production was live in Sydney, and a kinescope—a process for filming from live TV— was made for the other states.

The reaction was high praise. The Sydney Herald reviewed it as, "a masterful piece of work in which a predominantly young cast gave the play flesh-and-blood virility."

Thus began my intro to Sydney, a city I loved and which became home to me for the next seven years.

One minor gig of this time bears mentioning. Owen Weingott, the actor I so admired in *Macbeth* and *Merchant*, put together a small company to tour schools with a production of Oliver Goldsmith's *She Stoops to Conquer*, which he directed. I played Young Marlowe, and Tony Lumpkin was played by Reg Livermore. Introducing a classic to high schoolers was enjoyable, if not greatly remunerative.

News ran through the acting community that the Melbourne producer George Miller was planning to renovate an old movie theatre, and deck it out as a Victorian Music Hall. Here he planned to produce *East Lynne*.

Stainton died before Miller planned the Sydney production, so the piece was to be directed by Stainton's girlfriend, Betty Bailey who now claimed billing as Betty Bailey-Stainton. She was to play the girl pining for, and never getting the hero.

At the audition, I asked to read for the villain, the part my grandfather had played in the late 19th century. Miller and Bailey both considered me more suited to the hero. I begged to disagree and after much badgering on my part, read for the cad, Sir Francis Levison. I insisted that I would dye my hair black (as I had a few years before for *Watch On The Rhine*), streak it with grey at the temples, add an evil moustache and a little dissolute makeup under the eyes. Somewhat reluctantly, they gave me the part. And yes, I had to sing. There was much music in the production, the action being accompanied by dramatic piano underlining the joy, sorrow and tension of the plot, as in a silent movie. Appropriate songs of the period were sprinkled throughout. My number was an undercutting of the villainous exploits of Levison—the seduction of Lady Isabel, the lies, deceit and downright upper-crust oiliness—*I Don't Want to Play in Your Yard*, a children's song which went:

> I don't want to play in your yard,
> I don't like you any more
> You'll be sorry when you see me
> Swinging on my cellar door.

At least I was loud.

This was accompanied by a sophisticated soft shoe routine choreographed for me by Sydney dancer Keith Little who got my two left feet aiming in more or less the right direction.

We opened in November 1961. I was a month short of my 22nd birthday. Opening night, the paint was barely dry on the set, but the house cheered with approval at the final curtain.

My reviews were flattering in the extreme, and Miller and Stainton were relieved that I'd twisted their collective arm. The Music Hall, *East Lynne*, and I were a great success.

As the run progressed, I began to field the shouted comments from the audience aimed at the villain. I collected a repertoire of appropriate retorts.

Male Audience Member: You're a cad!
Me: What was that madam?
Male Audience Member: I'm a man.
Me: Your secret is safe with me.
Female Audience Member: You should be ashamed of yourself.
Me: (squinting at her table) Judging by the company you keep, so should you.

One night a cabbage was thrown at my feet. I picked it up and put it to my nose. "Whenever I smell this, I'll think of you."

And on another memorable night, referring to my trousers, which had been tailored tight, a drunken chap yelled: "Open yer coat and show us yer balls!"

I replied: "I'm an actor sir, not a juggler."

Every night, I made a curtain speech from a superior social height which began, "Ladies and gentlemen—and those less fortunate…"

The Aussie movie star Chips Rafferty came several times and I joined him and his wife for drinks after the show, as I did for the retired D'Oyly Carte grande dame, Evelyn Gardner who urged me to take up Gilbert and Sullivan.

I did fashion spreads for women's magazines—the villain glowering amid a bevy of fashion models. There were press interviews, one of which was given prominent space in a Brisbane paper. The headline ran: HOMETOWN BOY MAKES GOOD. My mother was unimpressed and said so to her GP. The doctor had been to Sydney, had seen me in the show and, in a letter, which I still have, disagreed strongly with her. I flew her, my father and brother to Sydney to see me and she admitted to enjoying the show. My sole regret to this day is that I never travelled my aged grandmother to see it, she who'd played Lady Isabel in her youth.

After I'd been playing Sir Francis for several months, Babette and Tom Stephens came from Brisbane to see the show. Afterwards, I eagerly awaited Babette's praise. But she gave me the Babette frown and said, "It was hard to know what your character was all about." I was astonished to hear this; I'd laboured long and hard to give my character the bearing of an aristocrat, the suavity of a congenital liar. Babette expounded. "You dashed through the dialogue so quickly so you could devote time to your devastating ad libs, the character became two dimensional."

It was Babette who, several years before, had warned me against letting a performance grow in a long run—against changing what I knew was right in the first weeks I'd played a part. She told me that the essence of the character was always evident, but that I, the actor, had become bored with the repetition of the script and too enamored of my banter with the audience. "There's a balance."

She was, of course, right. Never again, in a long career, have I ever let a performance grow or diminish due to the months' long repetition of eight performances a week. Often, I watched those around me embellish, and change delivery due to boredom. Once my character was established, usually within the first couple of weeks, I set it in stone, deviating only if circumstances demanded.

Apropos, there are three stories I cherish, two ancient, one modern.

George M. Cohan, the giant of Broadway in the early 20th century, left a successful production of his play, *The Royal Vagabond* to attend to another show of his elsewhere. When he returned after several weeks, he watched *Vagabond* from the audience, then went backstage to pin a note on the board:

"There'll be a rehearsal at ten tomorrow to take out the improvements."

Across the pond, at about the same time, the iconic Mrs. Patrick Campbell was playing the very first Eliza Doolittle in Shaw's *Pygmalion.* Every night, as the play progressed, she'd move a piece of furniture aside, or farther downstage, which enabled her to move farther upstage, so the rest of the cast were obliged to turn away from the audience to look at her. It's called upstaging. When Shaw saw the play after it had run a few weeks, he wrote to Mrs. Pat, "I've moved the sofa and chairs to their original positions and nailed them to the stage. You can do as you wish with the grand piano."

Thirty years ago, Maggie Smith had a great success in London and on Broadway with Peter Shaffer's *Lettice and Lovage.* It was directed by the great Michael Blakemore. I saw it in London and again when it came to New York and observed to Michael afterwards that the New York Maggie was so much more subtle than the Maggie I'd seen at the end of the West End run. His answer was an exasperated, "Maggie can't leave well alone. If she gets a laugh on a double take, tomorrow it's a triple take. If she drops a prop and it gets a laugh, by the end of the week, she'll drop it five times. Before the Broadway opening, I took out the improvements."

With George M. Cohan a forethought, no doubt.

EIGHT

MID 1962, *EAST Lynne* was in its sixth month when auditions were announced for a new revue at the Phillip Theatre.

I was tied to the success I was enjoying at the Music Hall and couldn't consider auditioning. Marion Beecroft, a Melbourne actress who played the maid brilliantly in the Sydney *East Lynne* accepted the call, but was a bundle of nerves. She asked me to accompany her to the theatre and run lines with her. We sat in the lobby, going over the pieces she'd chosen for her audition while others were herded in one by one. When the stage manager came to collect Marion, he recognized me and asked if I was auditioning. I said sadly I wasn't.

The auditions were being conducted by writer Ray Taylor, producer Bill Orr and Gordon Chater, and when the stage manager returned to the auditorium, he mentioned that I was outside. Gordon, whom I'd never met, insisted I come in and read. I had nothing prepared, and read a comic poem the stage manager shoved at me.

They offered me the show.

It was my dream to be in a Phillip revue, but I was committed to the theatre whose success I'd helped establish.

I discussed the situation with George Miller giving myself the feeble excuse that I'd played East Lynne for six months and the play could do with a change of scenery. He reluctantly let me go.

The revue was called *What's New?* - the premise, to introduce newcomers to a revue audience.

The cast were unknowns at the time—Maggie Dence, Arlene Dorgan, Reg Gorman, Janet Brown, Earle Cross and Noeline Brown. The material was lacklustre; the critics noted this and generally answered the question "What's New?" with "Not much." The run was short.

However none of the above names remained unknown for long.

Dot Mendoza the musical director at the Phillip was a stern taskmaster. Enunciation was paramount for revue songs where the words mattered more than the music. One vivid memory remains to this day. Janet and I did a parody of *The King and* I, and we cut a hectic polka around the stage. One evening, Janet caught the heel of her shoe in the hem of her crinoline, staggered, and fell onto me so that we were nose to nose. She uttered a rather un-Anna-like, "Shithouse!" into my face. I dissolved into uncontrollable laughter and not a word of the lyric emerged for the rest of the number.

Afterwards, Dot bore down on me with a fiery lecture on the evils of breaking up on stage. It took. It's happened a few times over the years, once to my eternal shame in London's West End, but the image of a fuming Dot Mendoza usually rose up to keep me in check.

For me, the bonus of *What's New* was getting to know the cast member who impressed me with her glamour, her wit, her comedy timing, and her dry baritone delivery. We were to work together often for decades after this show, and we remain. closer than friends to this day—more like family.

And that of course, is the one, the only, Noeline Brown.

One night during the run, Maggie Dence came to my dressing room, alarm written on her face and said, "Look out! Noeline Brown's after you!"

Indeed she was. While I was flattered, there was no way even Noel's advances could've caused me to change my innate orientation. It doesn't work that way. We took a year or so to figure that out, but the end result was a devoted friendship which remains to this day.

~

Hearing that the revue had closed, George Miller begged me to return to the Music Hall. The actor who had replaced me was discovered to have a drinking problem. It became obvious on his very first entrance when he walked from upstage to down, gradually getting lower and lower until he was on his knees at the footlights.

I returned to complete the year run of *East Lynne,* and when the subject of a new show popped up, the title, *Lady Audley's Secret* was bandied about. In its day the play caused a sensation; Lady Audley was the very first female villain in melodrama. The problem for George was that there was no villain role for me. I asked him to allow me to rewrite the play. He agreed and there followed weeks of plundering the Sydney Public Library for all the information I could find about Lady Audley. No internet, remember? I sat daily at a desk in the library, making notes, writing dialogue longhand, which I would then take home to my trusty portable typewriter. I rewrote the hitherto villainous Lady Audley as a badly-done-by heroine and wrote a smooth cad for myself: George Tallboys Jr. I delighted in writing the flowery dialogue of Victorian melodrama for the now heroine:

> Lady Audley (*clutching her breast*): Shame! Shame! And the curse of a stained escutcheon!

I added two comedy servants, a scene at an East End Music Hall where the villain is hiding out, and where songs of the day were performed.

Casting was a breeze. Rosalind Seagrave, a good friend from Brisbane theatre days, had just graduated from NIDA, and was a perfect fit for the tortured heroine, Sheila Kennelly the ideal Music Hall diva, and as the hero, the wonderfully talented actor who'd taken over the hero in *East Lynne* for the latter part of its run, Donald MacDonald. Donald projected all the qualities of heroism; in gesture, stance and delivery he was the very picture of an upright gent. The memory of him singing "Come Into The Garden Maud" makes me smile even now.

In act two of the plot as I wrote it, the villain sets fire to the Music Hall to avoid discovery. I rode onto the stage on a fire wagon singing, "Hold Your Hand Out, Naughty Boy."

For a touch of megalomania, I composed the florid overture for the show for the pit piano, and some of the incidental music to underscore certain scenes.

Lady Audley was a success and its long run assured. It was later produced in Melbourne with equal success.

John Faassen, who'd been brought in to direct *Lady Audley* suggested doing children's matinees of appropriate plays. *The Tinder Box* was chosen and Donald and I played the bickering villains—Donald padded up to look corpulent, and I wore a tight fitting costume to make me even scrawnier than I was. I wrote a song for us which we did with a cute soft shoe. I began: "I'd Rather Be Thin Than Be Fat."

To balance the insult, Donald's verse ran: "I'd rather be fat than be thin."

Even as I settled in to the long runs of the shows at the Music Hall, my association with revue was far from over. Some of the writing contacts I'd made during *What's New?* urged me to compose music to their lyrics for the Phillip revues, and Frank Strain's popular Downstairs Revue. Melvyn Morrow wrote literate, complex lyrics and Stuart Carmichael rather bawdier numbers. With Stuart's lyric, I composed the music for "Togetherness" which was performed first in a Phillip revue with topical lyrics changed every week. It was later appropriated for *The Mavis Bramston Sho*w as the weekly opener.

NINE

I SPENT A LOT of time with Noeline trying to evolve a comedy "something". We weren't sure if we were aiming at a cabaret act, a stage show or TV, but we were both dedicated fans of Mike Nichols and Elaine May and we wanted to build something on the foundation they'd laid. Their improvised sketches were, to us, the very meaning of comedy. Their routines hold up today as biting comments on society and social issues; they rely less on gags, than on character and situations, and are every bit as funny now as they were in the early '60s.

Noel and I discovered as we worked together that we were amused by the same issues, and as performers, we had a reciprocal sense of timing—a gift if two actors are going to perform comedy together.

We played a few of our recorded efforts for Terry Pritchard, a friend who worked in programing at radio 2SM. He played them for the powers that be, and Noel and I began recording snippets of comic comment, no longer than a minute apiece, which played in the afternoon shows.

The technician who ran the broadcast was a large, burly chap with a mop of untidy red hair. His name was Reg. And I doubt I've ever met anyone more Reg in my life—there was always a cigarette dangling from his lips which in no way impeded his droll, often monosyllabic observations.

He liked what we did and our tiny forays into radio became regular.

~

The next show for the Music Hall was *The Face at the Window*. I, of course, was to be the body associated with that face. The play called for a woman of the world, a villainous female colleague of the villain. Who better than Noeline?

We made a mean couple. I wore a handlebar moustache and a goatee, Noel wore a low cut gown, swung her hips around and smoked a cigarillo.

Once again Donald was the upright hero and it was decided he should be blond for the role. I had become used to my hair dyed black. Every Friday night after the show, Noeline, Donald and the music director, Bernadette Alam would come to my flat and Noel and Bernie would touch up Donald's and my roots. …Or, as Noeline put it so delicately, we'd "get rooted."

My first entrance was to rise menacingly in unflattering green light from a trapdoor in the stage. At the final dress rehearsal, the theatre was deserted except for the Millers, some of the money people and other invited dignitaries. Bernie Alam was at the pit piano playing shuddering dramatic chords as I rose into sight. The staircase from basement to the hole in the stage had been hurriedly built and as I rose, I bashed my shin painfully on one of the steps. Just as my head emerged into the light, I uttered a resounding, "Shit!" which echoed around the theatre. Bernie froze mid chord, George Miller let out a startled gasp, but the sound which saved my dignity was the roar of laughter from Noeline's dressing room.

I should acknowledge that not all was plain sailing in those heady Music Hall days. One of the actors, Barry Lovett, was a thorn in my side. He was brought on board by director John Faassen to play the detective in *The Face at the Window*. Barry seemed to have serious psychological issues, principal of which was seeing himself as the star of the show. He confronted me before the cast at rehearsal one day with the accusation, "You're always trying to steal center stage!"

My kneejerk reply was, "Wherever I am is center stage."

It was a glib thing to say, but there was more than an element of truth in it. I was fully aware that in these roles, I had the audience's attention whether standing still or doing cartwheels.

The situation went from bad to worse. Lovett would talk over my speeches, step in front of me in a scene, perform some distracting piece of business to pull focus, but always, I found a way to get around these antics without confrontation. One in particular I remember well. Barry complained to the director that I never looked at him when he was speaking. That evening, during a long scene we had together, I never took my eyes off him. Whether it was logical for the character or not, I watched his every move, sometimes inches away from him. By the end of the scene, he was running sweat. The subject never came up again.

This one actor's psychotic behavior was the only unpleasant element in the happy times with the many, varied casts who worked at the Music Hall in those early years.

~

In 1963, during these Music Hall years, I did two undistinguished half hour plays for ABC TV which bear no more than a passing mention. The better of the two concerned a scheming bank manager, me, who plots to rob the vault and is inadvertently locked in it by the janitor.

The other was a dismal piece written for the modestly talented Kessey Twins. In it I played the egotistical compere of a TV program which the girls eventually steal from him. The script was badly written, and apart from my being unable to come to grips with a character, it called for the twins to sing and dance. I saw the recording of this recently and shuddered, certainly at my own awful performance, but mostly in sympathy for Anthony Newley who wrote "Nothing Can Stop Me Now," the number rendered by the twins at the play's finale. The Sydney Morning Herald called the show "a disaster." They were kind.

~

The Music Hall demanded another children's show, this time it was *Beauty and the Beast*. I played the Beast, a transformed prince, and Noeline the beautiful maiden who falls in love with him. We were costumed as for a Victorian production of the play, Noel in a hoop skirt over long frilly pantaloons, and me in tights. At the dress rehearsal, Noel took a good look at my legs in tights and said, "You have no visible means of support."

I absorbed this devastating slight, and when I stopped laughing, I carried myself as if on oaks instead of saplings.

It was a terrific departure from the evil doings of our nightly shows at the Hall, and we loved the unrestrained involvement of the audience of kids. At the end of the play as the Beast grows weak and close to death, Beauty wonders how to save him. The cry from the audience was deafening at every performance: "Kiss him! Kiss him!"

By now, I was a known quantity in Sydney theatre and had a substantial following. I'd learnt a great, great deal about theatre, my range and my limits. The advice of Babette Stephens stood me well during this period, and in the years to follow in the business of which I was now an integral part.

~

There was no part for a traditional villain in the next play at the Music Hall, *The Evil Men Do*, so we agreed that I would write a part for myself as narrator of the story. This time I was relieved of the moustache and dyed hair. I wrote rhyming couplets to introduce scenes and characters. If you are old enough and as interested in theatre as I was, you may know the double LP recording Noel Coward made of his operetta, *Conversation Piece*, which starred Richard Burton and opera singer Lily Pons. Coward introduced each scene with marvelously intricate rhymes. Mine might not have been as intricate, but they amused the audience.

Noeline excelled as ever and we had a number together: "You Called Me Baby Doll a Year Ago."

~

During this run, I wrote an entirely original play for the next Hall production, a satire on TV westerns, *How The West Was Lost*. I used cliches from every western ever made: bad guys were cut off at the pass, a lone gunman spoke for justice, Scarlett made mint juleps for the ranchers, and frequent, brief appearances were made by a Native American I called Chief Running Gag. I wrote a part for myself as the bad guy and one for Noeline as the pulchritudinous saloon keeper.

Meanwhile, Noel's and my radio comedy snippets caught the attention of Festival Records and we signed contracts to make the first ever Australian comedy LP for them. With our idols Nichols and May uppermost in our aspirations, we started working on material.

At the same time, we were rehearsing *How The West Was Lost* during the day, while playing *The Evil Men Do* at night. And one of those nights was a game-changer.

TEN

CAROL RAYE ENTERED my life in the spring of 1964. Carol, a major British movie and stage star in the late 40s, and early 50s, married veterinary scientist Robert Ayre Smith, and after living for a stretch in Kenya, she took a producer's course at the BBC in London. She and Robert moved to Australia where he took up a post with the CSIRO.

Carol had been impressed by the blockbuster BBC satire program, *That Was The Week That Was* and was eager to produce something similar in Australia. The ABC, a non-commercial network, seemed the obvious choice, but they, in their infinite lack of perception directed her to ATN Channel 7. The general manager there, James Oswin, was an imaginative and enterprising man who was open to the idea. He offered a small amount of money for Carol to set up a pilot.

Carol conferred with various authorities in the business, all of whom decided that Gordon Chater, star of so many Phillip Revues, would be the ideal mainstay of a potential cast. Michael Plant, thirty-three year old wunderkind of Australian and American television was to be executive producer, while David Cahill, studio stalwart at 7, would direct the cameras. They needed a straight man, someone who took on the chores of David Frost in the BBC original. Gordon knew my work, as did one other on the production team, Jim Fishburn, who'd directed some Phillip revues. They recommended Carol should see me.

One night, playing my ever-so-sophisticated narrator in *The Evil Men Do*, I was aware of Gordon's bawdy laugh echoing over all others in the audience. A sly glance across the footlights confirmed he was indeed present, along with Jim Fishburn, David Cahill and a glamorous woman I later learned was Carol Raye. The next day, they asked me to join the cast of the as yet unnamed show. No audition was involved, the request came without qualifications.

When I read the rough draft of the script, I conferred with Noeline who thought, as I did, that such racy material would never survive on network TV. Australia was still a very conservative nation. There was an unwritten "White Australia" policy which excluded immigration from countries of any other colour, a right wing government which embraced colonialism and pledged undying allegiance to Queen and Crown. The Vietnam war was escalating and, far from divorcing Australia from it, the government blindly followed America and introduced conscription. Movies, particularly French and Italian movies which involved anything related to sex were heavily censored, and books such as Lady Chatterly's Lover were banned outright, their possession resulting in imprisonment. A popular satirical magazine, Oz, founded by three liberal university graduates, was prosecuted for corruption of public morals.

And of course, homosexuality was a prosecutable offence with prison sentences attached.

Many of these issues were addressed in the pilot episode of the proposed TV show.

I left the Music Hall for the second time. I abandoned rehearsals for my own piece, *How The West Was Lost*, and replaced myself with accomplished actor, John Unicomb.

Ken Shadie was a news writer at Channel 7, but a news writer with a wonderfully droll sense of humor. He contributed sketches for the pilot, and when the show went national, Ken became chief writer and script editor. Over the years we aired, he wrote some of the funniest and most biting sketches.

One line of his was the perfect example of his irreverently dry humor and remains uppermost in my memory. The Airforce's new jet fighter, the F1-11 with its almost invisible swept-back wings, kept crashing, often with fatalities. Ken's line? "If God had intended the F1-11 to fly, He would've given it wings."

Ken went on to write for Paul Hogan, and later wrote the screenplay for *Crocodile Dundee*.

The proposed TV show still had no name, and no female star. Gordon Chater suggested that we had the perfect candidate for a female star at the head of production. So, Carol did double duty as producer and star. A guest star was introduced to complete the cast of four: the greatly versatile June Salter.

Title? Many were bandied about—The Late Show, The Late Revue (which sounded like an obituary), and someone observed that we were doing a uniquely Australian show; it wouldn't surprise any of us if the management imported a no-talent American or a failed Brit to front the piece, as was the habit with J. C. Williamson productions. And that led to the idea that a fictitious female would be created, imported as the lead, and the show would be named for her; but when it was discovered that she had no talent, she'd be expelled—except that no directive would find its way to management to rename the show.

In that simple joke to establish a title, the show's first satirical comment was made, underlining the Great Australian Inferiority Complex—that foreign artists were more talented than Australian.

Mavis Bramston, and Valda Clissold were fictitious names one associated with genteel Australian suburbia. They'd long been joke names actors blamed if their audience was dull. "Mavis must be in the house tonight." Or, "Valda's out there."

So, the show became *The Mavis Bramston Show*.

We needed a Mavis.

I took Noeline with me to a cocktail party at Michael Plant's apartment where the cast was gathered with writers and the production crew. The big question, "Where do we find someone to play the no-talent Mavis?" came up. Writer Jon Finlayson's eyes lit on Noeline.

Flustered, and not entirely eager, Noel was pressed into service.

We taped the pilot before an invited audience in the Macquarie Auditorium in the center of Sydney. The response was encouraging. As we anxiously awaited a verdict, I had a phone call from someone whose work I knew, but had never met.

David Sale had written material for Toni Lamond on Melbourne TV and for stage revues. When, for personal reasons, he relocated to Sydney, a mutual friend gave him two phone numbers, one of which was mine. He explained he was in Sydney, searching for writing work. I invited him to the private viewing of the *Bramston* pilot. The whole gang was present, including the general manager of the Fairfax Newspaper empire, and ATN Channel 7, Rupert "Rags" Henderson.

Henderson's instant reaction to the pilot was an unequivocal, "Go!"

I introduced David to Michael Plant who asked him to submit some material. To the show's good fortune, he did so frequently for the entire run; to my personal delight, he wrote many musical numbers which suited my sprechgesang style of delivery. David went on to become executive producer of the show, and later, the mastermind, writer and producer of the equally groundbreaking series, *Number 96*.

ELEVEN

THE FIRST BRAMSTON show went to air in Sydney and Canberra on November 11th 1964.

The opening theme was "Togetherness", which I'd composed a couple of years earlier for the Phillip revue, *At It Again*. The satirical take on the week's news report which topped the show was provided by the writers of Oz Magazine, Richard Neville, Richard Walsh, and Martin Sharp.

Noel was a gloriously posh Mavis in an interview with Jon Finlayson, then performed "I Could Have Danced All Night" with sweeping gestures, great caution negotiating the staircase, and absolutely no respect for musical pitch.

We read poems by Aboriginal writer Kath Walker in which she decried the treatment of Australia's indigenous population by the government. November 11 was Armistice Day, so we did a parody of World War I songs, followed by the cast singing, "Friends and

Neighbours" illustrated with scenes of mob violence and Ku Klux Klan marches.

After the show, the ATN switchboard lit up with outraged protests, viewers horrified by the things they'd seen and heard. These, we soon discovered, were a very small minority. The greater public embraced the show without qualification and the press raves were unanimous.

TV Week wrote: "Whatever the critics do to Mavis Bramston now is insignificant. The step to adulthood has been taken. Other stations must follow to keep pace. It has taken a step that can never be recalled."

A rival studio was quoted: "ATN7 has taken a step that no one else has had the guts to do."

The Sunday Mirror wrote: "Oh Mavis, Never Leave Me!"

The first six shows were an overwhelming success in Sydney and Canberra and it was decreed that we'd go national in 1965. There were no seasons in those days, so this meant we'd do a show once a week, every week for a year. We totalled 45 shows in 1965.

The show was never live, contrary to some reports. We taped from the very outset, recording before a studio audience on Monday nights, the show going to air in Sydney on Wednesdays at 9 p.m. If anything relevant occurred on the Tuesday we had off, we were rushed back to the studio to record an insert.

Tape, in those primitive days, was not easy to edit. If we fluffed a sketch or a song mid segment, we couldn't simply repeat the song; we had to go back to the beginning of the entire segment, do every preceding sketch over, and beg the studio audience to laugh at all the gags again. One such disaster occurred in 1966 when Noeline had joined the show as a regular. The sketch went thus:

Noeline and I are discovered by a front door, in the moonlight after a romantic evening out.

Me: You know how I feel about you. Will you marry me?

Noeline: No, I'm sorry I can't.

Me: But why?

Noeline: You're too uncouth.

Me: Uncouth? Me? I've just taken you to the ballet, last week it was the opera, and the symphony orchestra, we eat at the best restaurants. So what's all this uncouth bullshit you stupid cow?

At the first camera rehearsal in the afternoon, we reached the point where I said, "Uncouth? Me?"... And I farted. Loudly enough to have the cameramen leave their cameras to double with laughter. Noel did likewise, and so did all the tech crew behind the glass in the booth.

We pulled ourselves together and got through the sketch.

That evening, the studio audience in place, we were taping the show. The sketch came in the middle of a segment. Moonlight. We walked to the front door, I turned to Noeline and said, "You know how I feel about you. Will you marry me?" And she collapsed in uncontrollable laughter.

The audience had no idea why.

Without detailing the reason, we explained we'd have to go back to the beginning of the segment, do the preceding material again, and then our sketch, and would they kindly laugh again in all the right places.

We started at the top of the segment, the other cast members did the preceding material, and we started the sketch again. This time I got only as far as, "You know how I feel about you," and we both dissolved into heaving laughter, as did the camera and floor crew.

By the third time we repeated this, the audience was entirely silent, having no idea what they were watching. We nailed it on the fourth, straining to keep straight faces.

~

There were never fewer than twelve writers on the show, and when news of its extraordinary success traveled around the world, submissions came in from British and American writers. One day in the production office, I looked through a few of these and came across a sheet of music with an accessible melody and a very sharp and funny lyric. I snagged it for myself at once, and asked to see any others from this writer, a New Yorker, Lesley Davison. A little research revealed she'd written songs for the famous Julius Monk revues at the Plaza Hotel, the long running Crystal Palace revues in Aspen, Colorado, for *Laugh In*, the *Dean Martin Show* and a long list of others. She also happened to be the niece of J. B. Priestley.

She, her orchestra leader husband Forrest Perrin, and their children would become my closest friends in the US when I relocated to New York, and in the '90s, Lesley and I would co-write a revue for the Off Broadway Triad Theatre which would run for two and a half years.

~

In November 2014, I met Australian documentary film maker Stephan Wellink. *Bramston* came up in conversation and I remarked that it was fifty years since the show first aired. I was disappointed that Channel 7 had done nothing to mark this gold anniversary.

It set the wheels in motion and Stephan got to work interviewing those of the production who were still alive. The result was an entertaining and truly informative film which covered the nature of the show, why it broke so much new ground, and how it changed Australia from a deeply conservative nation to one more open to the new, the different, the imaginative.

Pushing the Boundaries is superior documentary. If you haven't seen it, do yourself a big favor and find it!

TWELVE

THE 1964 CHRISTMAS issue of TV Week featured a picture of Gordon, Carol and me on the cover. First up in 1965, I signed a contract with Channel 7 for the national Bramston shows and noted a morals clause which stated that any breach of accepted public morals would result in immediate termination of my contract.

I doubt I realized the full significance of that clause at the time, but it would soon become alarmingly apparent that as a public figure, especially a leading man type, my private life would be under constant scrutiny.

To our disbelief the writers and creators of the satirical Oz Magazine who provided our weekly "news" reports were arrested for obscenity and sentenced to six months in prison with hard labour. Their conviction was later overturned, but this horrific attack on free speech stunned us all and only encouraged our writers to push the boundaries farther.

Just before Christmas, a benefit was held for the Oz three at Sydney

University's Footbridge theatre. Jon Finlayson, Noeline and I did a parody of Peter, Paul and Mary and sang their "Puff The Magic Dragon", with lyrics changed to "Poof The Tragic Drag Queen." We stopped the show. We were obliged to return for an encore, but in the fluster of the moment, could remember nothing of the harmonies and barely managed the lyrics. No one seemed to mind.

~

The national Bramston show, under Michael Plant's sure hand, was a ground and record-breaking success. The name "Mavis" went into the vernacular as meaning satirical criticism. It was accompanied in every newspaper article with the words, "sensational", "ground-breaking", "bold", "scandalous". Religious bodies took against us, as did the father of one of my primary school classmates who threatened to sue us for obscenity. The channel employed a team of lawyers for the specific purpose of staving off such threats, at every one of which the ratings soared; in fact, to this day, they remain the highest of any show in Australian TV history.

There were no recording devices in those days—you had to be at home, glued to your TV. If you missed the show, you missed it. Consequently, on the nights the show aired, the streets of major capital cities were deserted. In Adelaide, the night assigned to late night shopping coincided with the broadcast; the city was obliged to change late night shopping to a different night as nobody shopped when Mavis was on.

We found, much later, that a Sydney burglary group which became known as the Mavis Mob, robbed homes during the airing of the show. Their ploy was ingenious. While entire families were huddled in the living room glued to the show, The Mob broke into the house and cleaned out every other room by the show's finale.

As historians now confirm, the Bramston Show was instrumental in radical changes in Australia's hitherto narrow political views; we were the beginning of the conversion of a deeply conservative nation to one with a more liberal attitude. We questioned the racism of the "White Australia Policy," a firmly held agenda of prime minister Robert Menzies. We heaped scorn on the antiquated laws stemming from the generally accepted view that we were a colony and had to adhere to Victorian laws and morals. We attacked censorship in a beautifully realized sketch by John Michael Howson in which Gordon, as a member of the vice squad, asked to see what his wife, Carol, was reading. It was a book on flower arranging by home decorator Constance Spry. Gordon, claiming he was qualified to find filth in literature, read verbatim from the book—"select the longest stem as the centerpiece of your arrangement." And, "languid arrangements are best suited to the bedroom." The genteel Constance Spry suddenly became pornographic. When the usual complaints jammed the studio's switchboard, the simple explanation was that we'd read Spry's instructions word for word.

~

Gordon, Carol and I were treated like rock stars. On one of my infrequent visits back home, I took my mother shopping in the city. In McDonnell and East, a large department store in Brisbane, I was suddenly set upon by frenzied shoppers. My suit was grabbed from all angles, buttons pulled off my jacket, the tie yanked from my neck; the management eventually contained the crowd and got us out of the store. My mother became hysterical. Given her determination to deflect my career in show business, I was perversely satisfied by this.

Ken Shadie wrote a sketch to reflect this phenomenon.

Gordon, June and I are in armchairs relaxing and discussing our respective weekends.

> Gordon: I made a roast for Sunday lunch.
>
> June: I helped my son with his homework.
>
> Me: I got mobbed again.
>
> Gordon: Oh self, self, self! Can't you talk about anything besides yourself?

National notoriety came with more than a few such indignities. I returned to my flat from rehearsal one evening to find a pregnant woman sitting on the sofa in my living room. She'd climbed the fire escape to get in and claimed I was the father of her child. I fled and called the police to remove her.

One day at rehearsal at a large hall in Eastwood, a suburb adjacent to the studio, I was at the center of the room rehearsing a number, script in one hand, cigarette in the other. Three young people, two boys and a girl walked in; the boys took an arm apiece and dragged me from the room. I was so surprised I didn't resist, and cast and crew watched dumfounded and immobile. I was put into a car and driven across town, informed by the merry band that I'd been kidnapped by University students who wanted a charitable contribution as ransom.

Once settled in a student's flat with about a dozen other students, we had a pretty good time. We drank, we joked, and I have to admit it was great fun. But Wednesday was the night I usually dined with Gordon at his Paddington house and rehearsed the new scripts. I called him and told him I'd be unable to join him as I'd been kidnapped.

"Kidnapped? Kidnapped? I've got a roast in the oven! It'll be ruined!"

Gaining no sympathy there, I suggested a call to the general manager of 7, Jim Oswin. He was in on the gag, fully aware of the publicity value. My abductors asked for a reasonable ransom to return me. I heard Oswin's reply clearly. "Nah, keep him." But the channel did cough up later.

Eventually, I begged them to take me home assuring them I'd claim to the press that I'd been captive all night. A few of them came to my apartment for drinks then left me to a good night's sleep. Next morning, they picked me up and drove me to a suburban pub where it had been arranged for Michael Plant to "rescue" me—and of course, the press were there to take pictures. The Daily Mirror's banner blared in big black letters:

STUDENTS KIDNAP TV STAR.

It would not be the first time I made headlines, nor of such a pleasant event.

Another indignity occurred when I was coerced into a flying visit to my old primary school in Brisbane, Windsor State, where I spent eight moderately informative years of my childhood. I was guest of honor for the school's centenary. It was the dead of winter and I was greeted at the airport in an open car. As I was driven the eight miles to the school, it rained, which seemed to be a comment on my schooldays. A few of my old schoolmates were there and welcomed me, some thoughtfully with towels. Most guests knew me from the show and were effusive, though a few turned away as if my glance might taint them with my heathen views. None of the teachers remembered me at all, such was my invisibility as a child. The multitudes of children flocked around, had no idea who I was, but stole my scarf, gloves, mini camera, a book I was reading, and a pocket handkerchief. Nostalgia has its costs.

~

In 1965, Ampol Petrol assumed full sponsorship of the program, a first in Australian TV. Pictures of Gordon, Carol and me adorned every

Ampol pump in the country.

These early 1965 shows were probably the best we ever did, and disastrously, many of those tapes were later destroyed in a fire in the studio vault.

My fan mail was flattering and disturbing at the same time—flattering that my TV work was appreciated, disturbing in that some contained proposals of marriage, some just plain propositions.

I employed one of the office staff at 7 to help answer the mail. Wendy Hunter was fun and good humored about this weekly chore; some replies I dictated, some she wrote herself, always enclosing a photograph. There was the occasional piece of hate mail. One read, "You are going to Hell!" I advised Wendy to reply that was the best news I'd had all day.

Another wrote. "All my girlfriends think you are terrific and watch your show every week. If I didn't think you were a stuck up snob, I might watch it too."

I dictated the reply, "Dear sir or madam, I think you should know that some psycho is using your name and address to send insulting letters. I enclose the letter should you want to take action against this loony."

~

Saturday was a day of rest. With safety in numbers a forethought, several of us from Channel 7 met at the Southern Cross Hotel in Potts Point every week for lunch. My old friend Terry Pritchard, ex 2SM, was now in marketing at Channel 7. Wendy, Jim Fishburn, Patti Mostyn, who was then Johnny O'Keefe's assistant, and the producer Michael Plant, all gathered just to get the pressures of the preceding week off our minds.

On Saturday July 10 in 1965 when the demands of the show were at their most intense, our little band met as usual at the Southern Cross to blow off steam. Michael Plant, more than any of us, was showing the strain of maintaining the quality of a weekly show. After lunch, we said our farewells, Michael returning to his Pott's Point apartment to edit scripts. On Monday morning, I drove to Eastwood for rehearsal as usual and was greeted at the door by Carol, her face streaked with tears. She told me that Michael was dead, an accidental overdose of painkillers suspected. He'd been found by a neighbor, stretched out on his bed, surrounded by scripts for the show.

I was stunned. Death had never been so close before, and certainly not of someone I so respected and valued as a supportive friend.

Gordon rallied us to continue rehearsal. Jim Fishburn took over as producer, and somehow, we managed to be funny as was expected of us that week.

Changes needed to be made, and these would adversely affect the quality of the show in less than a year.

~

How The West Was Lost opened well. I was at the opening night and happy to see John Unicomb being as slippery a baddie as I'd hoped to be, and Noeline strutting her stuff with a couple of songs Mae West might have envied. And the laughs were in all the right places.

This accomplished, Noel and I went into the studios at Festival Records and put down twelve tracks for our comedy album. For general consumption, it was called *The Front and Flip Side of Barry Creyton and Noeline Brown*. But the album cover I designed said a great deal more. The pic on the front was of the two of us in evening dress, my hand behind Noeline's back; the title read "The Frontside of Barry Creyton and Noeline Brown." The other side of the cover pictured the reverse of the frontal shot revealing that my hand was in fact on Noeline's rear. The title on this side read, "The Backside of Noeline Brown and Barry

Creyton" with "Back" struck out, and "Flip" written over it.

In its first week of release, the album outsold the Beatles, the Stones and Presley—and every track, except one, was banned from broadcast by radio stations across the country.

We were a hit.

THIRTEEN

THE GREAT BRITISH movie director, Michael Powell came to town to film *They're a Weird Mob*. I'd admired his movies for as long as I could remember—and that was since my mother took me to a matinee of *Stairway to Heaven* when I was eight.

Occasionally, my mother traveled to The Valley in Brisbane to shop, then take in a movie before returning to the wilds of suburbia. Her movie-going habit was to arrive at any time in the middle of the screening, sit through to the end, then wait for the next session to find out what happened at the beginning of the movie.

Given my mother's movie-going habit, at eight years old, I had no idea what *any* movie I saw was about. So it was with *Stairway to Heaven*. We were shown to our seats while a massive fire raged on the screen. This emotionally wrenching scene led to a sequence of events which was totally incomprehensible to me, then, THE END, and the house lights came up. We continued to sit. The lights went down. A newsreel, a cartoon, a preview of a coming attraction, then the title, *Stairway to Heaven*. Again a totally incomprehensible series of scenes, until—the fire! We'd seen that earlier! Was it a similar fire to the one we saw a couple of hours before? The same? Perhaps if we waited, some sense would emerge from what followed this fire.

But my mother got up and we left the theatre.

Utterly mystified, I begged for enlightenment on the tram home. My mother offered little beyond: "David Niven keeps dying and going to heaven but comes back in the end."

I've seen the movie countless times since. When viewed from beginning to end, the plot is not only comprehensible, it's a treasure of a movie directed brilliantly by Powell. But for my mother, any old place in the plot was fine as long as she could sit and remove her shoes. Movie-going to her was nothing more than a rest for tired feet and chewing gum for the eyes.

When my agents asked if I'd be interested in playing a small role in *Weird Mob*, I agreed at once. Graham Kennedy and I were given guest star billing.

I played the receptionist at the King's Cross Hotel where immigrant Nino, played by Italian star Walter Chiari, books in on his arrival in Sydney. I worked only one day on the movie, but apart from the pleasure of being directed by this giant of British cinema, I had the educational treat of *watching* him direct.

The movie was an enormous success in Australia. I got to know one of the cast, a relative newcomer to the business, a young and extremely pretty Jeanie Drynan. All these years later, Jeanie and her husband, director Antony Bowman are close friends.

~

One day, as my cab pulled up at the 7 studios, a rather portly, housewifely woman approached.

"Hello! You don't remember me, do you?"

I didn't.

"Margaret," she explained in a melodic contralto. Her flowered dress was that of a comfortably-off suburban matron, the red hair conservatively styled under a pretty hat, and the handbag hung carelessly over a wrist.

"I'm doing a little work at Seven," she said, "so I'll see you around."

Her high heels clacked on the concrete driveway as she headed for her car.

I went into the foyer and found Terry Pritchard waiting for me. "You know who that was?" I shook my head. "Reg," he said solemnly.

My jaw dropped as I tried to correlate this vision of feminine gentility with big, burly 2SM Reg, he of the mussed red hair and dangling cigarette.

Many months went by and I was obliged to record a voice over at 2SM. There, behind the glass, cigarette stuck to his lower lip, was Reg—the Reg of old, the Reg of the untidy red hair, sloppy T shirt, and monosyllabic delivery.

I asked no questions.

Terry explained later that he got sick of being Margaret and went back to being Reg.

I dearly hoped surgery hadn't been employed in adopting either persona.

~

After Michael Plant's death, desperate for a guiding hand, Gordon suggested we import the famed revue writer Peter Myers. In London, his succession of "Sweet and Low" revues were popular in the '50s, but when Peter took the reins, the sharp satire of the show declined in favor of Peter's milder and rather old-fashioned style of humor. Funny still, but with little satirical comment or bite.

Nevertheless, one sketch of this period provoked a serious reaction from its source material.

We did a sketch outlining the rather nepotistic practices of the J. C. Williamson management. Gordon played Sir Frank Tait, Carol played Googie Withers, and I, with silver at my temples, played Googie's husband, John McCallum, now a manager of the Williamson empire. I have no memory of the content of the sketch, but it prompted a lawsuit for defamation from Williamson's. Thanks to the stash of lawyers employed by the channel for just such occasions, the suit was ultimately dismissed. But at the time that episode was broadcast, Googie was playing at the Theatre Royal in Sydney in *The First 400 Years*, in which she and Keith Michell performed excerpts from Shakespeare's plays. I took myself to a matinee, eager to see this presentation, and was not disappointed. They played with subtle charm in the comedies, great power in the dramatic plays, lighting every iamb with deep understanding.

After the performance, I was eager to go backstage and congratulate Googie, but the impending lawsuit caused me to hesitate. I decided to brave it—I'd make a quick congratulatory comment and flee.

At her dressing room door, she acknowledged my presence and gestured for me to wait as she chatted with other visitors. The visitors dismissed, she approached me and I braced myself for rebuke. Instead, she embraced me warmly, pulled me into the room and said, "Darling, in that sketch, you looked *so* like John! It was uncanny!"

We had a very pleasant visit and I was able to heap sincere praise on this extraordinary artist whose talent I'd admired since I was a teen.

~

Midway through 1965, Carol dropped out of the show to devote more time to her family. Miriam Karlin was brought from London to replace her.

Miriam was a towering figure in British theatre, also known for her starring role on TV in *The Rag Trade*. A certain strength was regained, but from late '65 the show began a slow but steady decline from breaking new ground, to going over old. Miriam was a powerhouse of comedy invention; she was unafraid to venture into new territory, and shone new light on some of the older Peter Myers sketches. She became a good friend, was supportive during the decade I lived in London, and was usually the first phone call I made on every trip to London thereafter.

Having said that I resisted fits of the giggles on stage, a couple of instances of breaking up on the Bramston Show are worth noting—both were due to Gordon's improvising.

A male fashion show sketch featured James Kenny, Gordon and me as the models and Miriam as the posh mistress of ceremonies. One item featured a "His 'n' His" outfit for "friends" modeled by James and me. We made it obvious, largely from Kenny's pained expression that I'd just broken up with him. The finale had we three "models" on stage as Miriam announced, "All our fashions are truly arresting, and since wearing them, all of our models have been arrested." Fine. Until Gordon decided to flirt with Jim Kenny and in a tight closeup, gave him an unrehearsed lascivious wink. Jimmy and I lost it and couldn't contain the laughter. Miriam tried to restore order with a censorious ad lib, "Naughty boys!" But we were goners.

The other was in the "Sportlight" segment in which I interviewed Gordon as Jack Frost, spokesperson for winter games. We'd rehearsed in full makeup for the cameras, but for the recording, Gordon added a little item of makeup he'd deliberately neglected to tell me about—a large icicle stuck onto the end of his nose. It's the one time on the show I surrendered my usual deadpan, and literally doubled over with laughter.

~

1965 was the year that morals clause hit me hardest, not for any specific event, merely for the sword it dangled over my head.

And here we get back to sex.

The clause gained alarming significance when I realized I had a substantial female following. I had a predominantly female fan club. The press began to label me "eligible bachelor." This was encouraged by Channel 7 for its indisputable addition to the popularity of the show.

While we were rapidly upending Victorian views and morals, one aspect of the Australian sensibility did not change, and that was the legal view of homosexuality. Also, this was not yet the age when movie and television stars could be honest about their sexuality without repercussions.

There were occasional, though very few, cautious no-strings hookups during this period of public notoriety, but for the first time in my life, they left me feeling shame, guilt, and no small measure of fear.

Noeline and I had a close working relationship and a deeply established friendship, and the press chose to misconstrue this as a romance. We made the cover of TV Week with banner headlines such as: IN LOVE? accompanied by our pictures. Every article about our comedy album hinted at a deeper relationship. While we never acknowledged romantic involvement, we neither confirmed nor denied it. It became a major source of embarrassment for both of us, and one we felt keenly when a young female reporter was sent to interview us about our comedy LPs.

The girl arrived at Noeline's flat with a photographer. She told us she'd been sent specifically to get a picture of me popping the question to Noel, and the front page of that afternoon's Sun was being held to feature the picture.

To say we were gobsmacked is a nice way of saying we were gobsmacked. We declined. The reporter burst into tears and claimed her job was on the line; if she failed to get this story, she'd be fired. She offered us the engagement ring from her own finger for the picture.

Noeline and I repaired to another room to discuss the issue. Denial by omission was one thing, an outright lie was another. Noeline, ever the voice of reason, questioned the girl's ploy and doubted her job was in jeopardy. We returned and told her "forget it." The tears dried instantly, we did an interview about the album, the photographer got his picture, and we were relegated to page three.

The overwhelming popularity of the show caused me to move from my cozy flat in Springfield Avenue at the Cross, to a house in Woollahra, less accessible to the public. I missed only one acquaintance at the King's Cross address: a high class call girl who lived on the ground floor. Her door was often open as I left for rehearsals in the morning and she'd call a cheery greeting and we'd chat as I waited for my cab. She admitted to cancelling clients on Wednesday nights so she could watch the show. "I wouldn't be surprised to see myself pop up in a sketch," she said with a broad laugh.

In between residences, I moved temporarily into Gordon's terrace house in Paddington. He'd just bought a house at Palm Beach and spent most of his time there, so I had the Paddington house—and the clocks—to myself. Gordon, for whatever Freudian glitch in his childhood, was obsessed with time and punctuality. The former manifested itself in his collection of antique clocks, all of which chimed several seconds, sometimes several minutes apart. Just as I got over the jangling shock of the hour, all the other clocks would follow suit at various intervals.

Apropos Gordon's passion for punctuality, while I'd always been a hardy professional about rehearsals and performances, one morning, for legitimate reasons, I was an hour late for a Bramston rehearsal. There were no cell phones back then, so no way to explain my problem en route. When I dashed in, apologies at the ready, Gordon pounced. He gave me a stern lecture on *never* being late for rehearsal, respect for one's colleagues, and the inconvenience to cast and crew. The tirade left an indelible mark on me. To this day, I'm never less than half an hour early for rehearsals, and not less than an hour early for performance, and if I'm invited to dinner at 7:30, I'm at my host's door no later than 7:28, my finger poised above the doorbell until the big hand reaches half past.

The downside of traveling by cab during this period was that every cab driver had seen the show, all were fans, and all were convinced that their jokes were funnier than any we were doing. Consequently, I often endured the trip from the Eastern suburbs to Eastwood battered with variations on, "Did you hear the one about the…?"

I took driving lessons.

In my teens, I desperately wanted a motorcycle. Guess who nixed that one. So, with those dreams a thing of my restrictive past, and with more money than I actually had, I bought a fully imported Renault sportscar, a Caravelle. The officer who conducted my driving test was a fan of the show, and passed me on that basis alone, not, heaven knows, due to my driving skills.

I insisted on collecting Noeline from her apartment and driving her the fourteen miles to rehearsal every day. Less from wisdom than from downright terror, Noel chose to wedge herself into the token back seat of the tiny car, rather than sit up front with me.

One afternoon, driving back to the city, I came to an intersection. The light turned to red. Suddenly confused as to which pedal to push, I yelled in a panic, "Brake! Clutch! Accelerator!"

From the back seat came an equally panicked, "Rosary Beads!"

~

Festival asked us to record another album. Noel worked nights at the Music Hall, I worked days rehearsing, so we spent our only mutually free time, an entire night, midnight to dawn in the studio recording the tracks. It made a good story for Pix Magazine that during this session, after I'd demanded the tenth take of a sketch, Noeline yelled, "I hate you!" several times. It wouldn't be the last time I'd try her patience when we worked together, but in no way did it lessen the sheer enjoyment we always had as a double act.

After *How The West* closed, Noel wanted to try her wings in London and I saw her off at the airport. We were besieged by press, most of whom wanted to know how I felt about Bishop Muldoon's announcement that he was selling his Ampol shares due to the immorality of the Bramston Show. With the management's warnings about dealing with the press in mind, I resisted comment for as long as I could, and finally said a flippant, "I'm surprised a bishop has shares. I thought they were more concerned with heavenly things."

Next morning as I drove to rehearsal, I passed a newsstand and noted the banner for the Mirror. In stark black letters, it announced:

TV STAR ATTACKS BISHOP.

I thought, *Great. Someone's had a go at the silly old bugger.* When I arrived at rehearsal, the producer showed me a copy of the Mirror. The "someone" was me. The front page article was light on substance, but accompanied by two enormous photos, one of Muldoon with a beatific smile, and one of me looking like an axe murderer. Ever since, I've approached press interviews with caution.

~

At this time, I met one of my idols and we became friends.

Vincent Price, well known for his horror movies, was one of the wittiest people I've ever known. He came to Australia in 1965 to record the voice over narration for a documentary series about the Australian penal colony. We met at a press conference at the Southern Cross, and I admitted that after seeing him in *House of Wax,* I wanted to be him when I grew up. He laughed heartily and invited me to dinner. We dined at my favorite restaurant at the time, the Four Canoes in King's Cross. It was an evening to remember, not only to get to know this celebrated movie star, but we both stifled laughs at the reaction of the other diners who, as one, were quite silent as they watched us both eat.

This chance meeting resulted in a friendship that spanned decades, in Los Angeles, New York, London and back in Australia when his wife Coral Browne accompanied him during the tour of his one-man play about Oscar Wilde.

FOURTEEN

GORDON LEFT THE show at the end of 1965 and went on to star in the popular sitcom, *My Name's McGooley, What's Yours?*

At Peter Myers' suggestion, the management imported a new "star" from London—the very practice we'd condemned in the founding premise of the Bramston show.

Ronnie Stevens was a minor figure in London revue and while he kept the show afloat for most of a year, he not only favored the dated material Peter Myers contributed, he was, quite frankly, an arsehole. The show lost its bite and continued a steady decline.

Noeline returned from London and joined the show as a regular. The cast also grew with the addition of the sparklingly talented Hazel Phillips, and Ronnie Frazer. June Salter and I were the only two original cast members.

June had become a close friend. Her marriage to actor John Meillon was going through a rough patch, so on many Wednesday nights she'd come to my flat after rehearsal to watch the show. We'd eat takeout—my cooking skills in those days were nil. We'd diss the new material, commiserate about our private lives, and bolster each other's contempt of Ronnie Stevens.

I should explain the reasons for our utter dislike of Stevens. June and I worked well together. In one sketch we'd devised complex comedy business. We rehearsed this carefully and did it at the final camera rehearsal before we taped. Everyone thought it valid and funny, particularly Stevens.

That evening, as we taped the show before a live audience, Ronnie Stevens preceded our sketch with one of his own—and performed our comic business, move for move. This left us with nowhere to go in our sketch. If we did the business, it would look as if we'd stolen it from Stevens; if we didn't, we'd have egg on our collective face. We were obliged to settle for egg.

At no time thereafter, ever, did we rehearse in the presence of Stevens and generally avoided him until his contract was up and he returned to England.

~

Good friends were not only a joy during this period, they were essential. Personalities who peopled the popular shows of the day often got to know each other and of these, several became valued friends.

Noeline and I remained close confidants, but there were others who were warm and supportive and understood the difficulty I had maintaining a public persona while burying the private. One such was the ultra-chic Dita Cobb, panelist on 7's *Beauty and the Beast*, newspaper columnist and an extremely witty woman. In her memoir, she referred to me as "one of the great loves of her life." I read this only after her death and was flattered and moved.

Another was Stuart Wagstaff, eponymous Beast of that show. Imported to take over the lead in the stage production of *My Fair Lady*, Stuart loved Australia and remained to become one of the most loved and respected actors and TV hosts. He became one of my closest friends in the world, and remained so until his death.

And glamorous Denise McLaglen, niece of famed Hollywood character actor Victor McLaglen, was a regular on Don Lane's *Tonight Show*. She had replaced Faith Dane as Mazeppa in *Gypsy* on Broadway, came to Australia, liked it, and stayed. We occasionally met up after our respective TV shows at the 729 club. One night we went somewhat berserk at the poker machines. On discovering we'd spent all our money—yes all—we had to borrow a handful of silver to pay the Harbor Bridge toll. I've never so much as glanced at a poker machine since.

And this is a good place for an entirely irrelevant anecdote concerning Denise's uncle. I relayed it to Denise and she thought it so funny, she asked me to repeat it so she could write it down, word for word.

~

In 1936, Mae West was filming *Klondike Annie*. Victor McLaglen was in the movie.

Mae had given a small part in the movie, one line only, to an ex-lover from New York. He was no actor, but down on his luck, so was grateful for the pay. He played an old sea hand and was to burst into the mission and announce to Mae, "There's a boatload of guns in the harbor!"

McLaglen was known for his practical jokes. He took the chap aside and gave him lessons in diction for his one line. "Consonants!" McLaglen insisted. "We must hear consonants!"

The man was schooled for hours by McLaglen until they called him to the set.

Take one.

The door burst open, and the old sea hand rushed in and, taking care over the consonants, announced, "There's a boattloatt of cuntts in the harbor!"

Before the director could shout, "Cut," Mae ad libbed, "Well bring 'em ashore honey. We'll open a sportin' house and you can be the piano player."

~

By mid-1966 the Bramston shows seemed to drag for the first time since we began. I missed Gordon's involvement greatly. Professionally, he was an object lesson in bravery—he'd do literally anything to bring a character to life, no matter how outrageous. He was the fuel that ignited the show.

By the end of the year, the outrageous *Mavis* had become a run-of-the mill variety show. It would endure for two more years with larger casts and milder sketches, and then died a natural death.

At the end of'66, I decided to quit. I hoped Channel 7 might develop a sitcom for me as they did for Gordon. Instead, 7 had the rights to a Jon Cleary novel, *You Can't See Round Corners* which concerned a young Vietnam war deserter and his girlfriend. They asked me to play the lead as a teenage conscript from the western suburbs of Sydney. I declined on the grounds that I'd be laughed off the screen as both a teenager and a suburban lout. They persisted, making the offer more attractive with each meeting. I said a final "no" but agreed to help them with casting. They tested many young actresses for the girl; none seemed right.

A few months earlier, I'd been to Brisbane to open a new theatre. The show I saw was the musical *Calamity Jane* and its lead was an eighteen year old of exceptional talent, Rowena Wallace.

Casting for *Corners* reached an impasse, I urged the producers to test this unknown actress from Brisbane. They were reluctant, but I offered to do the test with her. They flew her to Sydney on a Saturday afternoon, we did a scene together and they offered her the role on the spot. The boy's role went to a young Ken Shorter.

That left me with an empty calendar for 1967. But not for long.

Stuart Wagstaff was playing in a revue at Frank Strain's Sesame Night Club and was eager for a break. He asked if I'd like to take over his role for a few weeks. I did, and a few weeks turned into full houses for almost a year. One press review observed that I was obviously enjoying my escape from TV and a return to live theatre. I was indeed.

At the same time, I was approached by producer Bill Harmon to do my own TV series in Melbourne, a half hour a day, five days a week. It would comprise sketches, songs, interviews, and would be called *The Barry Creyton Show.*

FIFTEEN

PRODUCER BILL HARMON, an American, bore a frightening resemblance to movie heavy George Raft. At every meeting, I expected him to pull a gun on me. The antithesis was true. He was a forward-looking, enterprising man, of gentle mien. He was also extremely absent-minded. At one meeting, addressing the production team, he said, "I have great hopes for *The Barry Creyton Show*, and now that we have a talent like…" He gestured in my direction, clearly having forgotten my name. Someone piped up, "Barry Creyton."

"Oh yeah," Bill agreed.

The producer and director became valued friends and remained so long after the show died a natural death. Bob Huber, producer, began his career with such shows as *The Twilight Zone* in Hollywood before moving to Australia; Dick Gray, director, was the brother of the great Broadway star, Dolores Gray.

I had The Sesame Club to consider and offered to resign. Frank Strain was reluctant to let me go and offered a generous increase in salary to keep me. Eventually, it was decided I would play Tuesday through Saturday nights at the Sesame, then fly to Melbourne Sundays, outline the week's show, rehearse the musical numbers and peruse the guest lists. Mondays, I'd record the five half hour shows, back-to-back, at the Fitzroy Teletheatre; then after a production meeting Tuesdays, I'd fly back to Sydney, and go straight from the airport to the Sesame for the Tuesday night show.

This I did for most of 1967.

And lived to tell about it.

I was assigned two writers for my show—two very good writers, I add, but after I'd spent two years on Bramston with a minimum of twelve writers per show, the strain on my guys to come up with scintillating material every week was considerable.

I was blessed with the splendid musical director, Ivan Hutchison, and a good choreographer who despaired of my ever getting a routine right—fallout from those dance lessons my mother refused to allow me to take.

Bob Huber juggled names of regulars for the show until we narrowed the field to an actress recently off a US soap, Melbourne favourite Terry Norris, and a transplanted American actress who would become a cherished friend, and whom I'd later direct, Betty Bobbitt.

The guest list was always interesting—prominent international singers and actors, chefs, politicians, sports figures; my friend, singer Lana Cantrell, on a triumphant return to Australia, broke her contract with Channel 9 to sing on my show, international model Donyale Luna flaunted her feline grace in a long interview, June Bronhill and her husband Richard Finney discussed their dispute with Opera Australia. I'd usually do a solo number chosen by Ivan who happily plundered the songbooks of Gershwin, Berlin and Rodgers and Hart, and if there was a singing guest, I'd do a duet with them.

Denise McLaglan performed her Mazeppa number from *Gypsy*, "You Gotta Get a Gimmick", in tandem with two glamorous dancers from the Melbourne Lido. To Denise, later in that show, I sang, "You're the Woman for the Man Who Has Everything", which gained further relevance in that Denise was 6 feet tall, and when she stood on an out-of-sight box, I was singing to her ample breasts. That episode drew outraged protests from suburban matrons, I'm happy to say.

Many of the guest singers were local. A sister act appeared on the show and at the conference the next day, Bob Huber asked if I wanted to book the sisters for another show. I shook my head. "Nah, I don't think they were so great."

They were Olivia Newton-John and her sister Rona.

So shoot me.

Knowing I was often weary from the constant weekly commute, and the strain of putting on a happy face, Dick would occasionally plan a prank to keep me on my toes. I'd once told him over coffee of the hilarity I derived from the concept of girls' marching bands. So, as I opened the show one day with a few gags and the promise of guests to come, a band struck up backstage, the entire set parted, and a merry group of twenty uniformed schoolgirls marched in playing all manner of brass.

I fell to a sitting position on the stage in uncontrollable laughter.

On another occasion, mid opening monologue, a total stranger walked onto the stage with a large box. "Special delivery," he said, "sign here." I signed, mystified, and opened the box. A large python emerged hissing happily and proceeded to wrap itself around me.

And yet another. A cooking session was planned for a major Melbourne chef to instruct me on the cooking of a soufflé. I stood by him as he deployed the ingredients. When he came to adding the flour, he managed to spill an entire bowl of it onto my beautifully tailored suit. After a profound apology, and much wiping with a towel—which made it worse—he broke an egg which also found its way onto my suit. Then another. And yes, I was helpless with laughter.

I sang "Autumn Leaves" while leaves fell around me, eventually burying me. The leaves had been gathered from a local park and no one bothered to check them before implementing them as props. They were infested with worms and bugs many of which bit me during my impassioned rendition.

On another occasion, as I sang "Smoke Gets in Your Eyes", smoke crept onto the set, eventually fogging me out completely and members of the Melbourne Fire Brigade rushed in to put out the supposed fire as I sang gloriously on.

My writers' struggle to produce new material every week provided me with a few memorable lines. At the end of every episode, I delivered a thought for the day. One of these was cut by the censors; I'm happy to repeat it now and PC be damned:

Thought for the day: "Gynecologists get paid for doing what other people get slapped for."

~

Dick was married during the run and his sister Dolores traveled from Los Angeles to attend the wedding. I was an immense fan of hers, having seen all her movies, and reveled in that extraordinary voice on so many Broadway musical albums, so I was delighted to meet her and her husband Andrew Crevolin at Melbourne airport when they arrived.

The *Barry Creyton Show* was modestly successful, eventually finding its audience, but not soon enough to please the general manger of HSV who despaired loudly, bitterly and often over the early ratings.

When the ratings eventually rose, the normally mild-mannered Bob Huber went to the GM's office and said proudly, "We've upped our ratings, now up yours."

By November 1967, the show, and I, were exhausted, but all of us involved had become close during the preceding months, none more than the camera and sound crew. The shows began recording early Monday mornings, and after three were taped, we'd break for dinner. I often took the whole crew to a nearby restaurant and treated them to fortification for the remaining two shows to be recorded that evening.

On the final show, I sang an emotional, "Don't Like Goodbyes," and a tearful Betty Bobbitt insisted on holding the cue cards for me.

I left the Sesame in Sydney having played to full houses for many months, and contemplated a break, my first real break for six years.

Dolores Gray offered me her house in Beverly Hills for as long as I wanted to stay. She lived year round on the ranch she and her husband built in San Dimas, thirty miles east of LA, and used the Beverly Hills house only occasionally. I gladly accepted and flew to LA in late November of 1967.

SIXTEEN

DOLORES GRAY'S HOUSE was tucked way, just off the top of Benedict Canyon, Beverly Hills, just up the street where, less than a year later, the Manson gang murdered Sharon Tate. I shudder now to recall that I never locked either the driveway gate, nor the door of the house.

The Channel 7 bigwigs had given me an introduction to an executive at Universal Studios, Gil Rodin, and he was delighted to give me a personal tour. I marvelled at the organization of a big Hollywood studio, an entity which was soon to become history as the studio system died. Gil also took me to lunch at the famous Chasen's restaurant, chosen eatery of the golden age stars, and a shrine to W. C. Fields.

One of Dick Gray's friends invited me to dinner and I experienced, for the first time, the Hollywood social schedule: First, you drive many miles to the host's house for cocktails, then you drive as many miles again to the restaurant, then you drive all those miles back to the host's house to collect your car, then the miles to get home. It's a trek I've become used to in the thirty years I've lived in LA.

I spent weekends at the ranch with Dolores and the endearingly bucolic Andrew, who kept insisting that I had to find me a beautiful girl and get married. Dolores, with a long life in theatre behind her, allowed Andrew these exhortations then turned to me and rolled her eyes. Her nickname for me in those days was "Skinny." Right. Rub it in.

For someone who'd had a spectacular career in both the US and London where, at nineteen, she was the first Annie in *Annie Get Your Gun*, then in many MGM movies, she was earthy, larger than life, but with a glorious sense of humor. At this time, she had no need to work, but like any actor, if work is even hinted, the need suddenly manifests itself. A script arrived from her agent and she drove to the Benedict Canyon house and settled in the den to read it. It was a western, *Heaven With a Gun*. Her agent had tactlessly told her it was a toss-up between her and Greer Garson.

Dolores finished the script, tossed it aside, and said, "This one's for Greer."

As it happens Greer didn't like it either and the role went to Virginia Gregg.

~

And of course, I caught up with Vincent Price who drove me around LA, pointed out the sights, and gave me some history of the city. He was on his way to New York to star in a musical, a first for him, *Darling of the Day*.

In late December, with no firm plan in mind, I set out for New York. An old Brisbane friend was there on business at the time, and urged me to see the Big Apple, as did Lana Cantrell who was at the peak of her singing career at the time.

The American regular who'd appeared on my show generously gave me an introduction to an actor friend; this led to an invitation to stay at his Upper West Side apartment.

~

While being welcomed with a cocktail by the Actor, an extremely good looking Young Man called in and joined us. He was introduced as an "acquaintance," the intimation being that he was a passing acquaintance at that. I had no reason to believe otherwise as my Actor host did everything he could, beyond strutting around the apartment and spitting on the floor, to give the impression he was as straight as a quiver of arrows. But I sensed resentment in the Young Man at being described as a passing anything.

I took The Actor's swaggering display of manhood at face value and kept myself to myself. So when the Young Man made a pass during a sight-seeing tour of the city, I accepted gladly, and without compunction we began a short affair.

Meanwhile, my Actor host had been engaged to appear in a staged reading of a new play in Greenwich Village. He paced the apartment wondering if he'd made the right move, as the play was controversial and might ruin his career. The play was indeed controversial.

At his invitation, I attended the reading in Greenwich Village and was greatly impressed by writing and performances. So too were producers who mounted the play uptown where it ran for a year and a half. Considering the play's theme, a collection of bitter, bitchy gay men celebrating a birthday, this was no mean achievement in pre Stonewall New York where bars, theatres and clubs were raided regularly by vice police.

The play, of course, was Mart Crowley's revolutionary, *The Boys in the Band*.

My Actor host became aware of my affair with the Young Man, his "passing acquaintance", and his previously hospitable attitude became acid and contemptuous. The Young Man fessed up: he'd been in a relationship with the deeply closeted Actor and could no longer stand being a secret, a "back street lover."

Bludgeoned with too much information, I fled to a hotel.

Later, in London, I received a long letter from the Actor apologizing for his inhospitable behavior. No mention was made of the Young Man; he blamed his ill humor on the pressure of work. I thought it best not to reply. And I never saw him again, until…

Fast forward to early 2018.

I was at a dinner party in Los Angeles with well-known film actor James Karen and his wife. One of the guests was a colleague visiting from New York—the Actor at whose New York apartment I'd stayed forty-seven years before.

He gave absolutely no indication that we knew each other. Eventually, I said, "I'm sure we've met."

"Oh no!" he asserted vehemently.

"Are you sure?"

"Positive." Then, a total non-sequitur: he dragged out his wallet and removed a handful of pictures which he displayed for the host and hostess. "Have you seen these pictures of my wife and children?"

Okaaaay. I pressed him no further.

~

Back to 1968.

After a brief stay at the hotel, Lana invited me to stay at her apartment on the East Side. I happily attended many of her prestigious gigs, including a few performances on the Ed Sullivan Show and her opening for Sammy Davis Jr at the Copacabana. And one gig I will never forget.

Lana had an Afghan Hound called Christian. I often walked the dog in Central Park and it became apparent that this was not the brightest canine in the pack. One weekend, Lana was the star act at the Concord, a Jewish resort hotel in the Catskills and we decided to stay over after her show. Somehow, the hound broke out of the hotel room in the middle of the night and ran through the corridors. I chased after it yelling, "Christian! Christian!" little realizing what I was shouting, or where, until doors began to open and censorious Jewish glares were directed at me.

~

Dolores came to New York briefly and I was her date for a party at Joshua Logan's townhouse—a pretty starry do.

On the plus side of the five months I spent in New York, I saw Vincent and Patricia Routledge in the enjoyable, though not so successful *Darling of the Day*, Angela Lansbury in *Mame,* Brian Bedford in *Rosencrantz and Guildenstern are Dead*, and the glorious original cast of *Cabaret* which included Joel Grey, the unforgettable Lotte Lenya and a slight, attractive girl with whom I'd later work on stage in the UK—the original Sally Bowles, and to my mind the best of the long line of Sallys I've seen around the world, Jill Haworth.

After six enjoyable months swanning around New York with no real agenda, I set my sights on London and the pursuit of gainful employment. Weary of being perceived as a "personality" in my own country, I longed to be a working actor again.

SEVENTEEN

SEX HAPPENS TO be of considerable importance to chaps in their twenties, and after having spent the better part of my twenties in a virtually barren situation, my life under a microscope, it might seem that now was the time to break out and make up for lost time. But as I understood from my teenage reading of Freud, it doesn't always work that way.

The insecurities and fears of so many years of national exposure were still with me and would lead to a horrendous breaking point not too far down the line.

~

My first impression of London was not favorable.

I arrived late at night and slept on the sofa of a friend's flat in Notting Hill. Next morning, left to my own devices, I did the logical thing and turned on the TV. After the bright color sets I'd seen in the US, and the choice of so many channels, British TV screens looked like a twelve inch swatch of grey corduroy. And there were two channels. Two. The one I landed on was in a foreign language. I was told later it was Welsh. *Why, in the name of universal entertainment?*

I contacted Miriam Karlin and she introduced me to her agent. He managed to waive the usual preliminaries for Equity membership due to my track record, and I did my first TV gig, an interesting role in an episode of *The Expert,* a BBC series starring Marius Goring as a forensic pathologist. I played his trusty lab assistant.

Around this time, an acquaintance introduced me to the great actress Coral Browne and we dined in a Knightsbridge restaurant. Coral is now remembered largely for her film roles in such as *Auntie Mame* where she played Vera Charles, the moving *Dreamchild* about the aged Alice Hargreaves on whom *Alice in Wonderland* was based, and the stark drama of *The Killing of Sister George*. She was celebrated on both sides of the Atlantic for her performances in Shakespeare's plays as well as contemporary dramas and comedies; she was also celebrated for her extensive use of profanity. She dropped four letter words in much the same way the gentle rain droppeth from heaven—but more often.

She left her hometown of Melbourne when she was twenty-one and when I met her, hadn't returned for thirty-four years. On being told I was Australian, she greeted me with, "How are things in The Bush dear?"

~

I called Peter Myers who was casting a new musical he'd written with his long-time collaborator, composer Ronnie Cass. It was based on Aristophanes' *Lysistrata* and called *Liz*. Peter asked me to play the general of the Greek army.

The cast of subsidiary comic characters read like a Who's Who of British comedy movies—Danny Green of The *Lady Killers*, Bill Maynard of several of the *Carry On* series, Jerry Verno of the *St. Trinian's* movies, and the star was Ron Moody, who'd had a sensational success on stage as Fagin in *Oliver*, and won a Golden Globe and an Oscar nomination for the movie. The juveniles, Lysistrata and her boyfriend, were played by Sally Smith and Graham James.

The cast was some twenty strong and the production was designed by renowned cartoon ist and theater designer Osbert Lancaster. The augurs were promising.

I had the big number at the end of act one, "The War to End All Wars." As always, I made up in volume what I lacked in vibrato.

Given the terrific cast, delightful score and a witty book, it was expected we'd play briefly out of town, then move to the West End.

Not so fast.

We opened in Canterbury at the Marlowe, a theatre where travelling shows, either pre or post London, played short seasons. The audiences were greatly appreciative and Peter made frequent adjustments to the script, Ronnie to the score.

Babette and Tom Stephens were in London at the time and traveled to Canterbury, staying overnight to see the show. At supper afterwards, Babette was complimentary and pleased to see I'd adhered to her edicts about volume, clarity and consistency, but most of all, that I'd projected class. "You," she said with a satisfied smile, "were the only one of the comic characters who seemed as if he'd dressed down for the show. All the others looked as if they'd dressed up."

Next we played the New Theatre in Oxford, and there things began to unravel.

Peter had added dialogue whenever a new gag occurred to him, and the show was running just shy of three hours. Ronnie Cass, the voice of reason, begged Peter to make cuts. "People have busses to catch!"

Peter refused, and towards the end of the Oxford run, after a performance, he ventured into the orchestra pit for a post-mortem with Ronnie who, by now was at wit's end. The microphones had been left on, and the entire cast in their dressing rooms were hushed witness to the raging argument—Ronnie insisting on cuts, Peter refusing, Ronnie yelling he'd quit if changes weren't made, Peter sticking to his guns.

The money people came to see it, all three hours of it, and also asked for cuts. Peter refused, and *Liz* closed in Oxford never to see the lights of the West End.

~

By now, I'd spent a year abroad—six months in the US, six months in London, and the coffers were low. I had a call from Australia asking me to front a new TV series and, with the bank account a forethought, I accepted, assuring my London agent I'd be back in a couple of months.

It would be a year!

EIGHTEEN

THE SHOW WAS for Channel 7 Sydney, a topical weekly revue, as was Mavis, but of a much milder temperature. It was called *Hard Day's Week*. My old friend Donald MacDonald was in the cast and we made a fair, if unremarkable fist of things. During this show, I was approached by Perth entrepreneur Frank Baden-Powell to do my own show at one of his theatre restaurants. It was to be called, *An Evening With Barry Creyton*. A return to London with full pockets uppermost in my mind, I agreed.

If I'd thought the Sesame year was hard work, I wasn't quite prepared for what this year held in store. I flew the 3,000 miles to Perth to rehearse for a week, returned to Sydney to record the TV show, then back to Perth to continue rehearsing. Once the show opened, this commute became routine for several months—Perth Tuesday through Saturday, fly to Sydney Sundays, record the TV show Monday evenings, then back to Perth for the Tuesday performance.

A bright memory of that Perth gig was the moon landing. A lifelong science and science fiction junkie, I was glued to the TV, sleepless on the nights preceding July 16, when Neil Armstrong set foot on the moon.

The theatre restaurant show featured a bevy of bikini-clad chorines who flanked me and disguised the fact that I had at least three left feet. I did numbers, sketches and generally, a good time was had by all including the audiences. But—there had to be a but—I'd encumbered myself with one of the long line of disastrous relationships I was to have throughout my middle age.

In Melbourne for a TV appearance, I'd met an attractive young man, earthy, unsophisticated, and I clutched at him emotionally—the adult manifestation of my affectionless youth. He, like many to come, was a mistake; just how big a mistake was a year down the line.

I travelled him to Perth and got him a job at the bar of the theatre.

I'd been in Australia for most of a year, and a career into which I'd barely made inroads waited for me in London. I returned, and took this fellow with me.

~

It was late 1969, and I ran into Peter Myers at a National Film Theatre screening. Ever the optimist, and undaunted by the failure of *Liz*, he told me of a revue he was planning. I read the script and found some good material, enough to say yes. It dealt with the 1960s, the various changes in the world over that decade, along with "Swinging London", and the politics and the scandals of the time. It was called *Ten Years Hard.*

The cast was headed by renowned comedy songster, Michael Flanders, he of the best-selling Flanders and Swan albums, *At the Drop of a Hat*, and *At the Drop of Another Hat,* and the sellout theatre productions of the same names. Michael acted as narrator, introducing each year, putting his own spin on the subjects.

In the cast was Sally Smith, the ingenue from the ill-fated *Liz,* and a young newcomer, David Essex. David would go on to become a major star in popular music, writing and singing his own songs, many of them number one hits in Great Britain. He'd be awarded the OBE in 1999. In 1969, he was an exceptionally affable young man whose talent was obvious from the get-go.

The show was directed by Charles Ross who'd directed a 1960 revue called *Look Who's Here.* I had the album of this show and played it relentlessly in the Melbourne rooming house when I was 20. Berys Marsh and I listened to it so often, we could do most of the numbers. I was delighted to be working with the man who'd helmed that favorite of mine.

We played the Mayfair Theatre and the show was well received, albeit with some qualifications. The Evening Standard critic said, "This revue presents the best impersonation of Prince Charles, and the worst of David Frost."

I did both.

I told David Frost of this many years later and he offered to give me lessons.

The problem with *Ten Years Hard* was that it was meant to define a decade, and that demanded chronological order. In any revue, if a number misfires, it's replaced and the running order reshuffled for balance. This meant that if 1962 didn't work and was deleted, it couldn't be replaced with 1966, or vice versa. Consequently some inferior material had to be retained for the sake of the running order.

We had a respectable, but less than spectacular run.

~

When a throat infection plagued me, Miriam Karlin introduced me to her doctor, Patrick Woodcock. He was not only Miriam's doc, but also that of John Gielgud, Marlene Dietrich, Peter Shaffer, Tony Richardson, and towering above this galaxy of patients, Noel Coward. Sometimes the waiting room at his Pimlico surgery was starrier than a West End opening. Patrick became a close and supportive friend and wise advisor during the entire decade I spent in the UK, He saw me through good health and bad, and more than a few emotional ups and downs. He'd have his work cut out for him in 1970, where a cataclysmic down lay in wait for me.

Patrick had a passion for theatre, and a unique talent for getting like-minded people together. When he died in June, 2002, his obituary in the Observer summed it up best:

"Patrick was brilliant at mixing people of fame and achievement with younger and greener guests, and watching what would happen—he was a convener rather than an impresario. He admired the creative spark of his friends, and encouraged incipient talent to aspire high, while steadfastly refusing to be ambitious for himself. He was one of those rare and vital people who offer the young a chance to find excitement in social life, and who thereby exercise an influence which can never really be documented."

His constant companion was Gladys Calthrop, a wonderfully energetic woman who'd designed most of Coward's greatest hit plays. During my worst emotional downs, Patrick would add me as a third when he and Gladys went to the theatre.

He turned fifty in January 1970, and I was Miriam Karlin's date at the birthday party at his Pimlico house. We arrived at the same time as director Tony Richardson who'd just returned from directing the movie *Ned Kelly* in Australia. Miriam, a passionate Ozophile, greeted him with, "How lucky you are to have spent so much time in Australia!

Isn't it the greatest country in the world?"

Richardson replied, "I hated every minute of it!"

There followed an argument proportionate to Greek drama. As this increased in volume, Patrick came downstairs, grabbed my arm and said, "Come on up. There's someone who wants to meet you."

The "someone" was Noel Coward, recently Sir Noel. He sat at the far end of the living room, looking like a Buddah. I'd told Patrick of my admiration of his work and he'd relayed this to Coward. My awe at meeting this legend must have been apparent, but Coward put me at ease instantly and said, "Forgive me if I don't get up. Legs you know." He patted the sofa beside him. I sat. "Patrick tells me you've done some of my numbers. Which ones?"

I outlined the songs I'd done in cabaret performances, "Uncle Harry", "I Wonder What Happened to Him", "Bar on the Piccola Marina." We discussed mutual friends, and touched on the one play of his I'd done, *Nude With Violin*. He was eager to know if I'd enjoyed doing it. Was he kidding?

Throughout this brief and warm meeting in a crowded room, he gave the impression that I was the sole object of his attention. I said later, it was like meeting God, except of course, that Noel Coward had a better sense of construction.

~

Carol Raye, my other Bramston co-star, came to London and instantly put her entrepreneurial skills to work. She approached producer and playwright Ray Cooney with an idea for a revue featuring Australian material. He agreed and planned for us to open at the Palace Theatre in Westcliff; if the response was favorable, we'd transfer to the West End.

Carol and I led the billing; Australians Tom Oliver and Beatrice Aston were in the cast along with just one Brit, Neville Phillips.

Neville turned ninety-nine as of this writing, and remains a close friend. Johnny Whyte, past master of revue, was engaged to direct.

The show was called, *This, That and the Other*. As I remember, there was some good material and some indifferent. Of the good, I did a sketch as an outback Aussie at a bar relating his week on the sheep station. At regular intervals, I took a schooner of beer and drank it in one fell swoop. Each time, the barmaid filled it again, and again I drank the whole. This occurred about six times during the monologue. Of course it was a trick glass, but the audience reaction grew to gales of shocked laughter as I seemed to down gallons of beer during the sketch.

I also had the joy of singing a number David Sale had written for me in the Bramston Show, "Name Dropper." A complex lyric detailed lists of famous names I'd collected in order to impress peers, dropping the names of prominent figures in London, France and America. The final verses went:

> Travelled to Hyannisport
> Where the Kennedy's hold court
> Lunch with Jackie, Bob and Ted was very hearty.
> Henry Ford, the Rockefellers
> And that funny Peter Sellers
> Joined us with the Vanderbilts
> And they were all dressed up in kilts!
> Oh, what a party.
>
> So you see what fun I get
> Mixing with the famous set
> And to drop their names around is quite divine.
> But there's something that spoils the whole damn show:
> Nobody—ever drops mine.

Cooney ultimately decided against taking us to the West End, but Westcliff audiences had a good time and so did we.

And there, the good times ended.

NINETEEN

ON THE DOMESTIC front, things were disintegrating. Gordon returned to Australia, and the Melbournite and I took a basement flat in Fulham, ordered some furniture and settled in for the long haul.

To bolster the income, the Melbourne fellow took a job waiting tables at a Chelsea restaurant where, due to his attractive exterior, he was fawned on by—well, just about everyone. The result was that many nights, he arrived home several hours after the restaurant had closed.

Our relationship became acrimonious in the extreme and one night, erupted in violence. Somehow, the lies outstripped the infidelities, and when I called him on these, and indicated that the relationship was at an end, he attacked me physically, leaving me stunned and bloodied.

I left the flat and hailed a cab, which was reluctant to take me due to the state I was in, but ultimately dropped me at the Chelsea flat of my old friend, Terry Pritchard. He was now working in publicity at MGM's

London office, and once again, I relied heavily on his friendship and hospitality.

When, after three days, I'd not eaten and hardly emerged from his guest room, Terry realized there was something more going on than mere unhappiness. My depression deepened. At its lowest point, I felt I might not rise from it. There were days I lay in bed staring at the ceiling for hours, days when I didn't eat. When left alone in the flat, suicide occurred to me more than once. When he became aware of this, Terry demanded I see my doctor if he had to frogmarch me there personally.

I considered Patrick Woodcock a friend and didn't really want him to see me in this grim state, but from the moment he opened his door to me, he was warmly supportive and sat listening while I got it all off my chest.

He offered no pills—no antidepressants, he said these could be addictive and ultimately worsen my depression. But he did offer advice. The ill-advised relationship was merely the tip of a substantial iceberg, he told me. Years of public exposure, of virtually no private life, and the sheer weight of the workload over seven years, and now this destructive relationship—had all come down on me like the proverbial ton of bricks. He insisted that the way out of this would not be solved by drugs, but by supportive friends, exercise, and keeping a journal and writing about it which, to a degree, I did.

He assured me he was one of those supportive friends, and would always be available when I needed to talk. My talks with him averaged about one a month for a year. Always he offered good advice, even if I sometimes seemed unable to act on it.

Whenever I had a clear thought, which wasn't often, I'd reflect on my teen years, reading Freud and Jung, and I'd wonder what the hell happened to the supremely stable guy I thought I was then.

Three months passed. Terry, always upbeat and a constant stream of jokes and one-line gags, did his best to rally me. He held parties, took me to parties, played matchmaker, to no effect or interest on my part. Little dragged me out of the slump.

Aware that the Melbournite had moved out of the flat, on which I was still paying rent, I returned to find he'd stripped the place of furniture, for which I'd also paid. My few good friends suppled the essentials like somewhere to sit, and somewhere to sleep, and often came by, to cook, to talk, to try to elicit some positive reaction from me, with moderate success.

I had a phone call at this time. My mother called to tell me my father had died. I could do nothing but offer condolences. Given my state of mind, I was incapable of feeling any depth of emotion. Much later, I'd consider the life he'd led, the struggle to make his wife and children happy, to provide for us, with neither support nor gratitude from my mother, and I felt overwhelming sadness at losing him, more so at having kept such a distance from him for my entire adult life.

I lost more weight than I thought I could spare. I was chain smoking, but at least I hadn't hit the bottle; I know it's traditional in such tales of woe—after all, it's how Lilian Roth got started—so I'm not sure how I avoided alcoholism. Perhaps because I couldn't afford the booze.

Four months on, I ran out of money. My agent suggested auditions for various productions. I attended none. The prospect of standing on a stage reduced me to quivering nerves. It occurred to me, with neither shock nor surprise, that I might never act again. My agent lost interest in me, and I lost my agent.

I needed to pay the rent.

A hearty South African woman who lived in the flat above me was aware of my situation, having heard every blow of the fracas that prompted me to leave four months earlier. She introduced me to a temporary employment agent who, learning I could type, sent me for an interview at the London Hospital for Neurological Diseases; rather appropriate under the circumstances. They hired me at once, but feeling I was a little too grand for the typing pool, called me "Mister Creyton" and gave me an office of my own.

I typed up a storm for them—legal letters, forms, diagnostic charts.

It paid the rent, and I had a little to spare for luxuries which, curiously, ran to a few canvases and a stock of acrylic paints. Over the next few months, I set up an easel in the bare living room and painted, something I hadn't done since high school. Therapeutic, certainly—profitable, surprisingly. I sold several—a couple of large canvases to a visiting American who liked my pop-art-ish style.

A little more pocket money.

~

One bright spot occurred during this time. The temp agency needed someone with a theatrical background to take dictation from, and type personal letters for the great Michael Macliammoir.

I'd been devoted to his work since my teens when I saw his internationally proclaimed one-man show about the life of Oscar Wilde, *The Importance of Being Oscar*. I knew of his extraordinary background, his founding of the Gate Theatre, Dublin, his acting career on both sides of the Atlantic, his association with Orson Welles which led to his playing Iago to Welles's Othello in the film *Othello*, and I'd read the wry book he wrote about that experience, *Put Money in Thy Purse*.

I met Macliammoir and his partner Hilton Edwards for lunch at a restaurant in the West End. As I'd been warned, Macliammoir was wearing full stage makeup and looked a little like a Californian sunset. But beneath the maquillage was a witty man who was a treasury of anecdotes. I joined them later at their hotel and recorded the letters on a portable cassette recorder, then armed with a sheaf of his personal letter paper, returned to my tiny flat and typed.

I heard that he was happy with the result, but never saw him again.

TWENTY

THE MONTHS DRAGGED on and somehow I made ends meet. Patrick, ever supportive, had me to dinner at his house with celebrated playwright Peter Shaffer the only other guest. In my depleted mental condition, I had little to contribute to the conversation.

One evening, Patrick called and asked what I was up to. The answer was, of course, nothing. He insisted I take a cab, for which he'd pay, to an address in Belgravia. True to form, he was eager to put two like minds together.

The house was six extravagant-looking floors in Belgrave Square, so intimidating I almost turned the cab around and headed for home. But Patrick collected me, and took me into the grand house to meet James Knapp-Fisher, somewhere in his 60s, retired CEO of publishers Sidgwick and Jackson. The interest we had in common—music, particularly show tunes.

Patrick knew my love of musical comedy and my encyclopedic

knowledge of theatre songs dating back to the turn of the twentieth century, and Jim Knapp-Fisher's den sported an entire wall of 78 recordings of every musical show that had ever been produced on the British stage.

Patrick sat back with a satisfied smile as he watched us exchanging enthusiastic likes and dislikes, songs and singers—records were dragged out of paper sleeves and put onto a player. We listened, we dissected, Jim told of meeting luminaries like Ethel Levy, Gertrude Lawrence, Bea Lillie, Ivor Novello. At the end of the evening, Patrick packed me into a cab, happy that he'd taken my mind off things for a couple of hours.

The end result was a long acquaintance with Jim whose every meeting cheered me. He took me to lunch often at the historic Garrick Club.

The Garrick was founded in 1831, and named for David Garrick, whose acting and management of the Theatre Royal Drury Lane had come to represent a golden age of British drama. Having catered to such as Irving, Kean, Olivier, Coward, and writers Dickens, Wells, Barrie and Milne, the club's membership is restricted to this day, and applications must be approved by a board before one can set foot inside its hallowed doors as a member.

At the top of the grand staircase, its walls covered with grand paintings of famed theatrical figures, the bar is devoted to Noel Coward.

And that triggers an anecdote which still makes me smile.

On my first visit, after a couple of pre luncheon drinks, I asked directions to the gents. When I returned, Jim asked what I thought of the plumbing, specifically the urinals. I said they looked remarkably stark and modern in a bathroom that belonged in a more decorative era.

He told of one of the last visits Coward had made to the club in the late 1960s.The gents had just been entirely refitted, the old head-to-foot marble urinals, replaced with the knee-high porcelain ones of the hit-and-miss variety. This modernization had cost the membership considerably in raised fees.

Coward visited them, returned to the bar and was asked by a guest what he thought of the new urinals.

"Expensive, tasteless, and they make one's private parts look so shabby."

This story caused me to consider construction—of plays, sketches and jokes in general. The best, the most effective, come in three parts.

Even if a play of today is in two acts, or just one, the structure, if sound, is still in three parts: setup, establishment or conflict, and resolution. That doesn't necessarily mean beginning, middle and end. French movies in particular have a habit of ending mid conflict, leaving the resolution to the imagination of the viewer. But even that, in a way, is the third part of their construction.

And of course, Coward's best, often flippant remarks came in three parts: 1, "expensive," 2, "tasteless," 3, the tagline.

Comedy patter songs always structure the payoff line in three parts. Take Coward's "Bar on the Piccola Marina" which concerns a widow who, with family in tow, visits Capri and discovers Italian men in a big way. The tag goes:

> Her family in floods of tears cried "Leave these men mama!"
> She said, "They're just high spirited like all Italians are—
> And most of them have a great deal more to offer than papa…"
> In a bar on the Piccola Marina."

Similarly, the best revue sketches and even the broadest jokes are best when constructed in three parts.

Take one of the oldest jokes I know:

OLD COLONEL AT HIS CLUB: I was hunting tigers in the wilds of India. I came to a clearing and there, a few yards away, was a monstrous Bengal beast, ready to spring. I raised my trusty rifle and pulled the trigger. It jammed! The tiger leapt at me with a roar. RROOWWGHH! I shit myself.

YOUNG MAN: Under the circumstances, that's understandable.

COLONEL: No, no, I mean just now when I went RROOWWGHH!

Setup: Colonel illustrating the roar
Establishment: Young Man validating the illustration
Payoff: Colonel revealing the outcome of the roar.

And while bludgeoning the reader with my observations on wit, praise must be afforded the wisecrack. It's a particularly American art form and like all wit, is social criticism. It needs no three part construction to make its point. It depends on a knowledge of its roots for effect, and it comments on those roots.

Some of the best were written and delivered by Mae West. In *I'm No Angel*, she asks a potential lover if he's married.

MAN: I've been married five times.

MAE: Five times! Wedding bells must sound like an alarm clock to ya"

And in court, the JUDGE asks: Are you trying to show your contempt for this court?

MAE: No your honor, I'm tryin' to hide it.

Then there's the one-liner. Billy Wilder, who spoke no English before moving to the USA, wrote some of the best one-line jokes, perhaps because he came to the language as a stranger and saw objectively how funny the language was by its very nature.

In *Some Like it Hot*:

> MARILYN: Real diamonds! They must be worth their weight in gold!

Coward was all but incapable of uttering an observation of any kind without injecting wit. On being told a less-than-respected acquaintance had blown his brains out, he replied, "He must've been a very good shot."

These are as funny today as when they were first delivered because the subject on which they're based is pretty much always accessible.

There's no "new" comedy, there's just comedy. And of all the performing and written arts, it's the toughest to realize. An anecdote is attributed to the internationally celebrated British actor Edmund Kean. On his deathbed in 1833, a colleague observed on his debilitated state, "This must be very hard."

"No," Kean replied, "dying is easy. Comedy is hard."

Kean said a mouthful.

Good comedy, as actor, writer or standup, is the hardest of all forms of artistic expression.

Special mention must be given to graffiti. We all know that at its most banal, it sucks. Pardon the allusion. But at its best, graffiti is social comment and therefore, wit.

> The old favorite:
> "Jesus saves.
> Moses invests."

On a Melbourne wall in the '50s, some high-minded soul wrote:

> "What would you do if Christ came to Carlton tomorrow?"
> Under it was the reply:
> "Move Ron Barassi to centre forward."

In the old days, one's equipment was measured in inches—centimetres don't have the same salacious impact somehow.

> On a Sydney public toilet wall:
> "I have 8 inches. I'll be here - 4th of January 1955."
> Under it:
> "Waited but you did not turn up – 4th of January 1957."

~

And while I'm on a soapbox…

In the late '50s, the "kitchen sink" drama was born at the Royal Court Theatre in London, and the "well made" play pronounced dead; the critics hailed a new era in theatre. Actually, it was not the sink which revolutionized *Look Back in Anger,* it was the glaring presence on stage of an ironing board which drew shocked outrage.

The play was considered an explosive departure from generations of lighter comedies and dramas. The new breed of writers wrote exclusively of angst, hatred, anger, rage and despair. This had never been done before? So, *Medea* is a jolly romp through ancient Greece, and *Long Day's Journey Into Night*, a comedic curtain-raiser.

But British angst was suddenly the fashion of the era.

Prolific British playwright Neil Bartlett said it best, tongue in cheek, in his play *Night After Night,* he stated: "*Look Back in Anger*… that's what I call a proper piece of theatre ladies and gentlemen. It's in black and white, lots of ironing, and absolutely no musical numbers."

Again, I contend that there's really no "new" theatre, there is just theatre. There's room always for plays to reflect life, to project hatred, anger, and all manner of social criticism. There's also room for a well-aimed custard pie.

For all the talk of revolution in the late '50s, in today's West End, or any day for the past fifty years, there's little evidence of the kitchen sink, yet there are regular revivals of the "well made" plays of Coward and Rattigan.

Go figure.

Okay. That's off my chest.

~

With time on my hands, and poverty a fact, I decided to examine the best constructed plays of yore.

I went to my local public library, free to residents of the area, and asked if they had any plays by Coward. After searching the basement, they found first editions of the entire collection of Play Parade, six volumes which contained all of Coward's work from 1920 to 1960. *First editions*! They'd been so long forgotten, they had to be dusted before I took them. Had I been in my right mind, I'd have stolen them.

Over a period of three weeks, I read every play back to back and discovered a great deal about construction of dialogue, of character and story.

I was a fan of Ray Cooney's farces, and those of Philip King, Vernon Sylvaine, Feydeau, and Pinero. An idea for such a farce occurred to me, and over a period of about a month, in my isolated little room at the Neurological hospital, I used the office typewriter and all the spare time I had to bash out a first draft. I stashed it on a shelf and forgot about it. It was called *Dear Sir or Madam*.

TWENTY-ONE

ALMOST A YEAR had passed, and thanks to the patient efforts of friends who put up with my downs, I began to think seriously about what the future held for an ex actor. Two close chums, Valerie Miles, ex Australian dancer resident in London, and Finbarr O'Regan, a humorous Irishman, were invaluable, healing company in those bleak days.

I was thirty-one. A year had passed since the depression took over my life, and while the dregs of it were still with me, I was in better mental shape thanks to my friends.

Val and Finbarr often dragged me to a small local pub in Fulham, The Fox and Pheasant—which we knew as The Fuckin' Peasant. After one of these cheery evenings, I returned home to a ringing phone. It was Australian Bill Redmond. He'd heard I was in town and asked if I was available to play a part in the national tour of *Abelard and Heloise,* which he was directing. The play had been an enormous hit in London starring Keith Michell and Diana Rigg. I thanked Bill kindly, and told him I was unwell and couldn't consider the offer.

After I disconnected, Val and Finbarr virtually fell on me, forcing me to call him back and accept. I did.

The night before the first rehearsal, I was a basket case of nerves and downright fear. I told Val I intended to call Bill first thing next morning and cancel. She stayed the night and, next morning, forced me into a cab at umbrella point. I went to my first rehearsal for more than a year.

~

I knew no one in the cast except the pretty actress I'd come to know socially in New York, Jill Haworth, the unforgettable Sally Bowles in *Cabaret* on Broadway. She was to play Heloise to Terence Alexander's Abelard. I played Bernard, a randy monk, and was asked to understudy Abelard. Looking back, even though I rehearsed weekly, I didn't come to grips with the lead character and prayed to the gods of theatre I'd never have to go on. They heard my prayer.

It was a pleasant surprise to know Jill was in the cast and we fell into a comfortable friendship, each allaying the other's nerves at the first reading.

One scene had me semi naked in a tower with a town whore. Given that I was now skinnier than ever, it took all the guts I could muster to remove my clothing at the dress rehearsal.

The tour was a great success. We played the major theatres in York, Manchester, Brighton, Glasgow, Newcastle, Edinburgh and Bournemouth to appreciative audiences.

Theatrical touring companies, either pre or post London are all but a thing of the past in the twenty-first century. I was fortunate to participate in a couple such during my decade in the UK. The routine was common to all tours—Monday through Saturday in one city, Sunday on the train to the next city armed with the Sunday newspapers. Sondheim said it best in *A Little Night Music*, where touring actress Desiree and her theatrical company sing:

> Unpack the luggage, la la la,
> Pack up the luggage, la la la,
> Hi ho the glamorous life!

The word "glamorous" gives the lyric a touch of irony, believe me.

The large *Abelard* cast were warm and friendly and in a few cases, starry. Norman Wooland, Viola Keats and Valentine Dyall had substantial film and theatre credits. Two husband and wife couples and a few singles played the various nuns and monks.

In most long running theatrical companies, factions form. In ours, the older actors tended to stick together, the two married couples kept to themselves while Jill, actor Mark Johnson and I formed a group of our own and explored each new date, sightseeing galleries, and city landmarks.

While the older cast chose to stay in hotels, our little trio decided we should experience the great British touring tradition of staying in "digs", rooming houses run by colorful landladies. These establishments ruled the touring circuit for most of a century; they, like touring companies, are history now.

For the most part, theatrical digs were an amusing experience—the landladies, some eccentric, some indifferent, some poking noses into one's private affairs, were the stuff of legend in the business. But the digs in Edinburgh was a cautionary lesson.

We arrived late on a Sunday, and were greeted at the door by a portly, middle-aged woman with an almost impenetrable Scots accent, beaming with good will and hospitality. She explained she'd only recently established her business of taking touring actors for a week apiece, and her glow of interest and curiosity was as comforting as the fine meals she prepared for us. She welcomed us to her kitchen, made tea for us. The following Sunday morning she bade us farewell holding back tears.

Cut to five years later. I was on a pre London tour with a new comedy and decided to stay at this dearly remembered house with its warm and welcoming landlady. Gone was the beaming welcome, the "make yourself at home", or "have a cuppa with me". It was more or less, "There's yer room, no noise after eleven."

Clearly, five years of actors had taken its toll.

In Leeds, the local company invited the entire Abelard cast to a special matinee of their current pantomime, *Cinderella*. As is the curious British custom, Prince Charming was played by a female, and the Ugly Sisters by two men.

Out entire cast arrived at the Palace of Varieties that afternoon, joyfully anticipating an entertaining matinee. The show was unbearably, abysmally bad.

We gathered afterwards in the foyer where a reception had been planned, and we waited for the cast to join us. No one said a word. We were all racking our brains trying to think of a non-specific compliment to disguise what we really thought. Finally Valentine Dyall broke the silence with his sepulchral baritone and said, "Pantomime is where sopranos go to die."

One other incident bears telling. In Bournemouth, the theatre was a new, well-appointed venue, part of a complex which included a cinema where Ken Russell's *The Devils* was showing. The Russell movie borders on horror in its depiction of a 17th Century priest accused of witchcraft; it covers demonic possession, self-mutilation, a naked

Oliver Reed wearing a crown of thorns as he seduces Mother Superior, played by Vanessa Redgrave, who utters strings of four-letter words and masturbates with a candle.

The green room at the theatre was generally populated by cast members in costume when not on stage. Such was the scene when, during our Saturday matinee, two office girls who'd just seen *The Devils* came accidentally into the green room while searching for the exit. They'd clearly been shaken by the movie and both were pale and trembling. When their eyes became accustomed to the gloom, the sight of a bunch of nuns and hooded monks sitting around proved too much. They both became hysterical, screaming in abject terror. The theatre manager escorted them gently from the premises.

Oh, and did I say I believed in good behavior in that temple, the theatre? No cracking up, no pranks... except on the final matinee where pranks are traditional. In the famous nude scene, Abelard and Heloise, stark naked, approach each other on a dimly lit stage, kneel and kiss. At this last matinee, as Jill approached from stage right, Mark Johnson and I were in the wings stage left, where she usually aimed her gaze to avoid looking directly at Terence Alexander's genitals. Knowing we had her full attention, we lowered our underwear, lifted our monk's habits, turned and mooned her.

Jill played the tender consummation of the legendary love affair stifling chortles.

More than just affording me gainful employment as an actor again, the tour built my confidence after a year of despairing limbo.

TWENTY-TWO

BACK IN LONDON, I had no place to live. I'd given up the basement flat and stored my few possessions, principally books, none of which the Melbourne chap had considered worth stealing.

I accepted the offer of cast member Mark Johnson to share a small, two bedroom maisonette on the edge of the City of London. A little later, when Mark relocated to Australia to join Bill Redmond in managing a theatre company, I had the small house to myself. My first act of redecoration was to drape living room and bedroom walls completely with blackout curtains—decorative, but their principal purpose was to block the twilight. They were drawn every day at sundown. This phobia of my youth remained with me for quite some time, exacerbated during the year of the breakdown.

The terraced house was one of six built atop a warehouse near Old Street. A large open terrace was common to all. The other houses were occupied by an artist and his wife, an actor and his partner, a stage manager, a documentary director and his wife, and Jack and Marge—the only residents unrelated to the arts. They were my next door neighbors and while mystified by the comings and goings in my tiny house, of which there were many, were kind and supportive neighbors.

The warehouse on which we sat was built in the '60s on ground which had been bombed flat in the Blitz. The only building still standing in a once colorful street was a Victorian pub, the Marie Lloyd.

In the '70s, that part of London was no man's land. London taxi drivers are the best trained in the world and can drive directly to the most obscure alley without resorting to a map. But none of them ever drove me home without needing directions.

I spent seven happy, busy and ultimately remunerative years in this cozy house.

I was back there recently to visit the two remaining residents, actor Gil Sutherland and his partner Joop. The area is unrecognizable now—high rise offices and hotels, boutiques, upmarket restaurants and cafes now cast shadows on the street where I lived.

I found a new agent, not a very good one, but an agent. I did a few TV shots, one in the sitcom *Kindly Leave the Curb* for ITV, and another nice part, a drunken armchair philosopher in *Take Three Girls* for the BBC.

~

Getting back to sex, which I was, it's worth documenting the scene in London in the 1970s and what led to it.

Until its decriminalization in 1967, homosexuality was still a prosecutable offence. As far back as the late 19th Century, when Queen Victoria upheld criminalization of male homosexuals, she was asked why lesbians should not be subject to the same law. She replied primly that it was common knowledge women didn't do "that sort of thing."

Many famous figures suffered prior to the 1970s, most notably Oscar Wilde whose life and career were destroyed by his imprisonment.

Alan Turing—without whose code-breaking machine, Britain might not have won World War II quite so soon—was arrested and convicted of no greater crime than a homosexual relationship. He was open about it in court claiming he saw no wrong in his actions. In order to avoid prison, he was subjected to chemical castration, and two years later committed suicide—great reward for his services to crown and country.

In 1953, Sir John Gielgud was apprehended in a public convenience in Chelsea for importuning an undercover police officer. He was fined and released, but the arrest made headline news. He was appearing in a play, *A Day By the Sea* at the time, and on his return to the theatre, after vilification by the press, he nervously hesitated to make his first entrance. His co-star, Dame Sybil Thorndike, took his arm firmly. "Come along John! They won't boo me!" She forced him onto the stage where, far from being booed, he received a standing ovation.

In 1962, a very brave movie made a plea for tolerance. *Victim* told of a prominent married barrister who, due to a brief homosexual encounter, was being blackmailed. It starred Dirk Bogarde, a fine actor, but a rather cowardly man in that he loudly and defiantly denied his own homosexuality to the end of his life. Nevertheless, the film opened the way for a questioning of the antiquated laws.

In 1967, a member of the House of Lords, the eighth Earl of Arran, put forward two bills—one prohibiting the culling of badgers, the other a bill to decriminalize homosexuality. The badger bill failed, the homosexual bill passed. When asked why the votes had gone this way, Lord Arran replied, "Not many badgers in the House of Lords."

By 1970, there began a freedom, and an escalating acceptance. Venues for marginalized men and women became accessible; hitherto, they were like secret societies, associated only with guilt.

There were clubs, pubs, cafes, two newsreel theatres in the West End and a rerun cinema in Victoria which openly catered to gay men, as well as quite a few parks which were pickup destinations. Of these, leading in both popularity and notoriety was Hampstead Heath which, contrary to the police entrapments of the past, these days has a police presence to protect the bucolic homosexual.

Body and mind began to regenerate, but battle-scarred from the destructive relationship, I feared anything close. The multitudinous encounters of the next several years were, in a way, a protection against commitment to any one person.

~

In 1973, *Gypsy* opened in London with Angela Lansbury—a terrific performance in a great production. Lansbury left the cast due to work obligations in the US and was replaced by Dolores Gray. She gave a powerhouse interpretation of Mama Rose and that extraordinary voice ruled the West End again.

Carol Raye was in town and was my date for *Gypsy*. Unwilling to admit poverty. I'd saved every last penny to treat Dolores and her husband Andrew to dinner at a Covent Garden restaurant after the performance. We went to her dressing room after the show expecting to find her wrung out from the emotional tour de force. On the contrary, she was bright and welcomed me with open arms, and, "Hello Skinny." The nickname was now more apt than ever.

She berated me for missing the opening night which brother Dick had attended. I was working out of town and missed his fleeting visit—regrettably, as soon after he was the victim of a fatal car accident.

Dinner was a special joy, even if Andrew assumed Carol was the love of my life and treated her as such. Again, and often, Dolores merely let him assume, and rolled her eyes to me.

~

I was approached by choreographer Michele Hardy to play Nigel in a revival of the musical *Salad Days*. This innocuous, but enjoyable piece was an audience favorite and in its time, passed for British musical theatre. My disparagement aside, it was a huge hit on its first outing. Nigel is the "jolly good show" aristocrat who has to be taught "It's Easy to Sing a Simple Song." The accent bludgeoned into me by my mentor stood me in good stead and no one doubted my blood was royally blue.

The principal juvenile was played by Ted Merwood. Ted was a dancer with just one previous lead role, but his looks, personality and baritone voice made him an ideal Timothy.

Rehearsals were fun, the company friendly. Ted and I hit it off at once, his wry sense of humor always made me laugh. A friendship was forged and he remains one of my closest friends in the world to this day.

The show played the Belgrade Theatre in Coventry for six weeks, and we hoped it would transfer to the West End. It didn't. But that disappointment in no way diminished the joy we all had playing it.

Nearly forty years later, a leading member of the British Noel Coward Society contacted me and asked if I had played Nigel in that production. He revealed he was then a young intern who operated the follow spot on my musical numbers. Today, Stephen Duckham directs musicals throughout the UK.

My smoking habit began to take its toll. By the end of the season, after weeks of singing my heart out, my voice began to suffer. When the show closed, I quit cold turkey and haven't smoked since.

At this point, I was able to look back on my year of emotional depression objectively and I determined to make health a primary concern.

TWENTY-THREE

THE FARCE I wrote while typing letters at the Neurological hospital reached Ray Cooney's office. Cooney was greatly impressed, but given that it had a cast of fifteen, declined to produce it. Instead he commissioned a play from me—a play with a smaller cast. I accepted gratefully, though I had no specific ideas and my only inspiration was the advance payment.

At the same time, I was asked to do a summer season in Eastbourne. I'd never done weekly rep in my life, but nothing else was on offer so I accepted. For all his ineptitude as an agent, Vincent Shaw gave a glowing report of my credits and I had no need to audition. Once we'd opened I told Ray Cooney, and myself, I'd concentrate on writing the play.

I joined the resident company at the Devonshire Park Theatre, a gem of Victorian architecture, and met the other actors. It became apparent at once that years of working in close proximity with each other had split the company into factions. A couple of actors on opposing sides barely spoke to one another. I determined to remain neutral, take the money and run. But I made the fatal mistake of accepting the leading lady's offer of accommodation. She'd divorced well and lived in a very grand house on the hill overlooking Eastbourne seafront. Her mother and her teenage son also lived there. My room was pleasant and the daily walk to the theatre suited my new health regimen; but the downside of the arrangement soon became apparent. I was subjected nightly to her bitter complaints about the rest of the cast, her intense arguments with her delinquent son, and within days I realized her mother was a dipsomaniac of the first water—though water had little to do with it. At least she was an amiable drunk, but conversation was an obstacle course. To avoid the petty differences between cast members, and the domestic dramas at the grand house, once we'd opened all three plays, I took the bus daily to Telscombe Cliffs near Brighton and sat on the beach there. This was to avoid running into any cast members sitting on the beach at Eastbourne. I claimed writing as my excuse and took a backpack of notebooks with me.

Summer seasons were generally well-regarded and well attended by the locals in those days. The program comprised three plays in repertoire. We rehearsed the first for a week, then played it for a week; during that week, the second play was rehearsed during the day, then it played for a week. Then the third was rehearsed days and played a week. Thereafter, for the rest of the season, each play was given in rotation for three nights apiece.

I'd never worked on a play at such speed in my life. There was no time to wrestle with character or motivation, one had to fall back on well-worn tricks to make the character convincing as quickly as possible. Then the change of play every three days was a challenge. Some nights, without taking a good look at the set, it was tough to remember which play one was in.

The plays we performed were Agatha Christie's *And Then There Were None*, Ray Cooney's *Not Now Darling*, and the Frederick Knott thriller, *Wait Until Dark*. I had a middling role in the Christie, dying spectacularly at the end of act one, a small part in the Cooney which I can't even remember, and a major role in the Knott, playing Mike, the goodish guy of the trio of sadistic crooks.

The resident designer was a short, demented Irishman who'd found what he considered to be the "perfect staircase" at a junk yard. Consequently, he employed it in all three sets whether appropriate or not. It was certainly not appropriate to *Wait Until Dark* which was set in a London basement flat whose staircase might have been at most four feet high. This staircase was twelve feet high, giving the impression that the heroine lived in a subterranean bunker. Moreover, my death scene demanded that I topple from the top to bottom of those stairs. Kneepads notwithstanding, I often died with bloodied shins.

Every Saturday night I did my best to quicken the pace of whichever play it was, so I could catch the last train back to London and the comfort of a weekend in my own home.

These three months behind me, with the barest of outlines for a play scribbled into notebooks, I returned to London and my small black and white TV.

I'd been yearning for a color TV to complement my growing audio-video system, but those outranked my bank account. My system, advanced for its day, though primitive by today's standards, comprised an open reel tape recorder, a cassette deck, the first FM stereo audio receiver to go on the market, and audio tape editing equipment.

My agent suggested that the necessary cash for the color set might be earned at Southern Television in Southampton. They'd been putting out feelers for a newsreader. I got the job and a new weekly commute began.

The job paid well, demanded nothing of me but clarity of diction and that I observe the strict rules of broadcast news, which meant never commenting on an item by word or expression, and certainly not with my own opinion.

After several months I'd saved enough for the TV and a little left over for a rainy day. I wanted to quit the dull newsreading job, but had a contract. With the news rules in mind, I decided to break it in the nicest possible way.

I chose to be on duty Christmas day and into the evening where, live at eleven, it was my job to bid the viewer carefully scripted compliments of the season, and to sign off.

I embellished.

"Goodnight and a very happy Christmas to all our viewers." Then I added, "The season of goodwill towards men is now officially over—so if you've been loving your neighbor, stop it at once."

The engineer in the glass booth turned pale, and sure enough, next morning I was summoned to the general manager's office. What did I have to say for myself? I replied sheepishly that I thought a little humor would do no harm. Po-faced, the management pondered this for some time and with fingers crossed, I waited for the boom to be lowered. Eventually the manager said that they valued my work and would overlook the indiscretion.

Now *I* was po-faced.

I stuck it for another week before pleading to management that I couldn't be sure my sense of humor would not get the better of me again and it would be best to submit my resignation. They reluctantly agreed to let me go.

I had the color TV at last, and decided that this year would be the start of my earnest pursuit of good health. I was still self-conscious of my bony frame. Rather than expose it in public, I bought basic weights, a bench, barbell, dumbbells, a squat rack, and installed them on the upper floor of my tiny house.

Never an excessive drinker, I gave up alcohol completely. And this drew a sharp rebuke from Gordon Chater on one of his visits to London.

We went to several plays together. Gordon's habit then, as it was for most of his life, was a cocktail or two before the show, a couple at intermission, and a bottle of wine with supper afterwards. At the end of a week with three plays already under the belt, we were to see a play in Shaftesbury Avenue. As always, we met in the bar where Gordon's first question was always, "What'll it be?"

All week, my reply had been, "Soda."

Gordon said loud enough for the entire bar to hear, "Jesus, you are so fucking scintillating! Have a drink!"

I point out that Gordon's idea of healthy living was simple. And I quote: "Never pass an escalator or a pissoir without using them."

I began to look and feel better and, outgrowing my home weights, I bit the bullet and bought a membership to a large gym in Russell Square, close to the West End. There began my now lifelong preoccupation with exercise and diet. I was aware that progress was being made when some of my older shirts, T shirts and jackets would no longer fit and I was forced to contemplate the cost of a new wardrobe.

TWENTY-FOUR

BY NOW, THE play for Ray Cooney had taken form in my mind and I began to set it down. Different writers have vastly different methods of assembling a play. I've always valued that of Noel Coward, and the composer Saint-Saens, both of whom had the entire play, or symphony, constructed mentally before committing to paper. In my case, at the very least, I must have the end of the play, the resolution, firmly in mind, and written, before I begin.

Ray asked for a farcical comedy, a genre often pooh-poohed by theatre snobs, but one I'd always respected. A style of comedy which had its beginnings in the plays of Aristophanes and Plautus can't be all bad!

For anyone who's led a sheltered theatrical life, let me outline the cliched template for any farce. Example:

Two men are involved in some nefarious scheme. They await the arrival of a pivotal character who will set the operation into motion.

The catalyst's name is Carless. There's a knock at the front door. The butler answers to a man whose car has broken down and who asks to use the phone for assistance. The butler asks him to wait. As he stands alone in the doorway, one of the schemers spots him and asks, "Are you Carless?"

The stranger thinks about this for a moment and answers, "As a matter of fact I am."

Chaos ensues.

My play didn't fall far from this tree. In most twentieth century British farce, the protagonist is often hungry for sex, but due to the chaos of mistaken identity and cross-purposes, never gets it. I proposed a pretty well-trodden plot device in which twins, one of impeccable respectability and one a devious womanizer create the chaos. Both of course played by the same actor. The plot concerned a respected astronomer in line for a knighthood who brings his wife to their country house for their anniversary. His twin, believing the house to be vacant for the weekend, brings his secretary for a few days of sexual recreation.

The mix of characters included the prim spinster secretary of the upright twin, the men's wives, both ex Windmill Theatre vaudeville dancers, a Scottish nun collecting for the convent, and a minister from the Home Office who chooses this weekend to vet the astronomer for a knighthood.

Sheila Keith as the Scottish nun was exceptionally fine. She'd just come off a horror movie where she played an axe murderer, but couldn't have been a more convincing, or funnier nun.

I composed a musical number for the second act in which the wives of the twins perform one of their old numbers as fan dancers which listed what they wore for their act—two fans, one smile, and a drop of Chanel—this, accompanied by the nun at the piano, and in the stunned presence of the Home Office minister.

It worked well, the cast were universally terrific, but the play needed work and there was an obstacle. Thanks to Prime Minister Heath's "Three Day Working Week", London theatre was in chaos, some plays closing down prematurely due to power restrictions. Ultimately, the fractured economy won and it was decided not to transfer, and my play closed after a successful season in Westcliff.

~

Miriam Karlin and I were frequent theatre-going companions, and during the three day week, we went to the Old Vic to see Laurence Olivier in what would be his final theatrical performance, *The Party,* in which he played a controversial Scots politician. Miriam had worked with him in the movie *The Entertainer*, so went backstage after to congratulate him; I caught up with Dennis Quilley whom I'd known in Australia, and met one of my idols, Frank Finlay, a chameleon-like actor who could play any nationality, type or accent with utter conviction.

The three day week impacted travel as well. After the play, Miriam was to have supper at my house and when we finally found a cab, we were caught in a traffic jam and came to a dead stop. The driver got out of the cab to berate the other drivers. Meanwhile, Miriam was in an ecstasy of dissecting the play. She was well-known as a staunch left-wing activist and trade unionist, and *The Party* had touched all the right nerves; she talked of her vision of equality, and how the downtrodden worker must fight for his rights. Then she noticed the driver was absent; she got out of the cab and yelled, "Oy! You left your meter running!"

~

I kept comfortably afloat in 1973 with voice overs, and marketing interviews for MGM, thanks to my chum Terry Pritchard. I interviewed such stars as Rod Steiger, Mark Lester the young star of *Oliver*, Lionel Jeffries who'd directed a charming movie of *The Railway Children*, and Lester Persky, producer of *Fortune and Men's Eyes.*

I also spent six months playing a leading character in the popular BBC radio serial, *Waggoner's Walk,* and in a brief flirtation with theatre of the absurd, I played a military colonel in *Urban Guerilla Boutique* at the Soho Poly Theatre.

A friend was an announcer at the BBC World Service and suggested, as a casual broadcaster there, I might add to my income. I read for the chiefs and was offered a contract.

~

In those days, the World Service was renowned as the highest standard of broadcasting in the world. The Service occupied eight floors of Bush House in the Strand with production offices and studios dedicated to every spoken language. The studios were on the eighth floor, the seventh housed the vast complex of equipment which relayed the programs to the respective countries twenty-four hours a day.

No regional accents were permitted for the English Service at that time. The precise, "received pronunciation" of all BBC broadcasts was the rule. These days, the rules have changed to accommodate fashionable diversity, and regional accents render many of today's news broadcasts unintelligible.

Because the news went out live all over the world, items had to be read at a precise speed—British News to fill eleven minutes exactly, World News, fourteen. A two second silence was observed after every news broadcast to allow the complex relays on the seventh floor to switch channels depending on the country receiving.

Every month, announcers were subjected to a short test for accent and inflection. These were held by an elderly female speech expert whose edicts were law. Yet, in spite of the formality of the service, the announcers were a jolly bunch, and made fun of their own pedantry: A sign on the fire escapes read: IN CASE OF EMERGENCY. An announcer covered all of these with cards on which was written in marker: IN THE EVENT OF EMERGENCY.

A couple of the casuals were also actors and schedules were juggled to accommodate their theatre performance times. A double life such as this often resulted in fatigue, and this invariably led to fluffs and spoonerisms, some of them so hilarious that I approached the chiefs to ask if I might use the log records to compile a book of BBC Bloopers. Below I quote some of the best.

For six months of my second year at the Service I was in a play in the West End. I did night shifts after some performances, sometimes so tired I dozed off between bulletins. I also became a major entry in the log books due to the following:

Today in Borneo, armed elephants attacked an outpost…

Correction, armed *elements* attacked an outpost…

This morning, gales disrupted the services of cross flannel cherries between Dover and Calais.

A major accident caused a bottleknock on the M-1 Motorway…

And on three occasions, in three separate sporting broadcasts, I referred to "The Monaco Grand Pee." After the third, I apologized profusely to the producer who merely gave me a weary smile and said, "It conjures up such a surreal visual."

On one middle-of-the night session, I sat opposite another announcer, a celebrated joker, and we alternated reading news items. After completing each one of mine, I relaxed into oblivion, but he caught my eye and gestured that I should listen carefully to his next item. It ran:

"Today in typhoon torn Manila, part of an old dyke crumbled into the sea."

I was convulsed with silent laughter, so much so that I was incapable of reading my next item which concerned a mass murder in Northern Ireland. My co-reader snatched the page from me and read my piece while I slid under the desk to prevent audibility.

If my gaffs were awful, some of the worst far exceeded them.

> WEARY ANNOUNCER: The criminal was apprehended in a whoreshop in Teasham. Whoops! A *teashop* in *Horsham*!
> ANOTHER WEARY ANNOUNCER: The Kent constabulary was informed, and a statement was taken by a kenstable from Cunt.

And there was an old stalwart, Ian Fellowes-Gordon, somewhere in his late sixties, a dear man, only hanging on to his position as senior announcer to support the upkeep of the inherited family castle in Scotland. One night during a recorded transcript of a literary program, he dozed off at the desk. At the end of the recording, there was dead silence—the engineer in the glass booth had also dozed off.

Down on the seventh floor, the engineers monitoring the relays panicked at the, by now, minutes-long silence—this was the era of IRA bombings in London and they feared the worst. Weapon at the ready, a security guard was rushed up to the eighth floor and cautiously opened the glass booth. He woke the sleeping engineer, who dashed into the studio and shook Fellowes-Gordon into dazed consciousness. Not quite sure where he was, or why, Ian opened the microphone and said in his smoothest, most dignified BBC tone, "That was a program."

He closed the microphone, then thought this needed elaboration. He opened the mic again and added, "In a moment, we'll have another program."

I wanted to call my book of bloopers, "That Was a Program."

The powers that be vetoed the idea.

Age 3, still on good terms with my mother (1943).

Ada Creyton, the grandmother who always encouraged me (1948).

Age 8, with my brother Trevor, age 3 (1948).

Age 9 (1949).

Age 12, with my allegedly musical instrument (1952).

My pen and ink won the annual Brisbane State High School Art Prize and was featured in the 1955 Yearbook.

Age 16 with my parents (1956). Not necessarily a happy family portrait.

At age 17, I had never set foot upon, or spoken on a stage. By age 20 I was playing leads. I was a quick learner.

Twelfth Night, age 19. Malvolio–a little nose putty goes a long way (1959).

School For Scandal, age 19, as Joseph Surface. One of my first more substantial roles (1959).

As Cleonte, in Moliere's *Le Bourgeois Gentilhomme* (1958) with Nancy Knudsen. I realised at an early age that, Moliere notwithstanding, male juveniles are thankless parts.

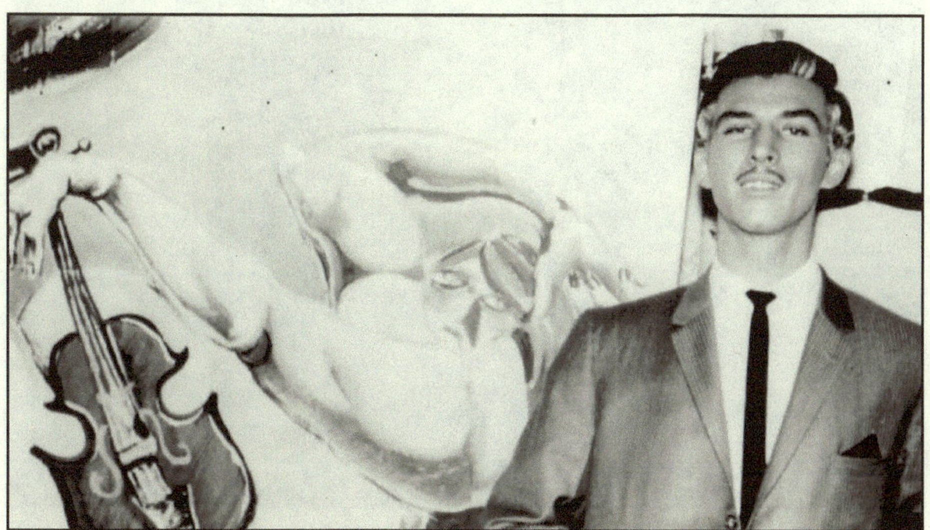

Noel Coward's *Nude With Violin*. My first leading role (1960).

The Merchant Of Venice, ABC TV (1961). As Lorenzo with Annette Andre as Jessica.

Winter Journey, age 20. With Clement McCallin, Noel Ferrier, and the great Googie Withers (1960).

Headshot, age 20 (1960).

The Patriots ABC TV, age 23 (1963).

The Philip Theatre revue, *What's New?* (1962). With Reg Gorman and Janet Brown.

Keep it Clean ABC TV (1967). I played a conniving executive with plans to rob the bank, and is inadvertently locked in the vault by the cleaner, Desmond Rolfe.

Age 21, *East Lynne* with Fernande Glyn as Lady Isabel. The show was an instant hit and established me in the Sydney theatre scene (1961).

Lady Audley's Secret. Terrorizing Rosalind Seagrave as Lady Audley, the put upon heroine (1962).

Lady Audley's Secret (1962). I rewrote melodrama's first lady villain as a heroine, and wrote in a villain for myself.

Villains by night, butter wouldn't melt by day in children's matinees of *Beauty and the Beast* (1963), with Noeline Brown.

The Face At The Window. Noeline joined me as the voluptuous Woman of the World (1964).

A NIGHT AT THE THEATRE

Now that the days are drawing in, thoughts turn to the after-five dress and more formal wear for later in the evening. These suits and dresses provide the answer, distilling the essence of good fashion—simplicity coupled with good fabric and meticulous attention to detail.

Sally Baker
FASHION EDITOR

A Night At The Theatre (1962). One of many commercial spreads I did as a result of my notoriety in the villain roles.

The Front And Flip Side Of Barry Creyton And Noeline Brown, Festival Records (1965). The first comedy album made in Australia. In its first week of release, it outsold the Beatles, The Rolling Stones and Elvis Presley... and was banned by every radio station in the country.

THE MAVIS BRAMSTON SHOW (1964 - 1966)

'The Mavis Bramston Show, *'Togetherness'*. I composed the music for the number which opened the show every week.

My album of numbers from *The Mavis Bramston Show*, Festival Records (1966).

A Bramston Show sketch defining me as the 'Rugged Indoor Type'.

The Mavis Bramston Show. The original Bramston team, Gordon Chater, Carol Raye, me and June Salter (1964).

The Mavis Bramston Show, with Noeline Brown (1965).

The Mavis Bramston Show, with Gordon and Carol–being outraged by the very material we were performing weekly.

The Mavis Bramston Show, the last get together. In 1996 I was in Australia to appear in Coward's *Blithe Spirit* for the Queensland Theatre Company. It was a tribute to Gordon at the Belvoir Street Theatre, the last time Gordon, Carol, June and I were in the same spot at the same time.

The Mavis Bramston Show. Ronnie Frazer, me as Postmaster Phipps, Gordon , Miriam Karlin, and Barry Humphries in an early incarnation of Edna (1965).

The Mavis Bramston Show with Carol, Gordon, me and June (1965).

The Mavis Bramston Show, rehearsal with June Salter and Carol Raye. I was most likely telling June a joke of dubious taste. Carol rehearsing a song with the legendary Tommy Tycho just out of sight.

The Mavis Bramston Show. Camera rehearsal prior to recording.

The Mavis Bramston Show, with Kathy Lloyd and Hazel Phillips.

On the cover of TV Times for *The Mavis Bramston Show.*

The Mavis Bramston Show, with Gordon and Carol on the cover of TV Times.

The Mavis Bramston Show, with Maggie, Haze and Gordon on the cover of TV Times.

Oil portrait by Peter Hanbury, (1965).

They're A Weird Mob (1965). A cameo in the Michael Powell movie. Graham Kennedy and I had guest star billing.

Duel at Diablo (1966). ATN sent me to the US for the premiere of this outstanding film, mainly for the publicity of hobnobbing with the world press. It was my first US trip and a great experience. This photo is from the movie set of a town built in Southern Utah.

Sydney Poitier, one of the stars of *Duel at Diablo*. I tried to steal focus, and failed.

With Dennis Weaver, one of the stars of *Duel at Diablo*. Weaver was a confirmed vegetarian and while we touched on the subject here, it took another seven years before I tried it for myself. Now, while not entirely vegetarian, diet is a primary part of my health regime.

With Eddie Littlesky, the baddie in *Duel at Diablo* stealing focus from me.

Host of *The Barry Creyton Show* (1967).

Head shot (1967).

The Barry Creyton Show (1967) with Betty Bob Bobbitt.

Old Time Music Hall (1970). Did I say I wanted to abandon the "personality" image and become a working actor again? Right off the plane, a desperate call from an old friend, Janet Brown, who was appearing in an evening of Old Time Music Hall. Their Master of Ceremonies was ill and would I step in?

Revue *This, That, and the Other*, at the Palace Theatre Westcliff, England (1970). With (L-R) Neville Phillips, Bea Aston, Carol Raye, myself, Tom Oliver, Barbara Angell and Roger Diss (seated).

Abelard and Heloise (1971), London. Post breakdown. Being lascivious with Dierdre Costello.

Headshot (1975).

Salad Days (1973), London. With Roberta Desti and Ted Merwood. Ted remains to this day, one of my closest friends.

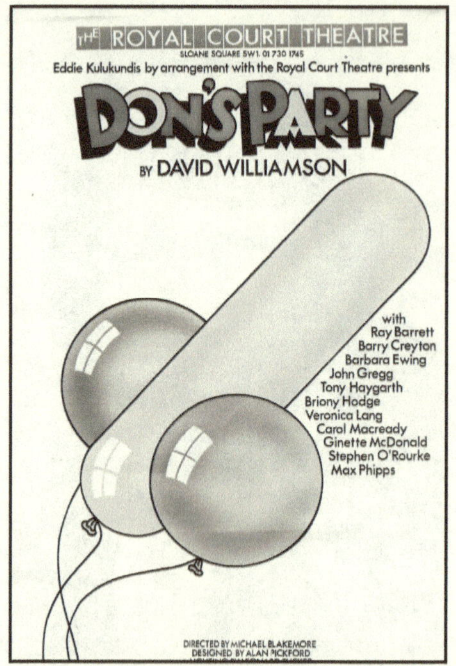

Don's Party, Royal Court Theatre London (1975). Directed by the great Michael Blakemore.

Rodger's Last Stand, London (1976). In spite of itself, it ran for six months in the West End.

Don's Party, Royal Court Theatre (1975). At my left, Veronica Lang, at the far right, Australia's great playwright, David Williamson.

Surprising Gordon Chater on his *This is Your Life* (1976). This was to be a few days in Sydney, then back to London, but the offers were hard to refuse. A three month stint in *The Naked Vicar Show* on stage turned into a 12 year stay.

Blankety Blanks with Ugly Dave Grey, Noeline, Graham Kennedy, Jon English, Belinda Giblin and Stuart Wagstaff.

Concurrent with *Blankety Blanks,* I flew to Brisbane every week to host *Stairway To The Stars* (1978).

Stairway To The Stars (1978) with Babette Stephens my loved and respected mentor from my teen years in theatre. A good friend and critical appraiser of my work as an actor.

Son Of A Naked Vicar (1977).

Bedroom Farce, Sydney (1977). With a stellar cast including inveterate giggler, Carmen Duncan.

Suddenly At Home (1979) with Sally Sander.

Much was made of my physical transformation on my return to Ausralia in 1977. After a year long illness in London, I determined to devote myself to health, and continue to do so to this day.

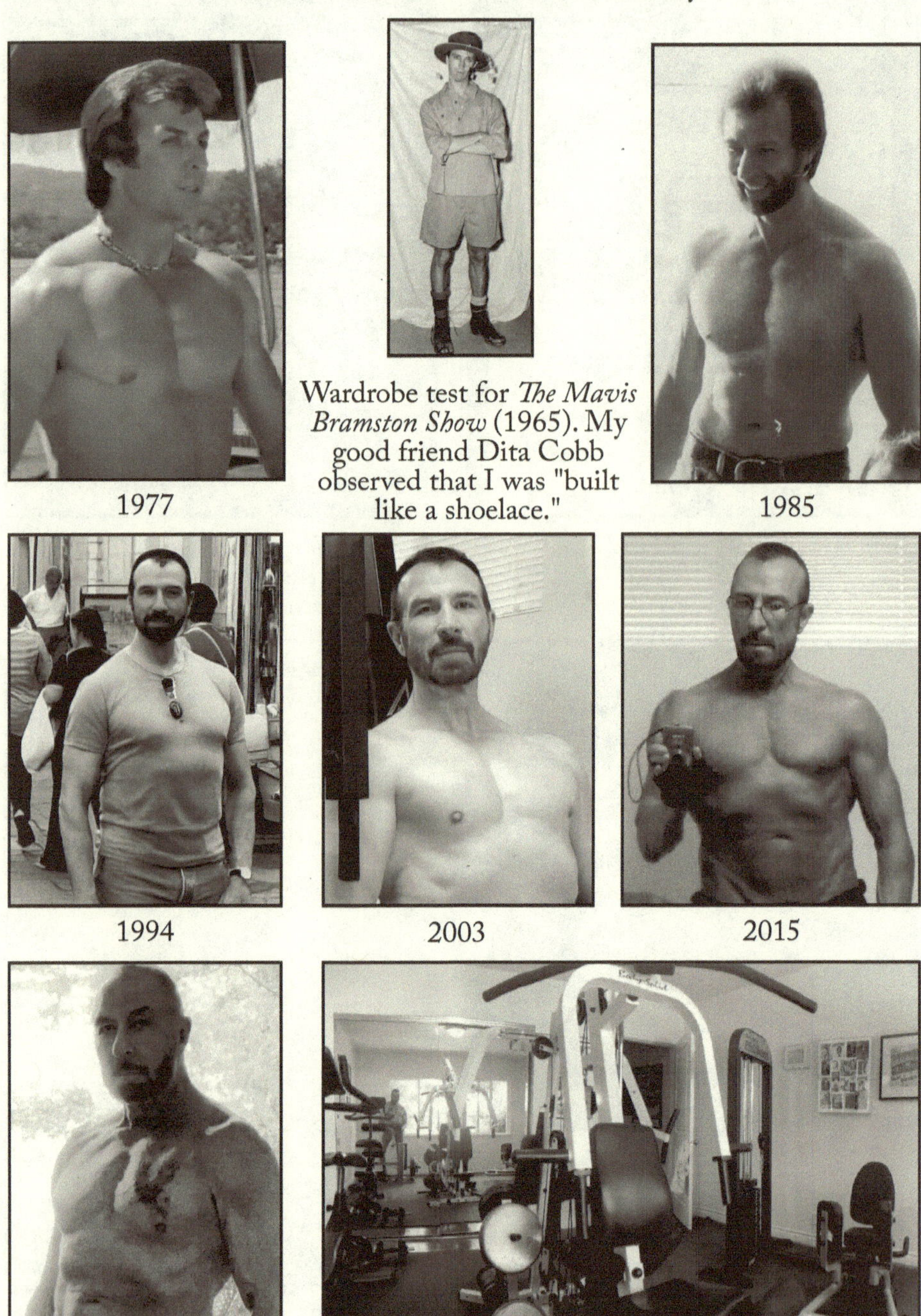

1977

Wardrobe test for *The Mavis Bramston Show* (1965). My good friend Dita Cobb observed that I was "built like a shoelace."

1985

1994

2003

2015

2024

Home gym.

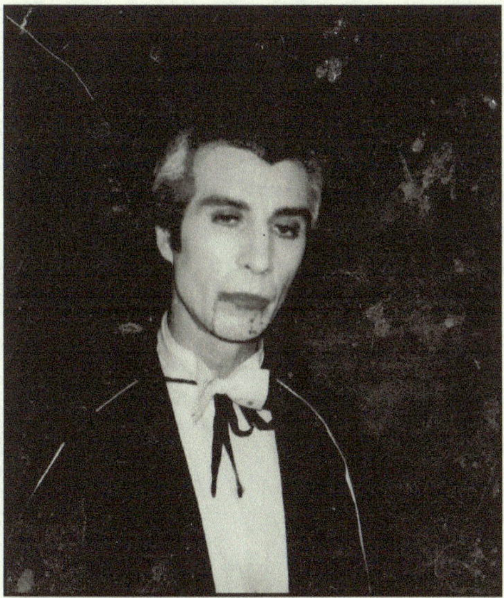

As Dracula in the unfinished movie, *Horror Story* (1980).

Side by Side by Sondheim at Marian Street Theatre (1985). Starring Judi Connelli, Bartholomew John, myself and Gaye McFarlane.

With Kerry McGuire in Ayckbourn's *Season's Greetings* at Marian Street Theatre (1984). Nominated for the Critic's Circle Award, I lost to Ruth Cracknell whose Lady Bracknell, in the view of Marian Street director John Krummel, caused one to think Lord Bracknell had married beneath him.

During the Brisbane run of *Noises Off* (1982), Stuart, Carol and I were guests of honour at Gold Coast Radio 4GG along with the legendary Phyllis Diller.

Noises Off (1982). Rehearsing with Stuart Wagstaff and the ever present danger of working with good friends... fits of the giggles.

Noises Off with Jill Perryman. Jill told me she kept a framed copy of this photo, as did I — but neither of us has any recollection of what it represented.

Noises Off caricatures of the cast by the brilliant cartoonist, Kentuck.

Pack of Lies, Marian Street Theatre (1985). As the cold MI5 agent.

Corpse (1986). I played twins!

My Honda 750.

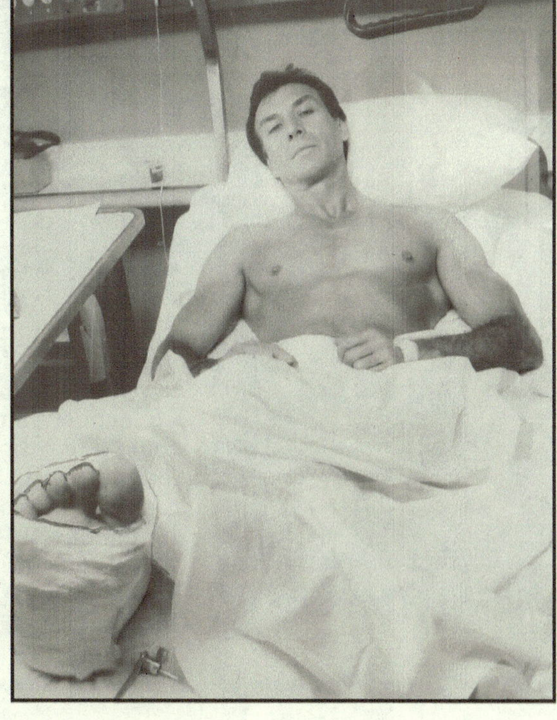

The motorcycle accident while playing *Corpse* in Perth. This picture taken by a sneaky news photographer the morning after surgery. Drugged to the eyeballs, I have no recollection of its being taken. Nevertheless, it featured in press all over Australia. I was in traction for a month, and a hip to ankle cast for another five.

During the hospitalization, I did two things - I drafted a play for Noeline Brown and myself, *Double Act*, and I planned the upcoming production of the musical *Nunsense* which I would direct. I bought the rights to this in New York and Mike Walsh took over production. I directed two companies running concurrently throughout Australia where for two years, it broke box office records.

And as soon as the plaster came off, I bought this Kawasaki 1100! I was directing the musical *Nunsense* at the time, and cast member Maggie King was a suitably terrified pillion.

I also directed the Dublin, Ireland production. Here, shooting the film insert with the Irish cast. With the author's permission, I wrote the short movie specially for each production–a western: *Nunsmoke*.

Maggie King, Betty Bobbitt, Geraldine Morrow, Robyn Arthur, Georgie Parker.

Double Act (1987) with Noeline Brown was the single most important milestone in my career after *The Bramston Show.* Not only acclaimed in Australia, it gave me international recognition as a writer, and has been produced in 25+ languages with major international stars. As of this writing, it is playing in Krakow, Poland, and in production in Budapest, Hungary.

Double Act – International Show Posters

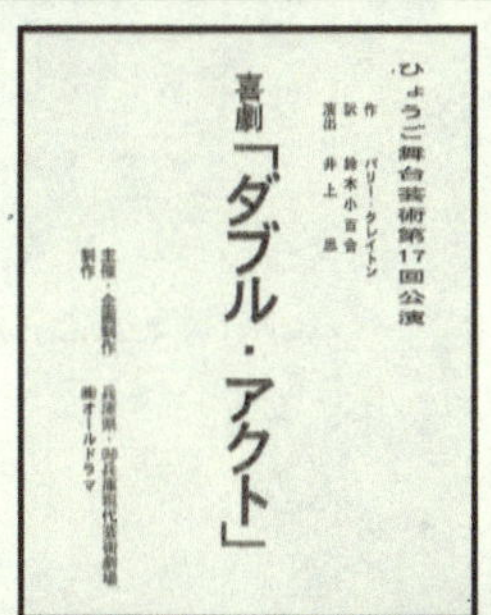

Noel Coward's *Blithe Spirit* (1996), Queensland Theatre Company. With Belinda Giblin as Elvira.

Valentine's Day (1998). A joy to be reunited with two of my oldest friends, Noeline Brown and Donald Macdonald.

Valentine's Day (1998). Noeline, Maria Venti, Judith Wright. I don't think much of the current craze for personal pronouns, but there's simply no way to think of the wonderful Maria Venuti other than "them" or perhaps, "those." She, and they, were a comic delight in this play.

Valentine's Day has been translated into only seven or eight languages. In 2024 it played Budapest and toured Hungary.

WEYHER-FILM-THEATER

VALENTINSTAG

Das Weyher Theater spielt
eine Boulevardkomödie
von Barry Creyton

Valentine's Day, Germany poster.

Valentine's Day, Netherlands poster.

Later Than Spring (2000). I wrote *Later Than Spring* for Marian Street Theatre, and specifically for my old colleague Donald MacDonald. Here with Donald and Katy Manning who pulled no punches playing the bitter character perfectly.

Glorious (2007), Sydney. Back in Sydney for a glorious reunion with Noeline in Peter Quilter's *Glorious*. Apart from a very convincing fat suit, I wore a toupee which changed position every time I appeared.

Glorious (2007) with Judi Farr.

Duets (2009). Another joyous return to Australia and the Ensemble Theatre. I delighted in joining Noeline again in these four one-acters by prolific playwright Peter Quilter, who came to Sydney for the opening.

Duets, Play one—a mismatched couple on a blind date. Another toupee, and a terrific set of teeth made specially for me by a Hollywood makeup artist.

Duets, Play two—unrequited love, ultimately requited.

Duets, Play three—divorced but stuck together.

Duets, Play four—marriage ill advised.

As Hector Hulot in Balzac's *Cousin Bette* for the Antaeus Company, (2009).

KING LEAR

by William Shakespeare

Adapted for audio and directed by Barry Creyton

℗ 2014 by Blackstone Audio, Inc.

Michael Winters and the entire Oregon Shakespeare Festival cast bring emotional freshness, ease, and clarity to the dense and heightened language and classic characters of this cornerstone of world literature

Well-mixed transitions, percussive music, and intense and convincing sword and battle sound effects add layers to the production, making it sound more film-like than stage-like.

A solid interpretation of a time-honored classic.

B.P. © AudioFile 2014, Portland, Maine

I adapted and directed these lavish, multi cast audio productions for Blackstone Audio, and LA TheatreWorks, all of which were reviewed flatteringly, substantiating my aim to make them sound like movies without the pictures.

At this end of my career, writing is my driving force–and unlike the stage, you don't have to look your best at a desk.

The View From Olympus Mons, NineStar Press (2022). Nominated for the Annual Goodreads Award for best novel.

Murder Is Fatal, CSpace Press (2014). An affectionate parody of the noir genre. "This ripping good read is a killer!" Tony Frankel, Stage and Cinema Magazine.

Phoenix, NineStar Press (2023). Now adapted as a six part limited TV series.

The Vengeance Of Zorro, BoldVenture Press (2024). This one came to pass thanks (if for nothing else) to Val Kilmer.

A final look at an item I never thought to love as much as my motorcycles, but in the Land of the Automobile, my vintage Thunderbird came close. Ford made only 60,000 of them and they became collectors' cars. But with no spare parts available, it's gone to the Great Car Yard in the Sky. Sadly missed.

When marriage equality became a fact in this country, my long time partner (of 36 years now) Vaughan Edwards and I took advantage of it and made honest men of each other on August 31, 2013. Certainly, respect, romance and sentiment played a part, but the two operative words uppermost were, "joint taxes."

At home in the San Fernando Valley, Los Angeles, California.

On holiday in Sorrento Italy with partner of 36 years, Vaughan Edwards.

TWENTY-FIVE

THREE YEARS AFTER the breakdown, I was in good shape mentally and physically.

I auditioned for a new play by the giant of Australian drama, David Williamson. It was *Don's Party* and was to play at the Royal Court, directed by Michael Blakemore. Make that the *great* Michael Blakemore. This is the man who won two Tony Awards in the one season, one for the Michael Frayn drama, *Copenhagen*, the other for a revival of the musical, *Kiss Me Kate*.

I read for the part of Simon, the stuck up right-winger at the left wing party. But thanks to my gym obsession, the muscles had kicked in by this time, and Michael saw me as the pugilistic Evan. We tossed it around, I read again, and Michael finally said yes to me as Simon—happily, as the Sunday Times gave me one of the best reviews of my life.

Simon was a dream of a character: uptight, a wine-tasting fish out of water, a right-winger in a violently left-wing, beer drinking environment. When Mal first catches sight of Simon, his query to the host is, "Who's the poofter with the poker up his arse?"

I used this as a guide to character, bearing and attitude.

I smoked a pipe, but unwilling to use real tobacco, I chose non-addictive herbal tobacco. The only problem with this was that it smelled like pot. So as the smoke drifted from stage to audience, row after row of heads turned upward to sniff in either horror or hope.

Rehearsals taught me a lot about the way a truly good director works. Michael had an overall view of the play from the start, but always allowed suggestions and encouraged discussion. He never became angry or impatient with actors. But there's always a first time, and it was provided by Ray Barrett who played Mal. Not only did Barrett prove difficult to direct, he spent each lunch break in the pub across the street, and returned to rehearsal the worse for several pints. One day, Michael snapped, and threatened to replace him if he preferred his drinking habits to the play. Barrett's afternoons were a tribute to sobriety thereafter.

One special bonus from this production was my lifelong friendship with Barbara Ewing, a New Zealand actress who'd been resident in London for some time. She played Kath. She'd done much TV, several movies, one for Hammer in which, breasts to the fore, she fled Dracula through a forest. She has since become a greatly respected historical novelist.

The play was greeted with critical praise and I had that particularly flattering notice from Harold Hobson of the Sunday Times.

It was planned to move the play to a West End theatre. But finally, while it was considered a little too commercial for the Royal Court, it was deemed not quite commercial enough for the West End.

TWENTY-SIX

ON THE ROAD again! Charles Ross, of the Mayfair revue, now invited me to join the cast of *Roger's Last Stand*, a comedy he was producing and directing. It was adapted from a Dutch play and, I thought, not the funniest I'd ever read; but the cast was stellar: Leslie Phillips the first name in light comedy movies as well as theatre, Roy Kinnear, well-known since *That Was The Week That Was*, Elspet Gray, known on stage and TV and later, as the queen in *Blackadder*, and Anna Dawson, star of many West End musicals. This lineup made the piece seem like a sure bet and I jumped in. Once again, I'd be wearing a bowler hat and sporting a furled umbrella.

I'd heard much about Leslie's temperament, and boy, did we experience it during rehearsals. For someone who spent his life playing light comedy, he was a singularly humorless man and gave the haughty impression of being far above the rest of the cast in knowledge and experience.

The plot concerned Roger, a respectable civil servant who tires of his mundane life and marriage, and abandons both to take up residence in an empty flat with only a mattress on the floor. Soon, another couple moves in with him, bringing their mattress, and Roger's wife arrives to try to make sense of the situation. I played an associate of Roger's who tries to bring sanity to his mid-life crisis and who, at the tag of the play, is revealed to be his wife's secret lover.

A pre London tour began in Leeds, then on to Edinburgh, Newcastle, Birmingham, Brighton and Bath. With the Edinburgh landlady a forethought, I booked into hotels for the major part of this tour.

Charles Ross, a seasoned director of comedy, was a font of invention and advice, but Leslie always knew better. During the Leeds run, Leslie demanded to take over direction of the play. The cast were less than happy at this turn of events, but as established professionals, we fell into line.

I should point out that as far as Roy, Elspet and Anna were concerned, I've seldom worked with such an agreeable cast and we four became close during the tour.

A few incidents lightened the gloom. In Brighton, we expected Elspet's good friend Honor Blackman at the Wednesday matinee. I longed for a glimpse of the glamorous Pussy Galore from *Goldfinger*. There was torrential rain that day and no Honor. We held the curtain while Elspet hovered anxiously by the stage door, and eventually Honor arrived on her motorcycle which she'd ridden from London, sodden to the skin. Far from being dashed, my admiration for La Blackman was greatly enhanced by this dramatic arrival. And how I envied her that motorcycle.

She was rushed into Elspet's dressing room, dried off, given a warm overcoat, and fifteen minutes later the curtain went up.

By the time we reached the Theatre Royal, Bath, the play was in better shape, but we were all weary of Leslie's constant demands. I remember greeting Roy one morning with, "How are you?"

He replied solemnly, "Just waiting for the insurance premium to mature." Roy was in no way a cynic, always open and jovial, but he did let one observation on Leslie's parsimony slip out over supper one night. "You know," he said in mock confidentiality, "Leslie has the first pound note he ever earned in a frame above his sofa."

In historic Bath I escaped the dramas by lunching every day at a pleasant restaurant near the theatre. It was co-owned by Roddy Llewellyn—the Roddy Llewellyn who shortly would be the fodder of tabloids for his supposed "affair" with a member of the royal family. He was a handsome man, about twenty-two at the time, very friendly and sat with me often. He asked about the play, about my workout program, and was highly complimentary of my physique. One day he said, "I'm having a few intimate friends in for supper tonight. Would you care to join us?"

You bet.

That night after the performance, I walked to the restaurant and found the street lined with Rolls Royces. The "few intimate friends" were Princess Margaret and her bodyguards.

I had the misfortune of being seated next to HRH.

There ensued one of the least enjoyable social evenings of my life. I knew the rules: don't speak unless spoken to; address her as 'ma'am'; wait until dismissed before leaving the table. I also knew she was known for playing psychological games—encourage the commoner to become familiar, and as soon as he does so, dash him to the ground by demanding to be addressed as "Your Royal Highness."

Perhaps she was a sadly damaged woman who took her personal grievances out on the rest of the world, perhaps she was deeply sensitive and unhappy with her royal lot, perhaps she longed for the simple life but knew not how to embrace it. Whatever. I found her to be a pain in the arse. A royal pain in the arse.

There was a guitarist and a few sycophants begged the princess to sing her favorite song. After a brief simulation of reluctance, she obliged and gave us the royal rendition of "Chatanooga Choo Choo." We were all prompted to join in. She nudged me during this and said, "Sing up! You're Australian aren't you?"

I failed to see the correlation, but I sang up just the same.

Later, during a lull in the conversation, she turned to me. "Roddy tells me you're in something at the theatre."

"Yes indeed ma'am."

"And what is the name of your play?"

"Roger's Last Stand."

"Very amusing," she said without the merest hint of amusement. "And who is your star?"

"Leslie Phillips."

"Oh, I've always thought he was very funny, with that little gap between his front teeth."

I thought, *she doesn't mean Leslie Phillips, she means Terry-Thomas.* But for the sake of Anglo-Australian relations, I kept my trap shut.

The evening wore on, and when she finally rose to dance with Roddy, I crept away.

Next morning at ten, weary from the social contortions of the previous night, I arrived at rehearsal in a foul mood. Leslie looked down his nose at me and said, "I believe you had supper with Her Royal Highness last night."

"Yes," I snapped. "And she thinks you're Terry-Thomas."

Leslie considered this with an incredulous frown. Anna stifled a smile, put her arm around Elspet and gently led her to the stage to prevent the smile from spreading. Roy excused himself, went to his dressing room and closed the door. But his guffaws could be heard clearly from within.

We opened in London at the Duke of York's Theatre in September of 1975. Of the mixed reviews, Harold Hobson of the Sunday Times was once again my champion, asserting, "Barry Creyton has more of the implicit insolence of British aristocracy than Leslie Phillips is capable of projecting."

Leslie didn't speak to me for three weeks.

But, to give him his due, his fans were loyal and the play ran for six months.

Another incident during the run incurred Leslie's wrath.

Elspet cared for the play less and less as the season progressed and began performing her lines by rote, but not so an audience would know.

In act two, my character, Richard, bursts into the room to find Roger downstage pondering something, while Elspet as his wife Lucinda is upstage gazing vacantly out of the French windows. As Richard enters, Lucinda swings around and greets him with an ebullient, "Richard!"

But, during this prolonged period of window gazing, Elspet, quite bored with the play, allowed her mind to wander to a luncheon she was planning the following day, and she ran over her shopping list—to herself, but absently whispering loudly enough for me to hear outside the door.

"A roast. Yes. A roast. I'll call the butcher at ten. A leg of lamb. Then the market for the veggies. Carrots, parsnips, potatoes. God knows what I'm going to do for dessert. Maybe a trifle..." And so it went.

My cue. I opened the door. Elspet swung round and uttered an ebullient, "Barry!" Then, after a moment's thought, "No, no, *Richard*!"

I broke into uncontrollable laughter.

Leslie gazed at me blankly for a while, then realizing I was unable to speak, approached, put an arm around my shoulder and said, "I know what you're going to say," and proceeded to quote my lines. This made it worse, and my giggles grew. After playing my entire scene as a monologue, he turned me gently to the door, opened it and said a fond farewell.

Later, I apologized profusely which he accepted more or less graciously, but things were never the same after that.

Apropos these shameful breakups, please note that in the original production of Noel Coward's *Private Lives,* Laurence Olivier playing Victor, found it hard to suppress the giggles and broke up frequently. Coward reprimanded him severely and, to an extent, cured him of the disgraceful habit. Whenever I flagellated myself mentally for giving in to chuckles on stage, I always managed to excuse myself by conjuring up an image of the great Sir Laurence similarly afflicted.

Roger closed in March 1976. Charles offered me the tour, but I declined; another six months of Leslie, even for money, was too much to contemplate. I suggested my friend Kevin Moore, who's made of sterner stuff than I, to replace me. Some months later, he returned to London with many anecdotes.

The year progressed with more voice over work, and the routine at the BBC as I waited for another acting engagement. I was financially comfortable so there was no desperation. I was urged by Bill Redmond to lecture visiting American drama students on the finer points of British drama, and in particular the history of London theatres. It was a gig he'd been doing for some time, and now, planning to return to Australia, he asked me to replace him.

This was an enjoyable task. Only once did I balk when, in describing British theatre of the 1930s, I quoted Noel Coward. None of the kids had heard of him. I moved on to Tennessee Williams and all of them glowed with recognition. It reinforced the contention that the US and the UK are two nations divided by a single language.

TWENTY-SEVEN

DURING THESE AFFLUENT years, I was a frequent opera goer. One performance I will never forget was Verdi's *Un Ballo in Maschera*, or as presented in English at the London Coliseum, *A Masked Ball.* The tortured heroine, Amelia, was played by Rita Hunter.

PC police, get out the handcuffs now.

I know, in these enlightened times, one is not supposed to refer to fat people as fat. But face it, Rita Hunter was FAT! No, *more* than fat, she was OBESE. She never flew first class because her behind wouldn't fit in a conventional airline seat. Instead, they removed the armrests of a row of three in economy and she occupied all of them.

When she sang *Norma* in New York, the headline of the Times review was headed, "Enorma."

Excuses of glandular problems are often made in cases like this. But in Hunter's case, it all came down to food. She loved it! Opera producer friend Don White told me of a day at rehearsal where at morning tea, she sent out for a dozen cream puffs. How nice, thought the cast, she's treating us. Nope, they were all for Rita.

The stories about her gastronomic indulgences were legion in opera circles. And when she sang at the English National Opera, the wardrobe department placed bets on guesses as to how many people could fit into one of her costumes.

Rather than try to get her to move, most directors simply placed her centre stage and moved the production around her.

At *The Masked Ball*, I managed to suspend disbelief for the first two acts, but in act three, at the ball, with the entire cast in masks, there seemed to be some doubt as to which one was Amelia.

At this point I started to chuckle. Come on folks, she's the only one on stage who looks like a roundabout on the M-1 motorway.

The chuckles became hysterical laughter. I was roundly shushed by the audience in my row, but I was a goner. Eventually, an usher flashed his torch on me and asked me to leave. I did so gladly, having had a thoroughly entertaining afternoon.

~

In September of 1976, I had a phone call from Channel 7 Sydney to ask if I'd be the surprise guest on Gordon Chater's *This Is Your Life*.

Gladly.

~

Sydney had changed in the years I'd been gone, but still felt like home. Gordon was duly surprised when I popped up, and the reunion was a joy.

I received two offers in the few days I was in town—one from George Miller to play the villain in a revival of *East Lynne* for a year, and one from Tony Sattler, Noeline's husband and mastermind of the popular comedy series, *The Naked Vicar Show*. He suggested three months in a staged version of the show.

I was tempted to play Sir Francis Levison, the role which established me in Sydney theatre, as I was now the right age for the part, but with my escalating career in London in mind, a year was far too long. I chose *Naked Vicar* and returned to London, to put the BBC gig on pause, alert my agent, and beg my neighbors to look in on my house for a few months.

Rehearsals in Sydney were hampered by my serious jet lag, and that Tony seemed to want me to impersonate Kevin Goldsby who'd originated the show on radio. I insisted I was better at impersonating myself, and once we'd cleared that hurdle, I was allowed to interpret the material as I chose. The show opened to universally favorable press, terrific audience reaction, and extremely flattering reviews for me, all of them welcoming me home as if I'd risen from the dead.

I was fortunate in my costar Tina Bursill, whose comedy was terrific and who was an unflagging delight to work with.

There was a moment in one sketch where I ad libbed nightly, and Tina struggled to keep a straight face—and always failed. I played a vet to whom she brings her goldfish for a checkup. The fish was plastic and as I examined it, I took a look at its underside, and commented, "Jewish." There followed nightly variations on this. On the final night of the run, Tina got her own back: Instead of the plastic fish, she presented me with a two pound flounder, fresh from the market, wet and slippery and very smelly. Needless to say, Tina and I became good friends.

Tempting offers of work were made, they multiplied, the sunshine got the better of me and my three months in Australia eventually turned into twelve years.

After the horrors of subletting my London house for a year, the owning corporation asked if I would like to buy it outright for fifty thousand pounds. I could certainly afford it at the time, but idiotically, I declined. That house is now worth more than a million pounds. I return to London frequently, and each time I visit my old neighbors in that pretty row of maisonettes, I lament my lack of foresight.

~

Noeline was on the panel of a new game show called *Blankety Blanks*, and suggested I join. For two years, I reveled in being a part of it. Thanks to Graham Kennedy's talent for outrageous ad libs, the show was a huge success and the weekly recording sessions were like a party. Graham was unique in his field, known throughout Australia as The King.

Of all the TV content the Grundy Organization produced, comedy and drama, *Blankety Blanks* was a jewel in Reg Grundy's crown.

Much was made of my visibly improved physique and Graham dubbed me "Muscles", often insisting I remove my shirt at the close of an episode. Unlike the days when flashing even the slightest glimpse of flesh reduced me to a blushing mess, now I happily exposed myself whenever asked. I posed shirtless for press pictures, was interviewed about diet and workout routine. And this led to my being stalked.

My stalker was a schoolgirl, later diagnosed with psychological problems. I was living in a hotel suite in King's Cross for this first year and I often answered a knock at the door to find her standing there, silent and staring. Berating reception did no good as she always found a way to slip past the front desk.

She turned up outside the gym where I worked out and stared; she'd appear at the windows of a restaurant and watch me as I ate. She found my mother's telephone number in Brisbane and would call her at two or three in the morning.

Eventually, her parents were located and promised the girl would receive appropriate therapy. I was relieved that they restrained her before she resorted to axe or chainsaw.

Graham Kennedy was an extraordinary talent. He could take a contestant's most innocuous word or phrase and instantly respond with a witty, often suggestive, always hilarious quip. I treasure his acceptance speech when he won the Gold Logie Award for the show. At a time when winners dissolved into tears of gratitude and thanked everyone from God to their pets, Graham said simply, "I'd like to thank myself for having faith in the Grundy Organization."

Meanwhile, the offers continued to multiply and Australia felt very much like home again.

Concurrently with *Blankety Blanks*, I traveled to Brisbane weekly to host a talent program called *Stairway to the Stars*. A bonus was that one of the panelists was my old friend and mentor, Babette Stephens.

A movie evolved from *Blankety Blanks*, featuring all the actors involved on the panel, as well as every other actor working for Grundy. It was called *All At Sea*, and aspired to be a screwball comedy in the *Carry On* vein. To be frank, it was pretty terrible, but great fun. They made full use of the body by stripping me to a swimsuit and underwear in several scenes. It was mooted that I should be nude when discovered in bed with Ugly Dave Grey (don't ask), but someone had the good taste to veto that suggestion.

~

I guest hosted several TV shows during this period. One of them was in Melbourne and it was announced that I would star as host.

A Melbourne reporter took vehement exception to this. "This game show panelist, with little to show in his background except his shirtless appearances on *Blankety Blanks*, has been hired to front a national TV show. The Australian television industry should be ashamed that they can't find someone of the appropriate experience for such a prominent task."

Either she'd been too young to see any of my TV appearances dating from the '60s, or had flunked reporter school. The producers replied on my behalf with the simple advice, "Do your homework."

TWENTY-EIGHT

I WAS APPROACHED TO join the cast of the popular soap, *The Young Doctors*. At the time, I was considering theatre offers, which of course were my first priority. I agreed to ten episodes only, as I did with every such offer in subsequent years.

Some old friends were in the cast, principally John Dommett, from my home town. I played the love interest to Cornelia Francis, and would ultimately jilt her—a nice story arc, but there were longueurs here and there when the dialogue sometimes seemed to mark time. I asked John, a seasoned soapie, how he made some of the more cliched lines convincing. "Easy," he said. "You take any sentence you like, pause anywhere you like in the middle, frown, then finish the sentence."

I asked him for an example. He suggested, "Today the sun is shining but tomorrow it looks like rain." Then read it thus: "Today the sun is shining, but…" Pause for deeply troubled frown. "Tomorrow it looks like rain."

I followed his advice whenever appropriate if I had trouble with a dramatic speech. Then came an episode where John's character had a life-threatening accident and my character was his surgeon. In the dramatic bedside scene, I was comforting him, assuring him he would survive. The dialogue was pretty banal, and as the scene progressed, we realized we were both pulling the same trick: pausing mid-sentence and frowning. And we broke into gales of laughter. So hard, we held up production for some time.

~

The Age of Aquarius passed me by.

I've often been asked why I never took recreational drugs. The answer is best illustrated by an evening during the *Young Doctors* run.

I was living in an apartment in Victoria Street, Potts Point, and worked out at the City Gym on William Street. I'd become friendly with two of the regulars, visiting Americans, and invited them to dinner. They were interested in the Sydney theatre scene, so I invited John Dommett to make a fourth.

I'd learned to cook by now and was rather proud of the dishes I'd mastered. I spent most of the afternoon preparing a sumptuous feast and welcomed the guests at 7:30.

Conversation during drinks and hors d'oeuvres went swimmingly. One of the Americans produced some weed which he announced as "Columbian Gold." This meant nothing to me, but when all three guests took a puff or two, I felt obliged to do so too. The chatter was animated, and as I checked the kitchen, another joint was produced. Again, I took a few hits.

As the evening wore on, conversation faltered and I thought, *This is the longest evening in the history of dinner parties.* I longed to wind things up so I could get some sleep. I turned to John and said, "You look very tired."

John had a streak of paranoia and responded instantly, "I must be going," and fled.

Conversation dribbled on for a while, until the Americans also said they should be leaving. "Oh really?" I said as I flung the front door open. They thanked me for a pleasant evening. I floated to the bedroom and passed out fully clothed.

Around three in the morning, I woke parched. Orange juice was my only thought. I stumbled into the kitchen and opened the fridge—which was full of food.

I hadn't served dinner.

At all.

Not a morsel.

And that, ladies and gentlemen, is why I never touched pot again.

~

In the late '70s, the horrors of the year from hell were way behind me, and as Patrick Woodcock predicted, I emerged in better shape mentally and physically than I had been in my life. As an actor, I was eager to take bold steps I'd restrained from taking in my youth. In the Bramston years, I'd felt hidebound to adhere to the "leading man" image the studio imposed, and as was accepted nation-wide. I was frankly terrified of exposure as anything else, and limited myself to "safe" interpretations of roles. In the '80s, all such restraints vanished and I became a much braver actor willing to change persona and outward appearance when a role demanded it.

Producer-Director Peter Williams asked me to join the cast of Alan Ayckbourn's *Bedroom Farce*, a London success which Peter intended to tour. Having seen little of Australia in my life, I agreed.

He assembled a splendid cast including my old friend Carmen

Duncan, Ruth Cracknell, Ron Haddrick and an actress who'd emerged during the decade I spent in London, Kate Fitzpatrick. The set consisted of three separate bedrooms indicated by three double beds ranged across the stage. Light moved from bed to bed as scenes played out. My character spent most of the play confined to bed with a back injury while my wife, Carmen Duncan, and I bickered.

Carmen was a much loved friend, and one of the worst gigglers I've ever encountered. Much worse than me! Once, when I forgot an essential prop, she brought it from my dressing room and presented it to me with an appropriate ad lib. Immediately on delivering both prop and ad lib, she dissolved into convulsive laughter and was incapable of delivering her dialogue. I found myself doing what Leslie Phillips had done for me in London. "I know what you're going to say…" I said to this guffawing jelly, and then quoted her speech. She was still incapable of speaking, so I added, "And if you *had* said that, I'd reply…" This, of course, made it worse, and Carmen left the stage in gales of helpless laughter leaving me alone to devise an explanatory monologue.

Actually, Carmen was probably the best laugher I ever knew. If she told a joke, she never reached the punch line, always doubling with laughter before she could utter it.

Many years later when we were both resident in Los Angeles, Carmen arrived at my house dressed in the peak of fashion for an event we were to attend. My car was parked on a steep incline by the street and as she opened the passenger door, it swung back and knocked her over. Carmen rolled, like a very glamorous ball, all the way down the slope into the gutter. When I ran to pick her up, it was almost impossible to get her to her feet as she was laughing uncontrollably.

Bedroom Farce was a great success and the tour moved off with a couple of cast changes. Pat Macdonald of *Number 96* fame took over from Ruth Cracknell and Belinda Giblin played my wife; Belinda and

I developed a rapport and a friendship and it was a pleasure to be on stage with her—a pleasure that would be repeated in 1997 when she played my wife again—my dead wife.

We began the tour in Brisbane. It was here that I abandoned myself to a fit of temperament.

The "bedrooms" were lit and blacked out according to the scene; though blacked out was an exaggeration—dimmed out was more accurate. And when dimmed, the actors were directed to remain frozen.

At the first Brisbane matinee, while playing one of my scenes, I was baffled by the lack of reaction and took a quick glance at the audience. No one was watching my scene; they were riveted to Pat Macdonald who could be seen clearly in her dimmed out bedroom, brushing her hair, remaking her bed, flicking through the pages of a book, applying makeup.

When the curtain fell, I lost it, berating her loudly and vehemently for pulling focus. I suggested that if she persisted, I'd be equally busy during her scenes, masturbating under my bed cover—let's see if she could pull attention to herself then.

After my tirade, the curtain rose on the cleaners weaving between the empty rows in the stalls to ready the house for the evening performance. As I stalked off the stage, I caught a glimpse of a solitary figure still sitting in the stalls—Babette. I'd forgotten I was taking her out for coffee. Once we were at the café, she said, "Enjoyed the comedy," adding, after a beautifully timed pause, "and the drama."

~

The tour covered Melbourne, Adelaide, Far North Queensland and finally Perth which I'd never visited, but came to love, largely thanks to the people I met there.

Barry Humphries was due to follow us into the theatre and came to a matinee. I could see him clearly from the stage. Every time we got a laugh, he turned to take in the audience. The gleeful expression on his face as he turned back to the stage was an indication of how much he enjoyed audience laughter.

One afternoon, we lunched at a nearby restaurant and examined the menu to find the special of the day was "Dhufish." Neither of us had heard of it. Barry asked the maître d' if it was a nice way of saying Jewfish. It was, the maître d' confessed.

I caught Barry's show before leaving town. During the intermission there were slides of parodied news items. One slide read:

DHUFISH DHUMPS OVER DHUMBO DHET.

I've said it often—I'll say it again: Barry Humphries was the greatest comic entity of his generation, perhaps of the century. There was no one else.

TWENTY-NINE

AUSTRALIAN SOCIAL ATTITUDES had changed by the late '70s, particularly towards sex and sexuality. There was an openness and an acceptance that made life less stressful for anyone in the public eye. No one enjoying this new freedom could surmise that, as Noel Coward put it, there were bad times just around the corner.

Freedom, defined as the power to act without restraint, is what led me to an acquisition I'd been sternly denied in my youth: a motorcycle. I was encouraged in this by a few of my non-theatrical friends who rode bikes.

These were a disparate bunch of guys in a wide swathe of professions—engineer, mechanic, teacher, restaurateur, woodworker, police officer—and it had become necessary in my life to have friends who talked some other language than theatre. My closest and most supportive buddies were Tony Shaw and Greg Smith—Tony an engineer and Greg, who'd piloted Chinoooks in the Vietnam war, eventually entered a seminary and became pastor of a unitarian church.

I was constantly berated by Stuart Wagstaff who said, "Real stars don't ride motorbikes." I quoted Honor Blackman and Sir Ralph Richardson who rode his motorcycle until he was well into his seventies. Sir Ralph called his "Bessie." I dubbed mine "Bruce."

The experience of riding a bike is hard to describe to the car-bound, but the word "freedom" pops up again. For a start, you're on the outside of the vehicle—air, scenery, all at 360 degrees around you; it's the closest sensation to flying you can get at ground level. Yet the rider must remain in total control; doze off on a bike and you cease to be vertical—or just cease to be.

I was asked in a recent interview if the leather gear attracted me. Yes, for one reason only: leather is a desirable intervention between rider and asphalt should one meet the other. Once on a camping trip with a few biker friends, I rode a dirt bike shirtless and came off it onto gravel. I still have the scars.

Hence, leather.

~

Peter Williams approached me about a delightful light comedy, *The Owl and the Pussycat.* It had been a hit on Broadway starring Alan Alda and Diana Sands and was filmed with George Segal and Barbra Streisand. The great George Segal would get to star in one of my plays later on. *The Owl and the Pussycat* would play in Brisbane at the Twelfth Night Theatre, an extension of the formerly amateur company, now an attractive professional venue of five hundred seats. Peter asked me to choose a leading lady. Noeline was busy with the TV version of *The Naked Vicar Show,* and it occurred to me that my then next door neighbor, Kate Fitzpatrick might be a likely Pussycat. Kate agreed and we rehearsed in Sydney, traveling to Brisbane for production week.

The play opened well with good reviews and appreciative audiences, but shortly into the run, it seemed to me that Kate decided the play was somehow beneath her talents and she began to show disdain for it.

But let's go back to the first week of the run when we were both still committed to the piece.

My old friend Vincent Price was in town at His Majesty's with a one-man play on the life of Oscar Wilde. We'd spoken on the phone in Sydney, but we'd had no chance to meet due to conflicting work schedules. In Brisbane we were playing the same performance times, so the only chance to meet was at supper after our respective shows. The manager of a city restaurant happily agreed to stay open late expressly to accommodate us.

Vincent's wife Coral Browne was with him on the tour, so to make up a four, I invited Kate. Unfortunately, Coral had chosen that day to fly to Melbourne to visit an ailing relative. So we were three for supper.

I hadn't seen Vincent for several years, and we had a lot of catching up to do. However, as we settled at the table, Kate entertained us for some time with stories of her prominence in Australian theatre. After thirty minutes, she excused herself to go to the loo. Vincent hadn't managed to get a word in so far, and as he watched Kate exit, he sighed deeply and said, "I *do* wish Coral had been here tonight." His implication was clear.

I relate the above for a good, if petty reason. I need to refute an assertion made by Kate in her 2004 memoir, *Name Dropping*. She claimed that during supper, Vincent told the story of how he introduced himself to Coral by lying naked on a bed with a ribbon tied round his penis, and how this revelation shocked me.

First, let's disarm the "shock" claim. Given the life I've led, I'm incapable of being shocked by anything short of world peace.

Second, the anecdote. The story of Vincent's introduction to Coral was well known throughout the business; it proved to be the meeting of two of the world's greatest wits and evolved into one of the happiest marriages in the history of Hollywood. But as well as a wicked wit, Vincent was a civilized, socially adept gentleman. There is no earthly way he would have told that story to a total stranger, and he certainly didn't that night at supper. In fact there's no way at all he would have told the story about himself. That it was widely told *about* him always amused him, but he was incapable of self-aggrandizement.

Perhaps Kate was thinking of some other evening she spent with Vincent, and another actor whose sensibilities were more delicate than mine.

Looking back on *Owl* from the distance of age and experience, it was a singularly unhappy experience for all concerned. The play deserved better—and may have had it if Kate had had a co-star of superior pedigree, or I an actress of lesser.

THIRTY

AGAINST MY AGENT'S cautions of lowering my standards, I accepted the leading role in the British farce, *Pyjama Tops*, costarring with British comic actor John Inman, well known for TV's *Are You Being Served*. I reveled in it. After the Brisbane experience, it was like a holiday.

The plot doesn't really merit going into; suffice to say I was a philandering husband with a blonde wife and a gorgeous redhead on the side.

John, a past master of farce, was great to work with—a consummate professional dedicated to extracting the appropriate laughs from his material, and greatly generous in his interaction with other actors.

My wife was played by Veronica Lang, my wife in the London production of *Don's Party*, and my mistress was played by glamorous Louise Howitt of *Young Doctors* fame. Louise asked me one night what my view of comic timing involved.

Tongue wedged in cheek, "It's simple," I told her. "If they laugh, don't talk. If they don't laugh, talk."

We played Sydney's Theatre Royal and Melbourne's Her Majesty's.

During the Melbourne run, I also did a guest spot in a TV special starring John. The premise was that I, as well as a star of theatre and TV, was a champion ballroom dancer, and would give a demonstration with my partner Joylene. At John's introduction, I dashed in apologetic—Joylene had been held up in traffic and couldn't make it. John insisted they'd already paid for the orchestra, so proposed he do the routine with me, he in dinner jacket, I in white tie and tails; we did the foxtrot, waltz, polka, cha cha, rhumba and a grand finale of jitterbug. Given that the only area of expertise I had in dance was a meagre soft shoe, after two weeks of rehearsing me, the choreographer was ready for a rest home. But the sequence was fun and a tremendous success.

~

Back in Sydney, I signed up for ten episodes of the popular series, *The Restless Years*. I played a ruthless businessman, partner to one of the lead actors, Noel Trevarthen.

Sidney Dalton was a nice role with some teeth, and I approached the part earnestly. But there was a day…

The story arc led me into an affair with Noel Trevarthen's teenage daughter which, of course, she was at pains to conceal from him.

The scene is Dalton's apartment, early morning. Noel, playing Jeff Archer, comes to my front door to discuss a business crisis. I open the door to him in a bath robe while his daughter hides in the bedroom.

JEFF: We have to talk.
(he looks into the room and sees items
of female underwear on the sofa)

	Oh, I see you're busy. I should come back later.
SIDNEY:	(opening the door wide) Not at all. Let's talk now.

Sidney does a business deal while Jeff's daughter cowers in fear and trembling in the next room.

I arrived on the set and noted the "items of female underwear." They included everything but a whalebone corset—there were panties, bra, slip. I went to the director and argued that surely, in this day and age, a teenager would wear no more than panties.

The director countered that the excess of undergarments was essential to indicate the presence of a woman in my apartment.

Okay.

Take one.

JEFF:	We have to talk. (he looks into the room and sees items of female underwear on the sofa) Oh, I see you're busy. I should come back later.
SIDNEY:	No Jeff, you don't understand. This underwear is mine. I wear it.

Noel roared with laughter, as did most crew, and yep, so did I. We did take after take before we managed to play it with straight faces.

During this stint, I was asked by a reporter for an evening paper how it felt to be doing a soap given my primary love of theatre. I replied, "Alfred Hitchcock once said that drama is life with the dull bits cut out. Did you ever wonder what happened to all those dull bits? They joined them all together and called them *The Restless Years.*"

I thought it a pretty good joke, but the paper quoted me verbatim. I wasn't asked to do another soap for some time.

On the tail of this departure from my claim of being a disciplined actor, I was asked to do a play at the Perth Playhouse, directed by Edgar Metcalf. This time it was not just I who fell prey to the giggles, the entire cast had trouble with a very creaky thriller.

The play was to be Anthony Shaffer's thriller, *Murderer*, but last minute negotiations broke down and it was replaced by *Suddenly, At Home*, an inferior thriller by Francis Durbridge. I'd seen the play in London starring my old friend Annette Andre and in spite of her fine performance, she confessed to reservations about the writing. I had the same reservations. But I was committed.

The plot concerns a smooth, villainous chap who murders his wife for her money only to be shot ultimately by his drug-addicted mistress—with a *lot* of talking in between.

For all my doubts about the play, this was an extremely happy experience. The cast were universally friendly, supremely talented actors and while there are only two still with us from that cast, we remain in frequent communication to this day: Sally Sander who played the doomed wife and Rosemary Barr the mistress.

On the first day of rehearsal, moving awkwardly around the room, script in hand, I made an affectionate gesture towards Sally, hooked my finger in her hoop earring and nearly tore her ear off. When we'd stopped laughing at that, I made a threatening move to Roz Barr, somehow managed to get my foot through her handbag handle and nearly broke my leg.

All this hilarity was a precursor of worse to come. As a thriller, the audience ate it up while the entire cast strained to keep straight faces. Many a line was delivered upstage to prevent the audience from seeing involuntary chuckles. So much exposition was delivered via telephone calls, *Suddenly, At Home* came to be known to us as *Suddenly, A Phone*.

But this run cemented my love of Perth and its people.

~

And here began yet another ill-advised relationship which would lurch through six years of desperate incompatibility. He had a PhD in the history of education. For all that, he was a deeply depressive person who bemoaned often and bitterly that he was living in my shadow. The whole thing deteriorated quickly, yet both of us hung in for six years from some kind of insane loyalty. I was relieved when he finally found someone whose shadow was shorter than mine.

~

I did a couple of guest shots for Crawford Productions in Melbourne in *The Sullivans* and *Cop Shop*, in the latter playing a millionaire businessman. I'd ridden my motorcycle to Melbourne for this one and the crew were amused that upon my arrival to the location on the bike, I was put into an expensive suit and thence, into a Rolls Royce for my first scene. Then back on the bike to return to the hotel.

After this, a guest shot was written for me *and* the motorcycle. I played a biker pimp doling out the services of David Franklin. I was obliged to slap his face in one scene and each take was followed by a prolonged pause as I asked anxiously if I'd hurt him. So much for The Method.

I was offered my usual ten episodes in a Crawford series, *Skyways*. At last, a part I relished: a psychotic husband and father who charms his way back into his family for the purpose of gaining custody of his four year old son.

The scripts were well written and production values were high, as they were in all Crawford productions.

My chum Tina Bursill was a lead in the series, and we had a

competition to see who could get to the office set first in the mornings. This was not so much from professionalism as much as it was about lighting. We often found ourselves in a desk-and-chair scene, one of us on the chair the other perched on the edge of the desk. The lights were overhead, so if sitting in the chair, one was looking up, fully bathed in flattering light. If sitting on the edge of the desk, one was looking down and resembled Mount Rushmore at noon. The race was to snag the chair position before one's colleague got to the set.

My final episode had the deranged man abducting his son and taking him on a flight to Berlin where Interpol arrests him as he suffers a breakdown. The episode was directed by Charles (Bud) Tingwell, a fine actor, a terrific director and an exceptionally nice person.

The four year old who played my son became very attached to me which was perfect for the father-son relationship in the show. When I arrived on set in the mornings, he'd beg to sit on my motorcycle which his mother cautiously allowed.

When we came to my final scene, I don't think his mother or Bud Tingwell had given him sufficient warning. As I emerged from the flight into the Berlin airport, international police seized me and wrenched the boy from my arms. I wrestled with the cops, screaming hysterically until they took me down to the floor and handcuffed me.

After the first take, the boy was inconsolable and kept asking his mother if it was real, had they hurt me, or was I just "tricking"—his term for acting. It took a lot of soothing from all of us to calm him down for a second take.

~

Around this time, a communicable illness began to afflict gay men. In the next decade, I'd lose many close friends, actors and writers as well as civilians, to what became known as AIDS. But in its early stages, it was the disease that dare not speak its name—or more accurately, the disease that authoritative bodies the world over refused to acknowledge. In America in particular, President Ronald Reagan refused point blank for years to admit there was a health crisis, let alone call it by name. It was as if gay men were dispensable, so the plague could be ignored, and research into containment could be delayed.

By comparison, note the astonishing speed with which science produced a vaccine for Covid—a communicable disease which affected everyone without discrimination.

AIDS wiped out a significant number of figures in the public eye: Freddy Mercury, Anthony Perkins, Liberace, Peter Allen, Derek Jarman, Brad Davis, Halston, Amanda Blake, Rudolf Nureyev, Arthur Ashe, to name *very* few. But in Hollywood, it could all be ignored, after all, everyone knew there were no homosexual actors in Hollywood. Then Rock Hudson died, and at long last, in 1985, Reagan was obliged to mention the forbidden word, "AIDS", and acknowledge that it was a national health crisis.

The most visible of those who became activists were playwright Larry Kramer, San Francisco city supervisor, Harvey Milk, and Elizabeth Taylor whose monumental humanitarian work was largely obscured by her celebrity. As a result of her good friend Hudson's death, she was the first globally recognized figure to raise funds for research and awareness of the disease. For her efforts, she was awarded the French Legion of Honor in 1987. But there were very few with her extraordinary humanity and bravery.

Today, thanks to the work of those who virtually forced governments to act, the disease is containable. Yet, down the line, in the "enlightened" 1990s, AIDS would affect my career irreversibly.

THIRTY-ONE

IN 1982, MICHAEL Blakemore came to town to direct *Noises Off*, the smash hit comedy by Michael Frayn which he'd directed in London and New York.

Noises Off is quite simply one of the funniest plays ever written.

Michael's direction was of course exciting, exacting and a joy to partake of. Again, as well as his solid, overall view of the play, he allowed invention. One small piece of business I suggested he thought worth keeping.

In act one, my character sits upstage with a box of groceries, while the director of the play-within-the-play is downstage arguing with the leading lady. Absently, I notice a banana in the box, take it out, peel it and eat it while watching the downstage altercation. Michael allowed it because it filled the scene logically without pulling focus from the central characters.

I did this eight times a week for eight months and for years after, was unable to look at a banana without wanting to throw up.

Carol Raye led the cast at first, along with Stuart Wagstaff and Frank Wilson and an actress with whom I became good friends, Anne Charleston. Later in the eight months we toured the play, Carol would move on to other projects and was replaced by Jill Perryman.

Wagstaff and I were the closest of friends—always a danger playing a dramatic scene.

At the top of act two, the set of the farce within the play is reversed so we can see what goes on backstage before a performance.

The play's stage manager is making a mess of the pre-curtain announcements: "Ladies and Gentlemen, please take your seats. The performance will begin in five minutes." A moment later, "The performance will begin in two minutes." Then, a moment after that, "The performance will begin in four minutes."

My character, Freddie, desperately insecure, is standing by the pass door to the audience as the director Lloyd, played by Wagstaff, bursts in, furious, and the dialogue went like this:

LLOYD: What the fuck is going on?
FREDDIE: Great Scott!

We opened in Brisbane and at the first Wednesday matinee, Wagstaff came to my dressing room deeply troubled.

"I just took a look at the audience. It's full of grey haired old ladies. I can't say 'fuck' in front of them. Many of them are my fans."

I became the righteous Voice of Thespis. "Are you kidding? This is a world famous play! Actors have spoken this dialogue in London, New York, Paris. You *must* honor the playwright!" I said from a great height.

Stuart nodded, and said, reluctantly, "You're right."

And we thought no more about it. Until act two.

My character Freddie is by the pass door as Lloyd bursts in.

LLOYD: What the *hell* is going on?
FREDDIE: Great fuck! …I mean *Scott*! Great *Scott*!"

And, of course, we were unable to look each other in the eye for the rest of the act.

If you've seen the play, you'll remember that timing of entrances and exits was vital. One night in Canberra, the door through which I was to enter jammed. Fearful of destroying the pace of the piece, I wrenched it open and it hit my left eyebrow with such force that blood flowed instantly. When I staggered on into the scene, the other actors thought, "Uh oh, blood. Barry's building his part."

At intermission, it was realized I'd done considerable damage and intermission dragged on to 30 minutes while the stage manager patched me temporarily.

After the performance, I was rushed to a doctor they'd woken from a sound sleep, and had four stitches in my forehead. The scar is still visible. I wear it with pride.

Oh yes, only one other incident ruffled the security of the company. Due to my gym habit, I sometimes left workout togs and jock straps in my dressing room. During the Adelaide run, I arrived one night to find all my jock straps had been stolen.

I don't even want to speculate on the motive.

~

Around this time I did a guest appearance on *The Mike Walsh Show*, a supremely popular TV variety show which was broadcast live around Australia. I wrote a parody of Noel Coward's *Private Lives* which I dubbed *Private Wives*. June Salter and I were Amanda and Elyot on their new respective honeymoons, regretting their parting—until she discovers that Elyot is now partnered with a man.

Upon the revelation:

AMANDA: A man! This martini doesn't seem very dry.
ELYOT: I must say you're taking it well.
AMANDA: So are you, obviously.
ELYOT: (*raising his glass*) Bottoms up.
AMANDA: I don't wish to hear the sordid details.

And later, on hearing Amanda's new husband is afflicted with jaundice:

ELYOT: Go then, go and be happy, you and your small, yellow husband.
AMANDA: And you and your tall, dark and handsome— husband.
ELYOT: Go! I'll turn the other way.
AMANDA: (*vehemently*) I don't wish to hear the sordid details!

Ten years later, the sketch was incorporated into a New York revue I wrote and was singled out for praise as a major highlight of the show by the New York Times, stating its "cheery salaciousness." And even later, it won me the Noel Coward International Writing Award with which came a considerable amount of cash.

Carol Raye, ever the entrepreneur, capitalized on the success of this sketch and approached Walsh's producers with a proposal that I write a sketch for the two of us to perform weekly on the show.

The first I wrote, *Prelude to the Falklands War*, depicted Margaret Thatcher on a fund-raising trip to Australia, prior to going to war in the Falkland Islands. The sketch was received exceptionally well, and thereafter, I wrote some eighty sketches for us which we performed live over two years. The Falklands sketch, though relevant to its times, still evokes warm laughter. You can find it immortalized on YouTube.

~

Once again, I found I was doubling the work load. It took my mind off the emotional vacancies in my life.

I was writing the weekly sketch for the Walsh Show for part of the time I toured *Noises Off*. I faxed the sketch to Carol (remember faxes?), then I flew into Sydney on Monday mornings, went straight to the 9 studio, rehearsed with Carol in a dressing room for an hour, then performed the sketch live, and immediately after, flew back to wherever *Noises Off* was playing.

~

I'd been eager to write something of substance for some time. In 1983, I approached John Barningham, producer of *The Sullivans* with a view to writing eps for a Crawfords series. At the same time, the casting director of a new series approached me about playing a regular role in *Carson's Law*. The series concerned a legal dynasty in the Melbourne of 1928 and was to star one of Australia's deservedly favorite actresses, Lorraine Bayley. They offered me the part of Robert Carson, the downtrodden son of the great legal eagle.

I declined in favor of writing for the show.

Over the two years it aired, I wrote a total of eleven episodes, just one short of the grand total of twelve written by principal writers Peter Pinney and Roger Moulton.

It was a pleasure to write for Lorraine Bayly, a splendid actress who always relayed the writer's words as if they were her own, and with a warmth that endeared her to her vast audience.

I also reveled in writing specifically for good friends including John O'May as a closeted homosexual which aberration, if discovered in Melbourne of 1928 was punishable by up to fourteen years' imprisonment. I wrote a character for Natalie Mosco, an American actress resident in Australia at that time; she played a drug-addicted silent movie star whose career was in decline. And a part for the wonderful actress Carol Burns with whom I'd later work as an actor in Coward's *Blithe Spirit*. Best of all, I invented a character for my cherished mentor Babette Stephens as the grand dame of a community theatre group. Art imitated life and she played it to perfection.

And of course, I wrote a guest shot for myself as a rather grubby playwright with an egg stained tie, and who, obsessed with Stanislavsky, determined to extract realism from an actor playing a tree.

One of the great advantages of my linear progression in the business of show was as an actor writing dialogue for actors. Instinctively, an actor/writer is aware of which phrases will flow from an actor's mouth, and which will cause a log jam. This is not always the case with a writer who's never had to speak his own words.

Example: While designing *CSI New York*, my partner Vaughan Edwards returned home one evening and related the plight of an actor playing a detective that day. The team were obliged to search homeless shelters, and the young inexperienced writer's line went, "We must institute a shelter to shelter search."

Try that five times quickly.

It took the actor ten takes to get it right.

THIRTY-TWO

THE LATE JOHN Krummel was a major name in Australian theatre in the 1980s. He was known as a risk-taking actor and a dictatorial director. He was also one of the most astute artistic directors I've ever known.

The Marian Street Theatre on Sydney's north shore was a delight to play. With a capacity of three hundred, there was an intimacy which bound the audience to the actor.

I'd heard horror stories about Krummel's treatment of actors, so was hesitant when he called asking me to replace an actor he'd lost from Ayckbourn's *Season's Greetings*. But the part was irresistible—Bernard, a feeble-spirited doctor with an alcoholic wife. This wimp of a man gives an elaborate puppet show each Christmas for his family's children who despise both him and his puppets.

I was given one of Australia's leading puppeteers to teach me the intricacies of operating stringed puppets.

Once I'd perfected the operation of stringed marionettes, I set about giving the impression of a modestly talented amateur. For instance, the puppet play was *The Three Little Pigs*, so I gave the same falsetto voice to all three so they were indistinguishable from one another. There was a dog—hard work for the puppeteer to operate four legs—to whom I gave a gravel voice for his frequent greeting, "Whassup, whassup?"

When Bernard, this poor defeated soul, gave his puppet show, the children were nowhere to be seen, so it played only to Ron Haddrick's curmudgeonly grandfather, and one of his daughters played by Suzy Roylance, both of whom observed the show devoid of reaction. The audiences howled with laughter night after night at the inept puppetry, all but one—Judi Farr's eight year old daughter was brought to tears and said this failure of a man attempting to entertain was the saddest thing she'd ever seen.

I often encountered Ron Haddrick in a radio studio over the years following this show; his greeting to me was always a gravelly, "Whassup, whassup?"

As for the appearance and the body language of the man, I gelled my hair flat and shaved above the temples to give the impression of a receding hairline. I hunched my shoulders and adopted the gait of a defeated man. I boast that the character was so convincing that Gloria Payten, my agent of twenty-three years, turned to her partner after my first scene and asked, "Who's that?"

I was nominated for the Critics' Circle Award and Krummel accompanied me to the ceremony at the Theatre Royal. I thought I was used to his eccentricities by now, but I underestimated his capacity for making his feelings known to the world. When the award went to Ruth Cracknell, Krummel clutched me by the shoulder and shouted, "*You've been robbed*!"

All eyes turned to us. It was refreshing to find I

still had the capacity to blush.

During this play's run, a blood vessel burst onto the retina of my right eye. It began with what seemed like flashing lights in that eye. When examined, the flashes were determined to be blood leaking onto the retina. A rush was made to save the sight—blood thinners, laser treatment—but the condition worsened. I was warned that I would lose sight in that eye quite suddenly.

The "quite suddenly" happened one night during the first scene of *Season's Greetings*. At the end of this scene, there was a total blackout, and in the dark, I was to follow a glow tape strip along the edge of the stage to the far side, to appear in the kitchen set when the lights came up. This was the point at which my vision decided to give up. The blackout, for me, was total and I could see no sign of the glow tape. As I crossed, cautiously, I stepped off the stage into the audience. Mercifully for the elderly couple who caught me, the stage was low.

And yes, I uttered my usual expostulation in such a situation: "Shit!" echoed through the darkness of the theatre.

In the dark the aged couple helped me to my feet and aimed me to the stage. I found Kerry McGuire's leg and climbed it—she played my wife and was seated at the kitchen table ready for the next scene. I felt for my chair, and sat just in time for lights up. Kerry did a double take; I had blood on my face. I mopped it with a table napkin and the scene proceeded.

The condition was irreversible. The retina was scarred and I lost central vision in that eye. One of the eye specialists advised that if I valued my life, I should abandon my much-loved motorcycle for a car. I considered this for a day or two, then on the next matinee day, I started out early and traveled the fourteen miles to the theatre slowly, making a mental note of every pothole along the way. And I lived to bike another day.

But the loss of central vision in one eye proved an even greater handicap than traffic or ill-kempt infrastructure; I'd never again be able to appreciate 3D movies!

~

I went on to do a succession of plays at Marian Street, each one a challenge and a pleasure to perform.

In the British play, *Pack of Lies*, about the pursuit of a Russian agent living in London suburbia, I played the cold, calculating MI5 operative who sacrifices a family's loyalty to capture the spy. Again I got to work with the terrific Judi Farr and as the alleged spy, Elaine Lee whom I came to adore, not just for her talent, but for her warmhearted sense of humor.

Side By Side By Sondheim was a pleasant interlude featuring many numbers by the master, Stephen Sondheim. Over the years, Graham Maclean designed half a dozen of the plays in which I appeared, and two which I'd written. His set for *Sondheim* was a glossy burgundy colored stage on which two grand pianos sat on separate turntables. I narrated the evening in a burgundy dinner jacket, while Bartholomew John wore a black dinner suit, and the two women, Judi Connelli and Gaye MacFarlane, were in aqua evening gowns. To describe the production as classy is a vast understatement.

During the run, Bart and Judi both fell prey to flu. Gaye and I stayed healthy somehow. Bart spent a couple of evenings dashing to the wings to throw up between numbers, and Judi was obliged to leave the show for a few nights. Powerhouse Geraldine Turner stepped in with virtually no notice and stopped the show with her every number. I'd certainly had reason to respect her talent prior to this production, but it grew a hundredfold as I witnessed the confidence and good humor with which she delivered the numbers.

Michael Blakemore was in town during this run and wanted to see the show. No way could I tempt him to pillion on my bike, so I took the car and drove him to the theatre. This is the director who was passionate about the golden age musicals and who won a Tony for his Broadway revival of *Kiss Me Kate*, so I wasn't entirely surprised when, on the drive back to Sydney, he shook his head and said, "Sondheim is bloody-minded. He never finishes a tune!"

One sad falling out marked this production. My agent Gloria Payten had, for twenty-four years, upheld my billing agreement—top billing, single line, above the title, and no less than half the size of the title. John Krummel delighted in shit-stirring; to him it was an essential theatre sport. So it was with a hint of delight that he informed me that, in negotiating contracts for *Sondheim*, Gloria had been pushing to bill Judi Connelli above me.

I took it up with Gloria querying her conflict of interests. Gloria argued that while I was merely narrating, the singing star of the production was Judi. I said I had no choice but to leave the agency. I was knocked more than a little sideways when Gloria burst into tears. But the decision had been made and I moved to ex-William Morris agent, Anthony Williams.

Krummel always honored my billing and when he asked me to play a significant part in just the first act of *The Philanthropist*, in which he played the lead, he gave me special billing in a box. Every bit as valuable as billing above the title.

It was during this production that I considered writing a play, a comedy specifically for myself and Noeline Brown. I spent the second act of *Philanthropist* for which I was idle, hard at work in my dressing room making notes.

The purpose was not only to write a comedy of some substance, but to give us both a virtuoso vehicle in which we could show off—

we relished each other's approach to comedy, our reciprocal sense of timing, and as the decades had proved, we shone when bouncing lines off one another.

THIRTY-THREE

AS WITH EVERY play, sketch or novel I've committed to paper, I wrote the final twenty minutes before I started the play. As I stated earlier, other writers have other methods which are every bit as effective, but those I know to be successful have a clear idea of where they're going before they begin. Coward had the entire play in his mind before setting words to paper—which made sense of the boast that he wrote *Private Lives* in three days.

Any would-be writer who tells you they have no plot in mind, but merely let their characters lead them along, doesn't have a play, they have a typing exercise. Just as anyone who claims, "I have a great idea for a play!" actually means they have a great idea for act one of a play.

I have to know where I'm headed.

If only life were like that.

I wanted my play to reflect two monumental plays about incompatibility, Coward's *Private Lives*, and Albee's *Who's Afraid of*

Virginia Woolf? both of which depict the comedy and tragedy of people who can live neither with nor without each other. These I actually referenced in my text.

I continued to jot lines, scenes, plot points for some time and took the skeleton of the play with me when I signed to do Gerald Moon's Broadway hit, *Corpse* with Gordon Chater.

~

The Gordon-Frost organization took advantage of a trip I made to New York

where I saw the play and collected the set design to bring back to Australia. It's a tricksy piece in which I played twins, with every conceivable device worked into the plot to make the audience believe there were two of the lead actor.

A couple of weeks in New York allowed me to spend much time with my now good friends the Perrins, Lesley and Forrest. Lesley, as Lesley Davison had written many musical numbers I did on *Bramston*.

I saw a little Off Broadway musical called *Nunsense* which I enjoyed so much, I bought the rights for Australia. I had no practical purpose in mind at the time, except that I knew it would be a success down under. Ultimately, I collaborated with Mike Walsh who took over production and I directed.

Gordon Chater was resident in New York at the time having had a triumphant success with Australian Steve J. Spears' one-man play, *The Elocution of Benjamin Franklin*—he won the Off Broadway award, the Obie, for this. I caught up with him and his roommate Tom Boyd who'd been part of the *Sugar Babies* company with Ann Miller and Mickey Rooney.

Press "pause" for a *Sugar Babies* anecdote of Tom's:

Ann Miller, undisputed queen of the nerve tap, was adored by the company. She'd been a movie baby so her theatre vernacular was limited. She flubbed a line one night, came offstage and said to Tom, "When I screwed that line, I had cheese all over my face!'

Tom said, politely, "Do you mean egg?"

Ann replied, "Egg, cheese—it's all poultry."

Back to *Corpse*.

Gordon flew in from New York on Air New Zealand and his first line as he disembarked was, a grumpy, "The airline is as boring as the country." He was greatly overweight and was eating and drinking far too much. It slowed the rehearsal process and, for the first and only time in our long relationship, we bickered over scenes. Director Edgar Metcalfe refereed and kept us on track. We were to tour Brisbane, Townsville, Rockhampton, Darwin and Perth before Sydney and Melbourne.

My first entrance into a dimly lit set was as Queen Mary. …And well you might ask. The play was set in the '30s and the Queen Mary disguise was employed by the down-on-his-luck actor twin in order that he could shoplift at Harrods with impunity.

Makeup took a good two hours prior to every performance, and much was made of my removing the makeup, stripping and donning male clothing in act one before Gordon's entrance as a bogus colonel whom my character would blackmail into murdering the rich twin so I could take his identity.

The only others in the cast were the delightful Maggie King and a bright young actor James Bean.

The plot included a duel between one twin and the colonel, and I took fencing lessons for three months prior to beginning rehearsals. Gordon decided to forego training and fake it, and one night, I nearly lost my sight completely at his sword's point, which struck me and drew blood just a quarter of an inch below my good eye.

For me, the swordplay involved a great deal of leaping from tall staircases and furniture. Gordon's weight prevented him from matching me, so I tended to look as if I'd been afflicted with St. Vitas Dance as I darted around him.

We opened in a heatwave in Brisbane at the Twelfth Night Theatre, which could barely accommodate the revolving stage on which were the two sets: the poor twin's basement flat, and the rich twin's sumptuous Art Deco living room.

In his physical condition, Gordon found it impossible to climb the stairs to a dressing room, so a makeshift room was constructed for him on stage level in the wings.

His habit of martinis with lunch, martinis with dinner, after the performance, and then a bottle of wine with supper, had made him constantly grumpy and one never quite knew what mood he was in at curtain up.

One matinee day, after my two hour slog of dressing and making up as Queen Mary, I waited patiently at the top of the staircase with Maggie King to make my first entrance. The company manager came to us and told us a party of high schoolers were still filing into the theatre—what should we do? It was my decision to make, so I told him to hold the curtain until they'd settled. I didn't want to play the quiet, eerie opening scene to kids finding seats.

After five minutes, Gordon stomped out of his dressing room demanding to know why the curtain hadn't gone up on time. I explained the situation.

He replied angrily, "Any actor worth his salt could hold their attention!" and he stomped back into his dressing room.

Maggie King burst into tears, and I was close. But once the audience settled, we started.

At intermission, the company manager Sid Piddington came to my dressing room in a sweat. “Gordon didn't mean that! He's not well today and his temper got the better of him.”

I considered this and said coolly, “Actually, he's quite right. The curtain must go up on time.”

“What about the latecomers?”

“Hold them until Gordon's entrance.”

For two weeks, I played my opening scene in utter quiet, then, a knock at the door which I flung it open to reveal Gordon. Instantly, ushers' flashlights went on all over the theatre, and latecomers shuffled noisily into seats. And not a word of Gordon's opening speech was heard.

Eventually, he apologized profusely for his hissy fit, I relented and it was business as usual from there on. And we always held the curtain for latecomers.

~

The play was greeted wonderfully on all the touring dates and Gordon and I received universally glowing reviews.

One of the dates was Alice Springs where I stayed at the same hotel as American star, Jason Robards Jr. He was in Australia to star in the TV movie, *The Last Frontier*. We breakfasted at the same time every morning, often together. He brought his two children to the matinee of *Corpse*.

The Gordon-Frost management were, for some inexplicable reason, against my traveling my own motorcycle to every city and arranged a deal with Honda to provide me with one at every date.

This worked pretty well—until we reached Perth. Here, the only bike Honda could spare was a dirt bike; not my favorite means of transport, and certainly not designed for reliability on hardtop.

Then, as Gordon told in his memoir, a funny thing happened to me on the way to the theatre.

The night before we closed Perth, with Sydney the next date, I was en route to the theatre. At an intersection devoid of any traffic, and doing no significant speed, I slowed for a red light; the brakes of the bike seized and I was thrown to the ground. The bike flipped and came down on my right leg. I guessed something was seriously wrong when, pain notwithstanding, I tried to lift the leg and my foot fell to one side.

Motorists stopped, one called an ambulance and the medics instantly shot me with something for the pain. My threshold for drugs of any kind has always been low, so that's all I remember until I was being prepared for surgery—a nurse was cutting my jeans off with scissors. My brain rallied sufficiently to warn her that as I'd been en route from hotel shower to theatre, I wasn't wearing underwear. It didn't deter her one bit.

Next, it was broad daylight and I was in a hospital room unable to move at all. A nurse explained that I'd broken both tibia and fibula close to the ankle. Happily (?) she explained, the breaks were clean. A surgeon—a very good surgeon I realized later—had spent most of the night aligning the bones, then drilling through my heel bone to insert a pin. From it, a cable traveled over a pulley to a weight, sufficient to prevent the bones from slipping past each other and shortening the leg as they knit. I was told I'd be in this bed, immobile, for a month.

When the extent of the accident hit me in full, I passed out, either from shock or the painkillers. I woke to hear muffled voices and found myself staring at a camera. Somehow, a news journalist and his photographer had managed to get past security and took pictures. Orderlies eventually chased them, but the pic appeared in the Perth evening paper and then around the country. It reached my mother before I did. She was convinced I was at death's door, and that theatre, as an institution, had done me in.

James Bean, who understudied me, took over for the final two Perth performances and was, I'm told, terrific. I've never had the opportunity to draw parallels with the immortal, if fictional Peggy Sawyer until now, but I can affirm that James went out there a youngster and came back a star.

The cast came to see me, faces as long as mine, and bade me farewell as they headed back to Sydney.

I heard nothing, absolutely nothing from the Gordon-Frost Organization—not commiseration, sympathy, ire. Not a single word. And not, I add, to this day. This somehow compounded the awfulness of my situation. To save the Sydney stretch of the tour, they had to replace me, but there was only one other actor in the world who was familiar with the physical intricacies of the twin doubling, and the mechanics of the production. Keith Baxter, who'd played *Corpse* on Broadway, was brought to Australia to replace me. I heard that rehearsal was tough on Gordon who had to cope with Baxter's considerable demands, and he finally had to give serious thought to the sword fight instead of standing stock still while his co-star ran around him.

The ongoing silence from the Gordon-Frost office was more than disappointing, more than hurtful, it was insulting. Chater, never one to hide his feelings or to mince words, said it best. Some years after the production, Ashley Gordon died and Frost called Gordon Chater to ask him to say a few words in tribute at the memorial. Chater's reply was simple. "I despised him when he was alive, I'm not going to say nice things about him now he's dead."

Weeks of immobility in a hospital bed lay ahead and I needed something to keep the neurons firing; I ran over my notes for a play. I had the hospital staff bring in my computer equipment which, in 1986, was rather more complex than today's laptops: the computer was a solid cube of eighteen inches, a separate monitor, keyboard, floppy disk drive and printer. These covered every square inch of the mobile bed table. A nurse watched with alarm as the pieces were deployed. "If we have to bring in life support, there's nowhere to plug it in!"

I worked daily on the play until I had a rough draft.

I sent out for a stash of vitamins and minerals which filled every other shelf in the room. Perth friends rallied and brought food and wine and lots of jokes to cheer me.

A month later, I was anesthetized again while they removed the traction and put my leg into a hip to ankle cast. A good friend, one of the many who were constant visitors, took me on my first walk around the ward to accustom me to the crutches, and cautiously to dinner at a restaurant, my first glimpse of the outside world for four long weeks.

Eventually, I was loaded onto a plane on the lift they generally used for food, and back in Sydney, my old biker friend Greg collected me at the airport in his car from which he'd removed the passenger seat to accommodate my cast.

I spent three months at home, miserable not just because of the confinement, but the relationship with Peter had deteriorated completely; I was as depressed by my situation as he was by nature.

After three months of minimal movement, the hip to ankle cast was removed and replaced by knee to ankle plaster which I was to wear for another three months. It allowed more mobility and encouraged John Krummel to ask me to do Ayckbourn's *Absurd Person Singular*. The play is in three acts, each separated by a year. I queried the validity of doing the play with a plaster cast, but Krummel considered that enough had been made in the press of my broken leg, that disbelief would be suspended and the plaster cast excused by audiences. And, to a degree, it was. But there was one night as I left the theatre, a patron stopped me and asked, "How come you had a broken leg for three years?"

THIRTY-FOUR

MIKE WALSH AND I agreed on dates for *Nunsense*, and once *Absurd Person* opened, I went about casting it. With author Dan Goggin's permission, I rewrote passages for Australian audiences. I decided against the conceit of the original New York production. There, it was played a little like sketch comedy, actresses were very much actresses playing nuns. In the three companies I would direct, I aimed for the impression of real nuns in a crisis situation obliging them to put on a show to raise funds.

We held auditions which were torturous, not only because I was hobbling up and down a theatre aisle with a leg in plaster, but due to my compassion for actors as a race, I hated saying no to anyone.

There was a wide range of auditionees, but the most curious of all was a sweet looking girl who came dressed in maid's uniform—black mini skirt and blouse, a little white apron and a frilly white cap. She gave her music to the MD, Michael Tyack, and winsomely began a golden oldie, "It's Been a Long, Long Time." Unfortunately, she had a lisp which rendered the opening chorus thus:

> Kith me onthe and kith me twithe and kith me onthe again,
> It'th been a long, long time...

She was so charming, that had a part been appropriate, I'd have cast her in a flash; but few plays spring to mind in which a sibilant maid is essential.

The first choice for Mother Superior was Joan Sydney. Sydney was a splendid actress and singer I'd first seen in an Old Time Music Hall cabaret in Perth where she sang the old Victorian number, "Are We To Part Like This, Bill?" and moved me to tears. As Mistress of Novices, I wanted Maggie King who'd been so good in *Corpse*. The rest of the cast were equally suited to the task: American Kelly Wells for Sister Amnesia, wonderful Robyn Arthur, whose unmiked voice could fill a stadium, as Sister Robert, and as the novice, Sister Leo, a newcomer, Georgie Parker. Georgie is now well known to Australian audiences for her lead roles in theatre and TV. Brilliant, witty choreography was devised by Dolores Dunbar.

In the original New York production, there was a slide show in act two, purportedly devised by the members of the order as a prank for Mother Superior. While in the Perth hospital, I wrote a short movie as an insert to replace the slide show in the original production. It was shot as a silent movie, *Nunsmoke*, a western, with the Lone Nun and Sister Tonto saving the township from the evil Sister Jessie Janes. It was filmed in glorious Convent Color—black and white—and supported by a short, amusing score by Michael Tyack, it stopped the show nightly.

I was still playing *Absurd Person Singular* at Marian Street when

Nunsense opened and Krummel generously canceled the performance that night and the entire cast came to the opening.

Mike Walsh and I sat together nervously, but fled and hid at intermission, unwilling to hear any opinion until the whole thing was over. We worried needlessly; the show received an ovation and the reviews were raves.

As the show progressed into its third week, one performance was growing, becoming busier and more vulgar. Joan Sydney was known to "improve" her performance during a run, and in this it became offensive as she progressed from being a real nun to a grotesque parody.

Night after night, giving notes, I begged her to bring the character down to where it had been on opening night. Joan refused point blank and one night slammed her dressing room door in my face with such force, that had I been an inch closer, it might've given me the nose job I'd craved in my teens.

Now that the show was a sellout success, Mike was inundated with calls from Joan's agent insisting that she was the star, and demanded top billing and a substantial salary hike. It was, in fact, an ensemble show and there was no "star". Confident that the show was an extraordinary hit, and mindful of Joan's disruptive behavior, Mike and I decided not to renew her contract when the initial six week agreement expired. We hired my old pal Betty Bobbitt to replace Joan, and the show once again became an ensemble comic joy.

Mike proposed a separate Melbourne production and insisted on a talk show favorite, Joy Westmore for Mother Superior. I was able to secure good friend Myra DeGroot as Sister Hubert, and *Laugh In* alum Chelsea Brown as Sister Amnesia. Three weeks into rehearsal it became apparent that Joy couldn't manage the musical numbers. A week before we opened, she pleaded ill health and dropped out of the show.

By now, the Sydney cast had begun a tour in Brisbane. I did a quick juggling act and pulled Betty Bobbitt from the Brisbane cast, upping Maggie King to Mother Superior there, and we opened at Melbourne's Comedy theatre with Betty's Mother Superior gloriously funny. Again, the show was a triumphant success.

These two productions played all over Australia for two years and broke box office records at every theatre in the country.

THIRTY-FIVE

THE PLASTER CAME off! After nearly seven months of confinement, I became a biped once more. Therapy began to get the now withered right leg back into shape. I hit the gym daily, a habit I'd missed. And you guessed it, I bought a brand new motorcycle, a Kawasaki 1100cc. A press pic of the new vehicle shows me in the saddle beaming, while the pillion is occupied by an alarmed Maggie King as Mother Superior. Though a lifelong atheist, I considered her presence in the photograph to be insurance. Just in case.

I rode the bike to the Southern Highlands to visit Noeline and her husband Tony Sattler. As I pulled up in their driveway, Tony took a good look at the bike and said, "So. You're going to commit Kawasaki now."

~

I needed a holiday badly and took off for Europe. I aimed first for an old friend's majestic villa in Malta. He'd inherited the Francia mansion built in 1740 and spent his life on its upkeep. Whenever I visited, I was given the upper floor of the north wing in the winter, and the lower floor in summer. After he died, having no heirs, he bequeathed it to the government and it served for a time as an official residence for dignitaries.

During the hours-long stopover in Rome airport while waiting for the connection to Malta, I was given a private room where I was able to employ my laptop—one of the very first in production—to work on the play.

I continued to work on it in the luxury of the villa in Malta, then a short hop to Paris, Amsterdam and London for a binge of old friends and theatre.

Back in Sydney, Stuart Wagstaff read the first draft of the play, and greatly enthused, he set up a private reading for his manager, Harry Miller. Noeline joined Wagstaff and Miller in my Double Bay apartment, and we read.

When we finished, Miller was silent for a moment, then said, "No one will go to see this. Too many words."

Seriously dismayed, I considered shelving the play. But a copy found its way to the Ensemble Theatre where director Sandra Bates was extremely eager to give it a home.

The prospect of working with Noeline again, aided immeasurably by Sandra's insight, made the tortures of a first production bearable. And there were tortures.

Here, I have to admit, in utter shame, to the way I behaved during rehearsal. All my previous writings aside, this was my first attempt at a serious comedy, one with a dramatic core, and a great deal was on the line. My anxieties were considerable and I became more than a tough taskmaster on myself—worse, I badgered Noel relentlessly: more naturalism, less visible emotion, more intensity here, less of something else there. Again, my Freud went out the window or I might have realized I was badgering myself, but taking out my personal insecurities on the person I cared most about in this exercise—my cherished professional partner, and more than that, my best friend.

One morning Noel came to rehearsal and saw me in conference in Sandra's office. She was convinced, due to my behavior, that I was asking to replace her. In fact, Sandra was giving me a much deserved dressing down for making life so miserable for Noeline. I felt like the world's greatest arsehole, and again Babette Stephen's wise advice came to mind: Pull yourself together.

The great Neil Simon once said, "all writing is rewriting." No truer sentiment has ever been uttered about the process. As we continued rehearsal, we found no cuts were necessary, but certain passages were awkwardly placed. To render the characters' emotional progression logical and seamless, there were days of literal cutting and pasting. Noeline observed that her script looked like a poultice. As far along as the last preview, we were getting an unwanted laugh late in act two, during the solemn scene where the protagonists part. I spent a night poring over the script looking for a trigger for this laugh—I found it in a single line in act one. Once this was cut, the solemn scene in act two was never again interrupted by so much as a cleared throat.

The opening was greeted with laughs the like of which I'd never heard before or since. And we always played the ultimate parting of the two lovers to absolute quiet, broken only occasionally at the midweek matinees when a sob or two escaped a few of the elderly female theatregoers.

Two days later, the reviews were due out. I biked to the local newsagent, bought the Sydney Morning Herald, and took it back to my apartment where I sat in the carport for some time before I was brave enough to open the paper.

Harry Kippax's review was an unqualified love letter. He praised the play, its wit, and our performances. I burst into tears. The relief at knowing it was a success was overwhelming. All the other press, magazine, radio and TV notices followed suit and were universal raves. We broke all time box office records for the Ensemble theatre, a feat we'd accomplish again when the play was revived a year later.

I was honored with the Norman Kessell "Glugs" Award for my contributions to theatre as actor, playwright and director. The award has since followed me around the world and now has pride of place over the fireplace in the den of my Los Angeles home.

In January 1988, after the Sydney season, Noel and I toured the play to Melbourne, Hobart and Launceston. Two American entrepreneurs, having read of its success, flew from New York to see it. One was fledgling producer Jay Cardwell, the other director Louis Burke. I had doubts about their plans. Burke saw it in a Broadway house, most of which seated more than a thousand. I insisted the play was better suited to an Off Broadway house of no more than five hundred. I agreed to meet with them in New York when we finished the short Australian tour.

While we were in Launceston, I said goodbye to two of my dearest friends. Dita Cobb had retired there and after we opened, we lunched and gabbed about "old times". We never became maudlin—I've found that innately witty people seldom do. But towards the end of our afternoon, Dita did say, wistfully, "The problem is your body wears out before you're finished with it."

It occurred to me that I was unlikely to be in that part of the world again, and saying goodbye was hard indeed.

The other treasured friend was Myra DeGroot, a great performer, singer and actress who was well known in London theatre before she took up residence in Australia.

I'd known her ever since I returned to Australia in the late 70s. Given the life of sometimes triple duty I led in those days, writing for one or two shows, and performing eight times a week in a theater, my friends respected my home life and always phoned before knocking on my door. There were three exceptions to this—actor friend since the early '60s Bill Reilly, biker friend Brian Waterhouse and Myra. They chose their times carefully, but if they happened to be passing by and knocked on my door, they were always welcome. If I was busy, they put the kettle on and made tea for themselves.

On one of these visits, Myra, ever energetic, announced that she'd booked Newcastle Town Hall for a one-night-only performance she called, *An Evening With Noel Coward*, starring just the two of us with a grand piano.

We chose carefully from the vast repertoire of Coward songs, and compiled a two hour show. We rehearsed for two weeks and played our one night to capacity, a standing ovation, and cheers.

While in Launceston with *Double Act*, I had a call from Anne Charleston who'd played my wife in *Noises Off*. She told me Myra was in a Melbourne hospital after surgery for bone cancer and wasn't expected to live. I flew from Launceston to Melbourne for the day, and sat for some time holding Myra's hand, running the past like an old movie, and indulging in laughter and more than a few tears. Late in the afternoon, half a dozen other friends arrived and Myra was caught up in happy conversation with them. This garrulous onslaught of well-wishers allowed Anne and me to move into the background. Anne was as cowardly about partings as I, and we both decided to creep out of the room, neither of us wanting to utter the actual word, "goodbye."

A few weeks later, in London, I had a call from Anne to let me know Myra had died.

~

Pause for anecdote.

Comedian Ronnie Frazer was incapable of saying something that was *not* funny.

My health and exercise regime was at its peak. Gordon Chater disdained my gym habit as dangerous: "All that exercise will kill you one day." And my vitamin and mineral supplements he bundled under the one banner, "kelp."

"All that kelp can't be good for you."

I had Gordon and Ronnie to lunch one day. When I served coffee, I left Gordon and Ronnie happily gossiping at the dining table and went to the kitchen to down my usual handful of supplements. As the sound of them dropping into a saucer "pinged", I heard Ronnie ask, "What's he doing out there?"

"Oh," Gordon said dismissively, "he's taking kelp. He takes a lot of kelp. He wants to live till he's a hundred."

Ronnie's mystified reply, "But he won't know anybody."

THIRTY-SIX

LONDON PRODUCER IAN Liston bought the West End rights for *Double Act* and I agreed to direct. Then Mike Walsh forged a deal to produce *Nunsense* in Dublin which I would also direct. In a way, Dublin made sense—Ireland is, after all, the Land of the Nun. But there was also an element of doubt as to how a broad comedy about nuns would be received there.

I planned ten days in New York to see plays, talk through *Double Act* plans with the New York producers, and to see my friends Lesley and Forrest Perrin, and Gordon who was back in New York and on a health binge—which, for Gordon, meant one martini before lunch instead of two.

I signed a lot of papers giving Cardwell the US rights to Double Act, but was uneasy about his plans to make it a "big" production. I dined with director Louis Burke whose wife had produced *Double Act* successfully in South Africa immediately after the initial Australian production. This was the first foreign production of the play, and its success augured well for further such outings.

Cardwell had already set about gathering financial backers. This seemed an encouraging sign until I met one or two. If you've seen Mel Brooks's *The Producers*, you'll get my trepidation. It's not that they were old, but Theatre with a big T was largely a foreign country to them; their sole interest was investment and return. One of them confessed to not understanding a couple of the bigger words in the play; could I change them?

Now I was nervous.

But this New York sojourn was significant for personal reasons which would affect my life from this point.

Of the plays I saw, one was by Terrence McNally whose work I admired greatly. *Frankie and Johnny in the Claire de Lune* starred Kathy Bates and for it, she won the Obie for best actress. Greatly impressed by it, I chose to have a drink and ruminate on it before returning to my hotel. I sat in an unremarkable bar on the upper West Side. A tall good-looking chap was also alone and somehow, we struck up a conversation. He'd just been to see the final performance of the monumental flop, *Carrie – The Musical*, and was still reeling from it. We swapped impressions of our respective theatre-going experience.

Vaughan Edwards, Welsh by birth, had been resident in New York since 1974. He worked in theatre design, often assisting the famed designer Tony Walton. He was breaking into television design and in three days' time, was due to travel to Dallas, Texas, to work on a mini-series. I too had three days before I left for London and the Dublin *Nunsense*.

We found we had a great deal in common, so much so, we were still talking when they closed the bar at four in the morning and asked us to leave.

We had dinner every night for those three days and agreed to keep in touch. We'd both been disappointed in relationships and were both resolutely single—and cautious. Neither of us was looking for, or in fact wanting a relationship. But there was something about this accidental meeting we both felt was significantly different.

~

My first meeting in Dublin with producer, company manger, musical director and stage manager for *Nunsense*, was encouraging. All were supportive and I felt I was in for a comfortable ride.

Sue Farrelly, Mike Walsh's right hand, joined me in Dublin as I cast the production. I'd known Sue since Carol and I did the series of sketches on Mike's show and always trusted her judgement, her taste and her friendship. I remember her wise suggestion during a production meeting on the original *Nunsense*: "Uh oh, he's getting grumpy—take him out and feed him." She knew me well.

We cast a few of the parts in Dublin, then I set out with the choreographer, an amusing, chain-smoking woman, on a drive across country to Galway for more auditions. We made a brief stop in Limerick to check out a preserved historic village where we were to shoot the film insert, "Nunsmoke". Here I braved the international exchange and called Vaughan in Dallas. We had, as we did in the many phone calls during this period, much to talk about, and much to laugh about.

Galway was everything the song promised, the bay picturesque, the people charming.

Finally, I had a cast of five terrific women who loved the piece, and rehearsals began with enthusiasm and laughter.

The venue was the historic Olympia Theatre, larger than I'd hoped, with two tiers of boxes and two balconies, but there was a warmth about it.

We opened on a Saturday matinee, and again Mike Walsh sat with me, both of us apprehensive—particularly as eight nuns settled themselves in the first stage level box. They were the real thing, of some order which demanded they wore white habits and wimples allowing only the bare essentials for seeing, breathing and eating to be seen. I clutched Mike's arm and hoped they hadn't brought tomatoes with them.

The first act was received with gales of laughter, but throughout, one of the pack of nuns in the box, an extremely old nun, clamped hand to mouth frequently and doubled over as if in pain. I was convinced she was expressing disapproval, and I was sure I was destined for hell.

On the contrary. At intermission, the nuns came alive with animated conversation, and I realized the elderly nun had been doubled not with pain, but with laughter.

The show was received well by press and public. I was due back in London for *Double Act* production meetings and left the day after *Nunsense* opened. I urged the cast to freeze the production—keep it exactly as it was on opening night. With Joan Sydney a forethought, I instructed the stage manager to make an audio recording of the show and play it to any errant actress if a performance started to grow.

On their closing night, immediately the curtain fell, the entire cast telephoned me in London to assure me they'd observed the rules meticulously and to wish me well with my play. In all, it was an extremely enjoyable exercise, the memory of which I treasure. Though, I must admit, after five weeks, the accent coupled with an abundance of Irish whimsy, started to get to me.

There was a short break before I was due to start rehearsing *Double Act*. It was the American July 4th holiday; so, emboldened by our many "keeping in touch" calls, I flew to Dallas for the weekend to visit Vaughan. The trip proved to be pivotal; we picked up conversation as if we'd seen each other just the week before, and the prospect of a serious relationship occurred to both of us.

And that weekend, folks, was the end of anything resembling happiness for the next six weeks.

THIRTY-SEVEN

I STAYED IN MIKE Walsh's pleasant Covent Garden flat as the cold-blooded torture that became the London production of *Double Act* began.

I argued casting with producer Ian Liston. Of the names put forward I knew the two I wanted—Gary Bond who'd played much sophisticated comedy including Coward's *Tonight at 8:30*, and Marti Kane, a feet-on-the-ground comedienne who'd starred in her own series, *Hilary*, for BBC. But Liston argued for two he contended were better box office implying that my absence from the London scene rendered me ignorant of who was "in". He insisted on Lisa Harrow and Simon Cadell.

"Who?" I hear you cry. And well you might!

From day one of rehearsal, I knew we were in trouble.

Lisa Harrow's great "comedy" reputation lay with just one production of *A Midsummer Night's Dream*. Try as I might, I couldn't quite imagine this humorless woman tossing comedy zingers back and forth, particularly if they were in iambic pentameter.

Cadell's claim to fame was a lowbrow TV comedy series set in a holiday camp, *Hi di Hi*. The point of my play was that the characters had to have a sexual chemistry. These two were hardly the stuff of Laurel and Hardy let alone Darby and Joan.

To cap things off, Liston gave me a designer who had the whole damn thing revolving on not one, but two turntables. So much for intimacy.

Harrow wrangled about depth of character until it became clear she had no idea how to play light comedy. She and Cadell insisted on replacing me with a director of their choosing. At this point, I should've pulled the play from production, but my agent was in Australia and I had no sound advice. Moreover, this was London's West End, and the prospect of having a play in a major venue there caused me to cave in. The director they chose was Harrow's brother in law, who'd hitherto directed only television.

I remember watching a rehearsal one morning, devastated by what I saw. Cadell strutted over to me and said, "What do you think?"

I muttered, "I guess it'll be fine once it gets up to speed."

Missing the point, Cadell drew himself to his full height, which was up to my chin, and said pompously, "You may not be aware, but there's a great deal of difference between speed and pace!"

I leant down to his height. "I think I gave that same lecture to someone when you were in short pants."

He huffed off. Harrow then confronted me with, "You've got no idea what your play's about!" To this day, I'm still trying to fathom the logic of that utterance.

The stars looked down on me. And I don't mean that in its romantic connotation. Both Harrow and Cadell considered me as incidental to the play I'd written. They made this clear to me in the least pleasant way possible and I felt like an intruder at rehearsals. I received no support from the director, and producer Ian Liston fled from anything resembling conflict.

Vaughan finished his Dallas job and flew to London to offer support—if not for my morals, at least for my sanity. And one small incident convinced me of the soundness of a prospective relationship.

He was aware of my growing anxiety with every torturous visit to the rehearsal room. He organized evenings at various theatres or restaurants to take my mind off the shit show I was watching every day, and he listened with understanding as I railed against all involved in the production.

I'm a neat freak. Vaughan's habit in those days was to leave things lying around. One night, as we returned to the flat after a show, there was a trail of clothing in his wake. I snapped.

"If you picked these things up, and folded them, and put them on a shelf, I wouldn't trip over them when I get up to pee in the middle of the night!"

He waited until I'd finished, the easy-going smile never leaving his face, then he said, "You know, when you get mad, you look like Cloris Leachman."

When I stopped laughing, I figured this guy was a keeper.

And I vowed never to get mad again.

The play opened in Windsor prior to London. The reviews were kind, but one of them wondered what these fine dramatic actors were doing in a light comedy.

So did I.

Lisa Harrow's lightest touch could've stunned an ox, and Cadell exuded all the sophisticated insouciance of an open garbage can.

I invited friends to the West End opening, but cringed as lines fell flat—lines that had stopped the show when uttered by Noeline and me. I sat next to pompous author Jeffrey Archer who didn't laugh once. To add insult to the considerable injury of the evening, at the drinks part afterwards, the two "stars" were dismissive of me while coddling any of the VIPs who'd had the guts to sit through the play.

The next morning, the reviews were mixed indeed. Only John Peter in the Sunday Times saw past the performances and understood that the play was well constructed and moved seamlessly from comedy to pathos. He said, in part: "A sulphurously hilarious two-hander. Creyton has set up a mood of his own—bitter, mordant, raucously funny, and humane."

Before I'd even finished reading the reviews, I was in a state of grief of the kind suffered when a good friend dies.

Vaughan understood my despair and the need to distance myself from the whole mess. That morning, without any conference, he booked flights to Nice, and the next day we were in the South of France.

We spent three weeks driving across the French Riviera, stopping for a night or two in randomly chosen hotels in Monaco, Antibes, Cannes, St. Tropez, to Marseilles, then back to Nice via Provence—Aix, Avignon, Grasse, Beau de Provence. We were sightseeing tourists and the break was exactly what I needed. So I was calm and fairly collected when news reached me that the play was closing after only three weeks. We got back to London just in time to see the second act on the final night. It was, if anything, more grotesque than it had been three weeks before. I went backstage out of obligation, but neither Harrow nor Cadell offered me warmth or commiseration of any kind or even a smile; somehow they blamed me for their failure. To crown this, Liston had organized a cast and crew party to which I realized, as they climbed into taxis, I wasn't invited.

Several years on, I heard from London friends that Cadell had succumbed to a fatal heart attack.

If only he'd died in preview.

Harrow later relocated to her native New Zealand, where at last, her accent was at home. I heard tell that in recent years she gave NZ audiences her *Queen Lear*, perhaps gaining all those laughs she lost in my play.

THIRTY-EIGHT

I TRAVELED WITH VAUGHAN to New York where I met his friends, and he mine. All seemed to think the combined "us" was a good idea. And so did we. We decided to give it a try. We searched for an apartment and found one in Greenwich Village in a building now known as *The Archive;* it was the old federal archive building which had been converted into loft apartments. It covered an entire city block near the Hudson river.

We were among the first to view the conversions and chose a two bedroom, two bathroom loft apartment on the top floor where every window had a view of New York Harbor, the twin towers of the World Trade Center and the Statue of Liberty.

The New York producer promised me a work visa and started to look at names to cast.

I called Sandra Bates to ask if she'd settled on the surprise Christmas production at the Ensemble. She hadn't. We decided on a revival of

Double Act. A couple of months in Sydney would allow me time to give up my flat, and top up the bank account by selling a little art just in case.

~

Back in Sydney, I stacked up the books, records, the art I couldn't bear to part with, and a few treasured objects and had the movers pack them for shipping. There was one item left over that I was reluctant to part with—my dining table. I observed to the moving guy that it must seem like a strange item to transport across the world. He replied on the contrary, "Dining tables are where people have the most enjoyable times. It's the bed no one wants to take with them." It served as a dining table in the New York loft, and traveled with us to California where it's been employed as Vaughan's desk ever since.

Naturally enough, my Australian friends frowned a lot, brought up every last one of my long history of disastrous relationships, and muttered warnings about leaping before I looked. But I felt hopeful if not entirely certain about things.

At the Ensemble, the play was received with as much warmth as in its first incarnation and once again, we broke records.

The comfort of playing it with Noel to the same enraptured reaction eased the disappointment of London. We played to capacity for the entire run, but the Thursday matinees were special. They were usually crammed to the rafters with white haired women and a sea of spectacles. Towards the end of act two, the two characters part, painfully, and this scene always reduced audiences to deathly quiet. At a certain point in this scene, we were both aware of light flickering over the far walls of the theatre. Noel and I were curious enough to glance beyond the invisible line dividing us from the audience and we realized the light was the reflection of rows of eyeglasses being turned upward so eyes could be dabbed with a tissue. A great compliment.

Beyond that invisible wall, the audience felt shielded from the onstage action; we actors however, were not shielded from the audience no matter how intense our concentration. One matinee, during that moving scene, Noeline sat at a small table about a foot from the front row. In a breathless hush at one matinee, the woman who sat within arm's reach of Noel turned to her friend and said, loud enough for the entire audience to hear, "She's kept her figure, hasn't she."

~

Liston, the London producer of the play, called my Australian agent. He talked of vesting, which is an option guaranteeing a contract for another year if a certain performance threshold is reached. Liston said, "I know we didn't vest, but I'm sure Barry will grant me the foreign rights."

Without a second thought, I said a simple, "No."

Immediately on the tail of this, I had a call from a prominent London agent, a force of nature, Patricia Macnaughton. She'd seen the London production, moreover she'd read the play, liked it, and asked if the foreign rights were available.

I thought *what the hell,* and said "yes."

It turned out to be the most profitable "yes" of my career.

Thanks to McNaughton's constant promotion, the play has been produced in more than twenty languages with major stars: In Canada, the movie star George Segal, and in a different production there, Sally Struthers, popular star of *All in the Family*; in Paris – internationally renowned Jean-Pierre Cassell and Spanish movie star, Carmen Maura; and in the US, Kier Dullea of, among many other starring roles, *2001 – a Space Odyssey,* and Tony Award winner Bonnie Franklin, all of whom were perfect. In Spain it ran for a year with TV star Lola Herrera; in

Berlin, TV star Anita Kupsch and theatre star Volker Brandt. I saw the Berlin production and was greatly impressed with their interpretation of the play and the slick production. Though I understood no German, the laughs were in all the same places as I remembered them when I played it. At the curtain call, Brandt called me up on stage for acknowledgement, and I was moved by the audience applause and cries of "Bravo" which, it seems, means the same in any language. During this, Anita leaned over and whispered to me, "Write something else for me before I'm too old!"

I add that in Germany, for more than twenty-five long years, there was not a single week when *Doppelfehler*, as *Double Act* was known there, was *not* playing in a major city. As I write this, it's playing successfully in Poland. It's been revived several times in Australia with major talents Tina Bursill and Rowena Wallace, and I was fortunate in seeing Australian stars Garry McDonald and Diane Craig who did the play perfect justice in a terrific production.

With no disrespect for any of the above, no matter how great the production, how impressive the international star, I have to admit that no production has ever given me the same complete satisfaction and emotional reward as that very first production with Noeline. It's a memory I treasure as a highlight of my career. Perhaps *the* highlight.

On every trip back to Australia over the years, I'd ask Wagstaff to be sure to let Harry Miller know how many more languages those "too many" words had been translated into.

~

There was a period of limbo after I gave up my Double Bay apartment and before I left for New York. I asked Wagstaff if I might stay at his house until I departed. His response was typical of his heavily guarded solo life: "You're welcome to stay—as long as it's no more than twenty-four hours." In fact I stayed for three weeks of laughter and the warm friendship we'd had since we met in 1964, and would have until his death in 2015.

Double Act closed at the Ensemble on New Year's Eve 1988. I said a sad au revoir to my partner in crime for so many theatrical ventures, Noeline Brown, and I was on the flight to New York the morning of New Year's Day.

THIRTY-NINE

NEW YORK WAS mid freezing winter. Vaughan and I took possession of a barren apartment on New Year's day 1989; wood shavings were still apparent on the floors from the renovation, but the space was promising—a separate lobby, leading into an open kitchen, dining room and living room off which was a bedroom and en suite bathroom. In the loft, a second bedroom and bathroom. And that view!

The day after I arrived, Vaughan was on a flight to Toronto to assist in the design of the movie of *Rosencrantz and Guildenstern Are Dead*, to be directed by the playwright, Tom Stoppard.

After the turmoil of shutting down my life and career in Australia, left to myself in an empty apartment, I had time to think. No doubt Vaughan was mulling the same questions in Toronto. Were we being hasty? Considering my history of disastrous relationships, was I in for yet another rollercoaster? But I lived in hope and the augurs seemed promising.

I stocked up on essentials and contacted friends of whom Gordon and the Perrins were top of my list, and Carmen Duncan was resident and playing the bad girl in a New York soap, *Another World*. They made me feel as if, empty apartment notwithstanding, I was welcome in this town.

Vaughan was gone for only two weeks when the production was shut down. When production resumed a year later in Croatia, Vaughan would take over as production designer.

My shipped goods arrived from Australia at the same time Vaughan took his out of storage. As we built shelves and deployed books, we discovered we had two of just about every theatre, film and literary biography as well as doubles of many CDs. This similarity of tastes somehow gave validity to the partnership.

Meanwhile, I continued to tangle with Cardwell and his efforts to raise money and find a venue for *Double Act*. My agent at the time was Peter Franklin of the William Morris Agency in New York; he bore a resemblance to silent movie comedian Harold Lloyd, but there the similarities ended. He was a wise font of good advice—and he too had his doubts about Cardwell as producer. Franklin wondered if I might be interested in pursuing my acting career in New York. I certainly was. But…

To work as an actor meant joining Equity, and that was dependent on one's having either a Green Card or Citizenship, and for these, a blood test for HIV was demanded. Under the republican administration of the time, no one, not even visitors were admitted to the US if HIV positive.

I was HIV positive, and in fact had been since 1983.

I add that I had no symptoms then, nor have I ever had any hint of illness. Now, of course, there's medication to neutralize the threat and render it undetectable. I'd been taking all the sane precautions since the plague began in the early '80s, and was healthier and in better shape than any contemporary. But no blood test meant no Green Card.

I found a canny and sympathetic immigration attorney, Kathy Gongora, who advised that while I was unable to work as an actor without legal residency, I could get a work visa as a writer without blood tests. I would have to renew these visas every two years until the restriction was lifted. It was not lifted until eleven years later in 2010. Ultimately, this meant that my prime years as an actor of my type, while at their peak when I was forty-nine, had diminished by the time I was sixty.

I considered writing as a sole means of income—a tough call, as I was never prolific.

~

What's not to love about New York? I developed a passion for the history of the city and whenever Australian or British friends visited in the three years we lived there, I'd take them on a tour of the sights.

Babette and Tom Stephens visited New York during my first year and came to lunch at the apartment. As always, it was a treat to see them and to catch up on news from home. They took an immediate liking to Vaughan and accepted him as family instantly.

~

Towards the end of that year, production resumed on the movie *Rosencrantz and Gildernstern Are Dead* and Vaughan was appointed to design the entire production.

They were to be shooting in Yugoslavia, now Croatia. We both traveled to London where I stayed a while to see friends, while he went on to Zagreb.

The celebrated playwright Tom Stoppard happened to be on my

flight from London to Zagreb, and knowing I was Vaughan's partner, was warm and friendly. This literary giant would later laud Vaughan's work in his memoir, and entertain us both to lunch when visiting New York.

While directing the movie, Stoppard's good humor was tried on a daily basis as the then young actors Gary Oldman and Tim Roth battled for first place as Chief Brat. Production was held up many times as they argued with each other, or with Stoppard. When this became a regular occurrence, seasoned actors Ian Richardson and Richard Dreyfuss would simply stroll off the set and wait patiently in their dressing rooms while Roth and Oldman settled their pissing contest and shooting resumed.

We celebrated New Year in Zagreb, and as the shooting rolled on, I did a lot of sightseeing with actress Joanna Miles who played Gertrude. News of the dissolution of East and West Berlin reached us; a member of the production team drove to Berlin and brought us back pieces of the infamous wall for souvenirs.

Vaughan's work on the movie was spectacular and triggered his run as one of Hollywood's leading production designers.

~

Double Act began its extraordinary history of production around the world. It played in Calgary, Canada, starring Sally Struthers in Noeline's role, and in Toronto with one of my idols, George Segal in mine. I saw both productions and my satisfaction was unqualified; good actors, *appropriate* actors and directors understood the play entirely. Segal was revered for his roles in so many movie comedies and unforgettable in particular for his Nick in Edward Albee's *Who's Afraid of Virginia Woolf?* He couldn't have been more perfect in my play, never missing a laugh, never sacrificing character for the sake of a laugh, and ultimately very moving.

These productions were enormously successful and made up for the misguided hell of the London production. As did the royalties!

One happy coda to the disaster of the Harrowing West End production was the first date instigated by the splendidly determined Patricia Macnaughton—a national tour of the United Kingdom. It starred two well-known and much-loved TV stars, husband and wife Jan Harvey and Stephen Yardley. I was encouraged by the many phone calls they and the director made to me during rehearsals to ask about various aspects of character and production. The tour was an immense success and Jan and Stephen became two close and valued friends as a result.

~

Movie producer Gerry Paonessa contacted me. He was interested in a screenplay of *Double Act* and I agreed to meet with his partner Charles Evans. I was asked to pitch the story of *Double Act* to the board of directors. Gerry's advice to me was, "Keep it short, maybe ten minutes. They have the attention span of a mollusc." Eager to give them detail, my pitch ran for more than two hours, longer than the play actually takes to perform. The board members were dropping like flies after ten minutes.

The prospect faded, not because of my pitch, but due to Evans's lack of real interest in movies. He made his millions in the rag trade, and was interested in movie production only to get one up on his brother, highly successful film producer Robert Evans. Charles Evans lost interest after producing one movie, *Monkeyshine*, and went back to the rag trade.

Likewise, prospects for the stage production started to head for the drain when it was discovered dubious use was being made of the investment money.

Did I worry? Not really. Not yet. New York was an adventure all by itself and I reveled in just being there.

FORTY

VAUGHAN WAS NOW a much sought after production designer and was frequently on location. Over years, I've spent time with him in far flung locales—Virginia, Florida, Texas, Nova Scotia, New Mexico, Georgia and South Carolina.

In South Carolina he was designing a movie called *They*, starring Vanessa Redgrave. I remember my first morning on arriving in Charleston. Vaughan took me to the historic Old Town where we intended to have lunch, but as we searched for a restaurant, shops were closing. We asked a woman why she closed at lunchtime. She replied, "We don't want to witness the march." And she locked and bolted her doors.

The march?

As we pondered this, six men ventured into the square wearing white robes and white hoods. Yep, it was a Ku Klux Klan march. They had a constitutional right to do so, but they were a forlorn lot. There were multitudes of protesters shouting insults, and ironically, the motorcycle cops protecting the marchers were all black. We stood watching, the only spectators in the square, fascinated by the spectacle. Then a protester threw a stone and hell broke loose. There were cops taking the protesters down, Klan men shielding themselves from blows, and police helicopters overhead. We got out while the going was good.

Here in this pretty town, the first shots of the Civil War were fired—a civil war which has never really ended in the United States. In 1865 it was a war between pro and anti-slavery. Today it's a war between left and right in a politically divided county.

~

If I sat resolutely on a political fence in my youth, I've become a fierce political animal in the thirty-five years I've lived in the US. I was a proud marcher among the seven hundred thousand who gathered in LA's streets for women's rights on the day after Trump's inauguration. It achieved nothing. Trump's far right appointees on the Supreme Court recently revoked the Row vs Wade ruling on abortion, and with it, women's rights to health care. In consequence of this, some far right states are now passing laws invoking the death penalty for any woman who has an abortion, or doctor who enables one. The same judges are weighing anti LGB decisions, banning books, forbidding schools from teaching black history in case it offends white students, and as the ultimate evidence of the puritan lunacy in Florida, a high school principal was fired for showing her art class a picture of Michelangelo's David. Why? One parent, one, deemed it pornographic.

Now we have a loaded and corrupt Supreme Court, whose far right appointees are reversing basic civil rights. Worst of the bunch is the fanatical Clarence Thomas, an African American who's married to an equally fanatical white woman. If he continues to reverse the rights of

Americans, his wife may end up owning him.

~

After three years, our prospects dwindled somewhat in New York. Vaughan was offered a movie in Los Angeles and I sold a screenplay to Hearst Television, who were also based in LA. We decided to go to California for three months to check things out.

Toni Lamond had kindly offered us the use of her presently empty house in Hollywood and we sublet our much loved New York apartment.

~

I remember loathing LA from the moment we touched down at the airport. I dubbed it "purgatory with palm trees."

For a start it was less like a city than a disparate collection of far flung suburbs. This was thanks exclusively to the insane political move post-WWII to tear up LA's streetcar tracks with a view to selling more tyres and gasoline. That objective succeeded beyond anyone's wildest nightmares, and LA became the land of the automobile. The downside was that downtown LA died. The actual city fell into ruin and remained a ghost town for nearly fifty years. The business establishments maintained their presence, but when they closed at five, downtown became a dystopian nightmare and was considered a dangerous place to be after dark.

Change began when the LA Metro began service. At first the subway system was regarded with suspicion by the automobile-indoctrinated citizens, and the service traveled virtually empty for its first year; but when it caught on, downtown was suddenly accessible after decades. The city gradually came to life again. In the past twenty years, some of the great movie palaces have been restored to their initial glory and are venues for live music, and retrospective movie screenings. Cafes, restaurants, boutiques thrive now, million dollar apartments have been built in the shells of long deserted buildings, and it's warming to stroll the streets now busy with pedestrian traffic.

~

Getting back to LA in 1991—three months turned into a year in which Vaughan was busy and I was in frequent discussions with my screenplay producer at Hearst, Peter Frankovich. Without warning, Los Angeles had become the city where we lived.

We needed someplace we could actually call a home, and we reluctantly let our New York apartment go. We found a rental, a house perched on stilts in the Hollywood Hills. The house was in the Spanish style, built in 1932. It boasted three bedrooms (one of which became my office), three bathrooms and a deck with a glorious view of the skyscrapers of downtown eight miles away.

Our landlords were former actors, Joy and Jay Donohue. Joy Rinaldi had been in the original Broadway cast of *Grease*. They became friends and remain so thirty years on.

The house had historical significance. Soon after it was built, it was rented by a New York actor trying his luck in Hollywood. As we know now, Humphrey Bogart's luck held good. The main bathroom was beautifully preserved exactly as it was in 1932, with original tiles and fittings. Every time I stepped into the bathtub, my principal thought was, "Humphrey Bogart's backside was in this tub."

We were not long settled when I had a call from Lesley Davison; she was writing songs for a new Off Broadway revue and asked me to write the sketch material. The show was to be called *Secrets Every Smart Traveler Should Know*. Given the theme of the Fodor book on which the revue was hung, I wrote a series of bogus travel tips and traveler advice on how to translate various languages; I included my Cowardesque "Private Wives" sketch on the premise: when you divorce, change your travel agent. Just in case.

FORTY-ONE

REHEARSALS WERE DIFFICULT. The next four weeks underlined the wry statement of Larry Gelbart: "If Hitler is still alive, I hope he's out of town with a musical."

Patrick Quinn was president of Actors Equity in New York and a first time director. The cast he chose were all revue veterans and knew exactly how to play their material, but it was the producer's idea that the musicians, particularly the bass player and the pianist should perform material of their own. I argued against this, not because their material wasn't good, but because they were both seasoned cabaret performers, and doing what was virtually their "act" would pull focus from the ensemble of actors.

And it did.

So there was grumbling among the actors and some of it was leveled at Patrick. After rehearsals, I often walked Patrick down 7th Avenue, part way to his home, and gave an ear to his woes, and such advice as I could offer.

When conflict reached critical impasse, Lesley had the idea of bringing in her friend Elaine Stritch to look at rehearsals. Again, I advised strongly against this as it would weaken the tenuous authority Patrick had.

And it did.

I was a fan of Stritch in the '50s when I first heard her sing "The Heart is Quicker Than the Eye" from the Broadway revival of *On Your Toes.* My adoration for her faltered in my London years when she did Tennessee Williams's *Small Craft Warnings.* She was a drinker in those days, and it was clear during the performance that she was as drunk as a skunk. She compensated by shouting every line. I was still shell-shocked from the onslaught of her performance when afterwards, I was introduced to her by a mutual friend. I had the impression of a deeply ingrained bitterness and anger lurking beneath the alcohol fumes. My fandom fell further when I saw *Company.* Okay Stritch lovers, get out the poison pens now. Certainly, she'd stopped boozing by the time *Company* reached London, but what Stritch regarded proudly as timing, seemed to me to be milking. Even Macready might've been taken aback. Much later, my respect for her fell totally when in her one-woman show *At Liberty*, she told a blatantly homophobic anecdote about Rock Hudson.

The night she came to rehearsal for the revue convinced me she was not only destructive, but that she'd missed her true vocation in life as an interstate truck driver.

After the chaotic rehearsal, I stayed back with Patrick trying to restore some of his confidence, but the poor guy was in tears. He'd just had the dregs of his authority, and his dignity, stripped from him by this gorgon.

The show opened at the Triad on 72nd Street, a well-known cabaret and revue venue and was successful enough to ensure a run. As I predicted, the musicians' solo turns were deemed highlights by the critics and much of the energetic work of the ensemble cast was overlooked.

My "Private Wives" sketch was singled out by the New York Times and a couple of other papers as the best of the material.

I attended the opening with my agent Bret Adams who was amused by my squirming at every one of my words uttered on stage—an amusement he'd enjoy again years later when he drove me to New Hampshire for the opening of *Double Act* there. He commented, "I've sat with a few anxious authors in my time, but you're easily the most entertaining!"

For all the trauma of the rehearsals, *Secrets* ran for two and a half years and has since been produced many times across the US.

When I returned to LA, I realized how much I'd missed this town.

~

Now settled in a city we called home, the one thing we should've expected happened. We'd had warnings since day one, but like all Angelinos, we ignored the minor tremors until the big one hit.

At 4:30 a.m., January 7, 1994 we were woken by a jolt which felt as if a giant hand had shoved the house to one side, and unsatisfied with this, shook it violently back and forth. The rumble was deafening; it was like being under an express train. The violent rolling of the house continued for 20 uninterrupted seconds—a long time—enough time to wonder if our house, already clinging to a hillside, would be down in the valley when it stopped.

The quake was 6.7 magnitude. Not quite enough to separate California from the rest of the United States, but enough to bring down a few freeways, several multi-story buildings and quite a few houses.

When the shaking ceased, a symphony of car alarms could be heard. But when they stopped, there was utter, eerie silence.

Power was out all over the city, so predawn, the blackness was total.

I climbed cautiously out of bed and checked for damage. The door to my office, was jammed shut. We realized later that every book in the room had fallen from shelves and piled up against the door.

I started downstairs to see if there was damage to the house. Every picture which hung on the walls of the staircase had fallen, making the steps an obstacle course of broken glass. There were cracks in the plaster walls of every room in the house.

I found a flashlight in the kitchen and checked that the gas lines hadn't been broken, then stepped out to the deck, pausing just before setting foot on it to make sure it was still there. Below us, in the valley, the blackness was broken by multiple flashlights and we heard neighbors calling, "Are you all right?" to other neighbors.

When dawn broke, we gazed downtown to see the skyscrapers enveloped in what looked like smoke—it was actually thick clouds of dust which had been stirred by the quake.

The Spanish style houses such as ours survived—wood and stucco bend in earthquakes. Bricks don't. Our brick chimney crumbled completely, as did every brick structure in the neighborhood. Just a few blocks away, an all brick house was now a pile of rubble.

We were due to dine with Toni Lamond that night. She was visiting from Australia and staying at the Ramada Hotel in West Hollywood.

After checking that all our friends were alive and well, we drove to West Hollywood staggered to see some of the older buildings on Hollywood Boulevard showing bare rooms, their front walls lying in piles of rubble in the street below.

Some areas were lit, some still blacked out. The Ramada was in total darkness when we arrived, but the receptionist gave us a candle and directed us to the third floor. Here we found Toni, sitting inches from her dressing table mirror, lit only by two candles, desperately trying to attach eyelashes.

FORTY-TWO

I RETURNED BRIEFLY TO Australia, to see friends and family, and to renew my work visa which I was obliged to do outside of the US every two years. In Brisbane, I went to a performance of *School for Scandal* by The Queensland Theatre Company. Babette Stephens was playing Mrs. Candour. The production under the sure hand of Alan Edwards was splendid. As well as Babette, who was in fine form, Carol Burns for whom I'd written an episode of *Carson's Law* was a wonderful Lady Sneerwell.

After the performance, I waited in the bar for Babette but was first assailed by artistic director Alan Edwards asking if I'd consider playing the lead in Coward's *Blithe Spirit* come January. I learnt later that during the performance, Alan had lamented to Babette that he'd lost their lead actor and needed to recast. Babette responded with a smug, "You know who's sitting out front tonight?"

I needed time to think about this and on returning to LA, conferred with Vaughan who insisted I commit to it. He was on a TV series, and would be free to travel to Brisbane for the final night at the SGIO theatre and perhaps join me for part of the tour of Queensland that followed.

~

I was still considerably jet lagged at the first readthrough, but delighted in the terrific cast: my old chum from *Bedroom Farce*, Belinda Giblin as the ghost of Elvira, Carol Burns as Ruth, and Sheila Bradley, a friend since the early '60s, as Madame Arcati.

Also in the cast, locals Elaine Cusick, and David Clendinning as the Bradmans. And the designer was the splendid Graham Maclean, a friend and much needed drinking buddy during the four weeks' rehearsal.

Clendinning invited me to dinner during that first week, along with John Dommett who'd returned to live in Brisbane. A charming gesture, I thought—until midway through the first course when Clendinning launched into a bitter denouncement of the Queensland Theatre Company for importing an actor from the United States (me), to play a role he was more than capable of doing himself.

John's paranoia kicked in and he had to be restrained from making a run for it. I accepted the criticism as graciously as I could, finished dinner, and decided to steer clear of Clendinning thereafter. A tough call when you're in the same play eight times a week for three months.

I was delighted however to renew acquaintance with Elaine Cusick, a contemporary of my teenage theatre days in Brisbane, and an actress I admired. I think in those early days, my close friends Ron Finney, John Larkin and I were all a little bit in love with Elaine and enthralled by her freshness of approach to whichever role she played.

This delight evaporated when, as the tour progressed, Elaine began pulling focus during the dinner scenes by uttering an unscripted "Oh", or "Ah", or "Mm" in the middle of other actors' speeches. When I asked if she might refrain, she took it as an affront and not only increased the interjections, but stretched them to the point of ludicrousness. Some of her interjections stretched over an entire octave of inflection. It played havoc with everyone's timing and threw the balance of every scene she played.

For me, the joy of the production lay with my co-stars, Belinda who'd done her homework on the character, and read Coward's own words on how she should be played, and was splendid; the wonderful Sheila Bradley's dotty Arcati was treasure, and I had the thrilling experience of working with the sublime Carol Burns. Carol and her husband of thirty-six years, composer Alan Lawrence became valued friends during this production and we later joined them in London during a mutual vacation and hosted Carol at our house in LA. Vaughan and I were devastated by her untimely death in 2015.

The opening was fine, the play received well; Babette was present and Noeline and her husband Tony Sattler flew to Brisbane for the event.

Vaughan arrived for the final Brisbane performance and joined my brother and sister in law in the theatre.

Vaughan set out on the short tour of Queensland with me.

Back in Brisbane, I lunched with Babette before heading home. "How was the tour?"

I complained about the hotels, the flights, the busses and as a capper, told of the childish behavior of Cusick to which Babette replied a tart, "Well, she played a bunny rabbit when she was five and never got over it."

She allowed me to mull this before asking, "How did Vaughan enjoy the tour?"

"Oh, he loved it every minute of it."

"Well, of course. He's a much nicer person than you are."

This was accompanied by a raised eyebrow and a particularly smug grin.

FORTY-THREE

IN 1995, *DOUBLE Act* found its way to a Miami producer, Arnold Mittleman, who had grand plans for it and requested a restricted contract, meaning he had the right to further it for Broadway production and TV.

I signed. Ultimately, I regretted.

His chosen stars had my approval, one by first hand contact, the other by reputation. I met with Sharon Gless of *Cagney and Lacey* fame at her LA apartment and read the script with her. She was an actress of greater range than her TV roles, and extremely eager to do the play. The male choice was a mystery beyond his featured role in the series *Hill Street Blues.* James Sikking was certainly enthusiastic and took me to lunch in Beverly Hills to impress this on me.

Then, the Harrow-Cadell Curse descended. In the first week of rehearsal, Gless became ill with encephalitic flu and was hospitalized. Two days later she discharged herself from hospital and made a determined return to rehearsal with a drip feed inserted into a vein; she wheeled the dispenser around the rehearsal room with her. But a week before opening, she collapsed again and they were without a leading lady. Mittleman called me in a panic and I suggested the New York actress who'd played opposite George Segal in Canada, Alexandra O'Karma. Since that highly successful production, I'd maintained contact with Alex and her husband.

She was rushed to Miami, rehearsed for a week and the opening loomed.

Vaughan was working at Universal's Orlando, Florida studios at the time on a series called *Seaquest DSV*. We arranged that I would fly into Miami for the opening and he would drive down from Orlando. We planned to meet in the lobby of the theatre before the performance.

Flashback a day: I went for the regular checkup with my LA doctor and he was eager to do a series of blood tests which required me to give up coffee and alcohol for a time. Never a great drinker, this meant putting a stop to my one modest martini in the evening. I told him I'd be gone for two weeks, most of which would be spent on holiday in Orlando with Vaughan, but giving up booze for that length of time was no big deal.

So, in Miami, prior to curtain up, Vaughan had his usual Manhattan and I had a soda.

Then, the play.

Mittleman had clearly had ambitions far beyond the intimate necessities of the play, and his design had sets trucking on and off stage like freight trains. The scene breaks were so long, even I lost track of the plot each time living room changed to bedroom and back again.

James Sikking, far from the energetic eccentric he played on TV, played the supposedly sex-addicted George of my play like a languid jellyfish. And Alexandra, making up for the lack of chemistry, played all out farce. It was as if actors, designer and director were all doing different plays.

At intermission, the promise to my doctor abandoned, I had two very large martinis and told Vaughan, "I'm not going back."

He argued, "You're in the house seats. They can see you from the stage, You have to go back."

I did. And had two more martinis after the final curtain.

Backstage, the stage management found me first and apologized profusely for the longueurs between scenes. They would be fine, I was assured, by tomorrow's matinee. Then Sikking apologized for not being able to get a grip on the character. I murmured encouragement, assurances. Mittleman, on the other hand, was convinced he'd produced a bound-for-Broadway blockbuster. I could think of nothing appropriate to say to him. He urged me to return for tomorrow's matinee when the show would be vastly improved.

We supped with Alex O'Karma who, having worked in a good production with the great George Segal, was fully aware of the deficiencies of this one. I merely urged her to pull back on her broader choices and see if Sikking could manage to rake up some sex appeal. He never did.

Next day, at matinee time, I was nowhere near the theatre. I was at a Miami South Beach restaurant gazing at the sea over yet another martini. That afternoon, Vaughan and I drove to Orlando where I spent two blissful weeks not thinking about the play. And not drinking.

As a bonus, my brother Trevor was in Orlando on business and he joined me on a trip to Cape Canaveral. My lifelong passion for science was rewarded by exhibits of the giant Saturn 5 rockets which propelled astronauts into space, and an interior tour of a Space Shuttle.

~

By now, "heading home" had substantial meaning; Los Angeles had become very much home.

I coasted for a couple of years, traveling to London to renew the work visa, then one day, John Krummel, artistic director of Sydney's Marian Street Theatre, called and said simply, "Here are the dates, write something."

That was all the incentive I needed.

I recalled the years in our smart apartment building in New York, and some of its eccentric residents and began a farcical comedy.

Valentine's Day concerns two middle-aged, but diametrically different men—Lewis a failed novelist subject to mood swings, Nick a wannabe tough guy with tenuous ties to the mafia. Both have been divorced respectively by the same woman who's cleaned them out financially. Nick hires one of his mafia buddies to put a hit on the now wealthy divorcee.

As ever, I wrote the final scene first, knowing just how the mayhem of mistaken identities should resolve, and I created Lewis specifically for Donald Macdonald who rewarded me with a beautifully fleshed-out character and one of the funniest performances I believe he ever gave. I also wrote Noeline in as Nick's long-suffering fiancée, and at Noel's suggestion, cast singer Maria Venuti as a predatory widow who goes after Lewis.

I had a terrific cast, in one of my favorite theatres, and a great design by my old chum Graham Maclean. Krummell supervised my direction, though, to be honest, his main contribution was to watch rehearsal convulsed with laughter.

We played to packed houses and the laughs were long and loud—so much so that on opening night, mid act two, there was such a prolonged laugh at a particular situation, that Donald and I had to invent considerable business to cover the stretch in which we were unable to resume dialogue. This reaction occurred every night of the run and, I was advised, in every other production world-wide regardless of the language.

The play was performed once or twice in other parts of Australia, but like *Double Act*, found its wider audience in Europe where it's been produced in half a dozen languages. The Rome production was so successful, it was revived a year later.

FORTY-FOUR

AFTER NINE HAPPY years in our rented aerie in the Hollywood Hills, we decided to buy something more permanent, and after a short search, we found the house we'd call home for the next eighteen years. Built in 1950, it had a vast high ceilinged living room which opened onto an equally vast stone terrace, a long, gated driveway with parking for at least six cars, a rare commodity in LA. There were four bedrooms, two of which we kept, the third became a library and the fourth a well-equipped gym. The office was separate from the main house, linked by a glass covered atrium.

It was in a particularly historic part of the Hollywood Hills. Just two doors from us was the magnificent Lloyd Wright house built in 1928 for movie star Ramon Novarro, the first Ben Hur. Beyond it, at the top of the rise, was the 1930 house which Cary Grant and Randolph Scott shared early in their careers. And the neighborhood was still pretty starry: when we moved in, Diane Keaton lived in the Novarro house,

Vince Vaughan just down the street and Brad Pitt at the cul de sac end.

After we'd made a few renovations and taken care of cosmetic details, the house was very much our haven. We were on a ridge in a canyon, surrounded on all sides by trees, so privacy and silence were guaranteed. The house also happened to be built on a trail from nearby Griffith Park, a trail which had never quite been eliminated by the decades of building, so our first sighting of deer grazing on the hillside by our driveway filled us with a great appreciation of nature. Weeks later when they'd eaten a hibiscus tree, several sapling lemon trees and an entire flower bed to the ground, I began to consider antlers on a plaque over the fireplace.

In spite of the fences and wire barricades we put up, they still found a way to invade—as did skunks, families of raccoons, coyotes and the occasional lost dog which, by some canine intuition, knew I was a sucker for dogs, and always found their way into my office. One belonged to a neighbor, Christina Ricci. On its return, she rewarded us with a four feet tall orchid.

We always welcomed guests; many of Vaughan's and my chums from England came to stay, and the list of Australians is more or less a Who's Who—Carol Raye, Noeline Brown, Simon Burke, Andrew McFarlane, Carol Burns, Tina Bursill, John O'May, Belinda Giblin, Stuart Wagstaff, Ross Skiffington, Graeme Maclean, Phil Scott, Michael Huxley, to name very few.

~

Once again, a call from Krummel: "Here are the dates, write something."

Again I put those thoughts I'd stashed in the back of the mind into action and wrote *Later Than Spring*. I loved the work of American playwright A. R. Gurney and treasured the original production of his drawing room piece, *The Cocktail Hour*. I aimed for a similar kind of family drama played in a drawing room.

Set in the upper echelons of New York society, it told of a father returning to his estranged daughter, a New York socialite, to tell of his impending marriage to a woman thirty years younger than himself. The daughter does everything in her power to prevent the marriage.

I particularly wanted an actress I knew well and had worked with often for the snobbish daughter; but with only one of the two acts written, she turned it down because she hadn't seen act two—fortuitously as it happened. Krummel suggested an actress I had never considered, Katy Manning.

Katy was a memorable Jo Grant in the greatly popular BBC series, *Dr. Who*. She turned out to be much more than a good choice, she was ideal. And so were the rest of that memorable cast. Once again, I wrote specifically for Donald MacDonald, was delighted by Michelle Doake, Kelly Butler, John Allen and the quite wonderful Elaine Lee. I played the errant father and directed.

The set by Graham Maclean was spectacular and entirely appropriate to upper class New York, and every night on lights up, drew spontaneous applause.

This was one of the most pleasant theatrical experiences I can remember. We looked forward to gathering at Marian Street eight times a week and always had gossip to exchange before the performance began. Later, Elaine told me this was the most enjoyable theatrical experience of her entire career.

Elaine was a gambling addict, and a very successful one. I admitted I'd never been to a casino, so she insisted on my dressing up—tie, jacket—and one night took me to the Star Casino at Darling Harbour.

I had no knowledge of blackjack, the game at which Elaine excelled. "It's easy darling. Watch me and do exactly as I do."

I did. I went in with 50 bucks and came out with 3,000.

But never again.

The reviews for *Spring* were extremely positive and the audiences appreciative. I expected it would be disseminated to foreign producers by my London agent, but the powerful Patricia Macnaughton who'd given *Double Act* and *Valentine's Day* such long lives had died, and her agency taken over by inept underlings. While they were happy to let *Double Act* and *Valentine's Day* find new audiences unaided by their promotion, they had little interest in pushing a new play. So *Later Than Spring* sat on their dismal shelves for some time until Frank-Thomas Mende, the German translator of my other plays discovered it. He immediately set about translating it for production in Berlin.

FORTY-FIVE

IN APRIL, 2000, Babette Stephens turned ninety. For her lifelong contributions to theatre and its inhabitants she'd been honoured with AM and an MBE. A lavish ceremony was planned and I was given a number of the reception venue to call. Babette answered and we spoke at some length. I'd seen the guest list and said it sounded like a pretty starry event. She replied, "Why not? It's not every day I turn ninety."

We reminisced briefly about our long friendship and she was called away to greet guests and have photographs taken.

She died in February of the following year leaving a chasm in the Brisbane theatre scene of which she had been an integral part for seventy years. She knew volumes about theatre, about acting, about how to elicit the best from actors she directed; she knew about audiences, their likes and dislikes and as a mentor, there was no one to match her. How lucky I am she was a part of my career and my life.

I owe her an incalculable debt.

I wrote the foreword to a splendid biography of her, *Never Upstaged: Babette Stephens, Her Life and Times* by Jay McKee.

~

Vaughan and I did a few "Grand Tours" in the next few years—to London and Paris on an almost annual schedule, then to Athens, Santorini, Malta, Barcelona, Berlin, Rome, Naples, Capri and Pompeii. We did the glorious Amalfi Drive on two occasions, lunching both times at Ravello where one of my literary and political idols Gore Vidal lived for thirty-four years. In the library of our present house I have two memoirs by Vidal, signed personally to me. They are supreme treasures.

I'd always been fascinated by Pompeii, having read many histories from childhood and seen many pictures; the real thing was no disappointment. The volcanic eruption which destroyed the city in 79AD left a virtual time capsule. Many buildings, while minus walls here and there, still had vibrant murals and mosaics; even the voluminous graffiti were preserved on many walls.

Political:

If honest living is thought to be any recommendation, then Lucretius Fronto is worthy of being elected.

Elect Gaius Julius Polybius to the office of aedile. He provides good bread.

Commercial:

To let, in the estate of Julia Felix—elegant baths for respectable people, shops with upper rooms, and apartments.

Lost property:

A copper pot went missing from my shop. Anyone who returns it to me will be given 65 bronze sestertii. 20 more for the capture of the thief.

And downright salacious:

Celadus the Thracian makes the girls moan!

Restituta, take off your tunic, please, and show us your hairy privates.

And at the House of the Poet, we saw the perfectly preserved mosaic depicting a growling Mollosian dog with the inscription: *Cave Canem*—Beware of the Dog.

Mollossians, a now extinct breed, were the ideal guard dog—big and mean.

Today, Pompeii is dog friendly. There are many strays, dusty, scruffy mutts, wandering the ruins. All are friendly, all welcome a pat on the head and a snack of whatever the tourist has in his backpack.

In the late afternoon, after walking the ruins for an entire day, we settled at a sidewalk café just outside the city walls for coffee before taking the train back to Naples. Here we gained a friend and an inspiration. A small black and white dog approached our table with the best begging act we'd ever seen. He sat, and raised his eyes to us with a practiced soulful expression and turned his head slowly and questioningly to the cookies on the table. We gave him one which he devoured politely, no snaffling. Then a waiter came outside and chased him. He vanished around a corner. When the waiter had gone back inside, the little black and white head appeared at the corner, and cautiously, he came back to the table and repeated the act.

On the train, Vaughan said, "The Dogs of Pompeii sounds like the title of something."

We agreed it was a good title. And we thought of all the dogs we'd petted in the ruins: a happy, tail-wagging mongrel who followed us around for no greater reward than our company; a large dog taking a nap inside the Stabian baths, in spite of the crowd of tourists who "oohed" and "aahed" at the murals; independent dogs who simply ignored the tourists as if it was beneath them to acknowledge humans.

We found that when a Neapolitan family tired of their pet, rather than take it to the pound where it would be destroyed, they sneaked it into the Pompeii ruins at night where they knew guards and tourists would take care of it.

We started to make notes for a young adult book featuring those dogs, in particular, the small black and white beggar we called Nero.

We returned to Pompeii a year later to make specific notes. We searched for our little black and white pal, but the only evidence we found was a small pup of exactly the same markings napping near the same café, perhaps our dog's offspring.

Vaughan had time off between series and we used it in the office of our house to write *The Dogs of Pompeii.*

Our heroine was a fifteen year old girl from New Jersey who visits her archaeologist uncle. He's unearthing a mysterious villa on the outskirts of Pompeii, and runs afoul of a diabolical millionaire who's determined to turn Pompeii into a theme park. The dogs, led by our little black and white friend, join forces with the girl and her Italian boyfriend to save the day and preserve history.

It was published by Random House Australia to extremely flattering reviews and positive reader reviews which ranged in age from thirteen to eighty. It was also highly recommended by the Queensland government for school reading. The marketing blurb read:

AN ACTION-PACKED ADVENTURE STARRING A GIRL, A BOY AND A STREET DOG WITH A PROUD HERITAGE!

A breathtaking series of adventures—a kidnapping, a motorcycle chase on the Amalfi Cliffs, and a fight for their lives suspended above the flames of a blast furnace. It's a race against time to save Pompeii, its treasures, and THE DOGS OF POMPEII.

A sequel was requested, so we wrote *Nero Goes to Rome*, in which our dog finds himself trapped in a van en route to Rome and manages to circumvent skullduggery in the theft of a priceless Vatican artifact.

The blurb:

Caroline, Gianni and Nero are reunited in another action-packed adventure which culminates in a life-or-death climax played out in the maze of catacombs far beneath the Eternal City.

This one was published while I was on a trip to Sydney. Vaughan joined me during this trip and without telling him why, I drove him from the airport directly to Dymock's Bookstore in the city and led him to the Young Adult shelves. There was a row of the newly published *Nero Goes to Rome,* with glowing reviews, and a card of recommendation by the bookstore staff, headed "Nero is my Hero!"

FORTY-SIX

I WAS IN AUSTRALIA in 2004 to renew my US work visa.

In Sydney I stayed with my old chum Tony Shaw while I negotiated the necessary biennial inspection at the US Embassy. This done, I was to travel to Brisbane the following day to see my brother Trevor, his wife Liz, and my mother who was ailing and suffering dementia. That evening my brother called to tell me our mother had died. Trevor organized the funeral and asked me to speak.

It was a small affair, attended by Trevor, his wife, a couple of my mother's friends and two cousins, Marion and Murray. Against my mother's express wishes, the organizers had allowed an open coffin.

The appearance was of someone sleeping peacefully, a passive, vulnerable attitude I'd seldom seen in my restrictive youth. Not for the first time, I felt an overwhelming sympathy for this woman who'd had no understanding of the world I longed to inhabit, and did her best to impose the Victorian values of her own childhood on mine. There was no sign of the bitterness, the anger. Certainly, during my adult years on the occasions we were together, there was laughter, perhaps because she realized she could no longer dictate a lifestyle to me, and finally understood that I'd created my own life and rules.

And I wondered, as my brother and I have since her death, how greatly did the insanity of her grandmother weigh on her? In her entire life, she never mentioned the awful murder-suicide to us—Trevor found out about it long after she died.

At the service, I spoke principally of the great good-hearted benevolence of my brother. When I left home to seek a career, he'd stayed behind and was there for our mother throughout her life.

Afterwards, I stayed in Brisbane for a few days to catch up with Trevor. He spent a day driving me to all our childhood haunts—our junior school, my high school, the house we knew as children, the seaside town where we had Christmas holidays, and eventually, we visited the small house in which my mother had spent most of her life.

We sorted through possessions and came upon a box of photographs. There were our parents' wedding photographs, holiday photographs, and pictures of them early in their marriage.

In every single photograph, she'd scratched out the image of our father.

FORTY-SEVEN

I WAS IN NEW York in 2005 and saw a wonderfully funny play by a friend, Stephen Temperley, *Souvenir,* a two character play about Florence Foster Jenkins. Judy Kaye was brilliant as the wealthy socialite who had ambitions to sing opera, with no idea of pitch or key, and was nominated for a Tony for her performance.

The play was bought for Australia and Stephen asked me to direct. But as we conferred on production plans in Los Angeles, I had calls from both Noeline and Sandra Bates asking if I'd play the boyfriend of Florence Foster Jenkins in yet another play about her, *Glorious* by Peter Quilter. I jumped at this request, though I realized sadly, this production ruled out plans for Stephen's play.

~

Rehearsals for *Glorious* were a joy with, thanks to Sandra's analytic direction, something new discovered every day. Noeline's singing as

Jenkins had to be heard to be believed. I mean that! Judi Farr was the befuddled friend of La Jenkins, Jono Gavin her pianist, Cosme McMoon, and Cris Parker gave a splendid tirade against tone deaf singers in fluent Spanish.

The text referred to my character, St. Clair, as a failed British actor, a ham who liked his food and liquor. I decided he should be overweight, of ruddy cheek and with a toupee that changed position at his every entrance.

Costume designer Mark Thompson engineered a very convincing fat suit with a high collared shirt to disguise the incongruous slimness of my neck.

Katy Manning and Barry Crocker were at the opening night. On my first entrance Katy turned to Barry and whispered, "Oh my God, he's let himself go!"

After learning of this, on every subsequent night, I was out of the fat suit, into my slimmest T shirt and in the bar before the audience had a chance to leave the theatre. Vanity lurks behind every character actor's paunch, overbite or wig.

Vaughan was designing *CSI New York* at this time, but flew to Sydney for the weekend to see the production. For the weekend. The following Tuesday, at the studio, his staff were discussing their various weekends—played basketball with the kids, a picnic in Griffith Park, shopped at the local mall. Vaughan was greeted with awed silence when he announced he'd been to Australia.

The prank.

At the final matinee, Jono Gavin was the target.

In our scene together, Jono's character Cosme, asks St. Clair, "Why did you come to America?"

St. Clair answers in pompous Shakespearean tones, "I came here to be—a star!"

And that, in Quilter's script, was that.

At the final matinee, it went like this:

"Why did you come to America?"

"Why do you ask?"

After a startled silence, Jono managed a barely audible, "Just curious."

I launched into a resume of my career: "I came here to be—a star! I came over with a boatload of nuns. But that's another story. In London, I was in *A Midsummer Night's Dream.* Noel Coward saw my Bottom and said, 'You must take that to America.' And so I came with great recommendation and untrammeled ambition." And so on.

In the wings, Noeline was preparing for her entrance. But as I launched into this story, she sat and said to her dresser, "Take it easy. He'll be a while."

~

LA is a movie town; theatre is the poor relation.

This is to Vaughan's benefit—less so to mine. Vaughan has seldom stopped working since we moved here. As well as many TV movies, he designed *CSI-New York* for 8 seasons, and thanks to his skill, none of it was actually shot in New York. He created New York streets on the back lot, Central Park in the winter which demanded eighty tons of ice to be processed as snow and sprayed onto the set, and a Statue of Liberty so realistic that when the lead actors were seen rappelling down the face of the statue, a New York Times critic, convinced that the real statue had been employed, railed against the city officials for allowing such a scene when terrorism was such a threat in the city.

In LA, while two or three mainstream theatres carry the tours from Broadway, little original work is performed at these. But there are any number of fifty to one-hundred-seat black boxes, fringe venues, which cater to theatre lovers, and some just to the friends and relations of the actors performing there.

Of them all, a bare handful produce anything like legitimate theatre, and many disdain anything remotely commercial. One standout is the Antaeus Theatre Company which initially set out to produce classics, and they gathered a company of accomplished actors and adhered to the "classics" label for many years.

Shakespeare has always been a hit-or-miss target for small theatre companies, yet Antaeus managed good productions of some of the Bard's greatest hits. Chekov was also a favorite of the company, but the most valid for me have been their productions of American classics—Tennessee Williams, William Inge, Lillian Hellman.

I'd been interested in their work and their mission since arriving in Los Angeles, but as a spectator. I was not eager to commit as an actor to a company that performed only four performances a week.

However, they were producing a respectable adaptation of Balzac's *Cousin Bette*, and close to opening, the actor playing Hector Hulot, Arye Gross, broke an arm. The artistic director, the late Jeanie Hackett asked me to take over. Now that I was a card-carrying citizen of the United States, I took the plunge and in spite of the limited performances, enjoyed every moment of playing the dissolute Baron who sacrifices family name and fortune to please his mistress.

Shortly after this, Jeanie asked me to workshop an obscure play by Noel Coward, *Peace in Our Time*, "perhaps throw a few of his songs in there," was the directive. The theatre had been given a grant by the Coward Estate to develop the play.

FORTY-EIGHT

PEACE IN OUR Time was produced in the West End in 1947 and ran for only one hundred and sixty-seven performances. It's a "what if" play centered in a London pub after the Nazis have won the war and occupied Britain. Fiercely jingoistic, it details the family who own the pub and their clientele, all of whom form a resistance movement against the occupation.

The original has a cast of thirty-six characters. Antaeus wanted a large cast, but not that large. I cut thirteen characters. Next, I considered songs. Old London pubs often had a well-trod upright piano in the bar. I chose nine of Coward's songs of the period that were about the war, about patriotism, about love and loss, which were performed by various characters—a night club singer, the piano player, an elderly couple asked to do a turn, the bartender. In order that these could be integrated, I cut about forty-five minutes of dialogue, mostly the political polemic of its period which meant little today and less in America.

Director Casey Stangl employed two voice coaches who were able to differentiate between upper, middle and lower class London accents, and at my specific request, the precise difference between South London and Cockney. Tom Budewitz's superb set, at floor level in the theatre, was so realistic, audience members wandered onto it at intermission, perhaps expecting to order a beer at the bar.

The production was an overwhelming success. Reviews were paeans, audiences crammed the theatre for the entire season. It won me the Ovation Award, the LA Weekly Annual Award citing Best Adaptation and was included in the LA Times ten best theatre events in world theatre.

Every review, in press, radio or TV offered unqualified praise. Modesty prevents me from quoting all of them, but it won't stop me from reading just a few!

Beautifully adapted. Creyton has expertly trimmed and massaged the original script with obvious tenderness and a keen understanding of how best to communicate Coward's story to a modern American audience.

WEHO NEWS

Creyton has shown an astute understanding of his material and its history—the inclusion of 9 of Coward's own songs, like Creyton's edits have been rendered seamlessly into the fabric of the play. Creyton's adaptation could, and perhaps should, become a standard for all future productions of this work.

FRONTIERS

Members of the Coward Estate and the Coward Society flew into LA to see the production and wild promises were made of finding a theatre in London. But ultimately, the cast of twenty-three for a straight play, worked against it in an era when even juke-box musicals balk at a cast of ten.

FORTY-NINE

ABOUT THIS TIME, due to my involvement with the Anteaus Company, I was asked to join a large cast of accomplished actors for a staged, rehearsed reading of a new TV series by director Ron Maxwell.

A few words about Ron Maxwell: He's best known for his obsessive movies about the Civil War—*Gettysburg*, *Gods and Generals* and *Copperhead.* He's also an eccentric of the first water—blow a bugle and he'll recite the entire screenplay of *Gone With The Wind.*

This project was no less obsessive—a life of Joan of Arc, a mini-series totaling six hours and a cast of thousands. We were a cast of about twenty, and the performance took place at the Stella Adler theatre in Hollywood. Part one, three hours, was performed one night, then part two also of three hours the next, then repeated thus for two more nights.

I shared a dressing room with a very talented, very bright young actor, James Parks—he played the Dauphin, I played the Inquisitor.

At the climactic end of the piece, the executioners piled wood around the soon-to-be immolated Joan as she was tethered to the stake. The vast cast were required to gather in the wings and to shout appropriate encouragements such as "Burn the witch!" "Death to the heretic!" "Kill her!" etc., as she prayed to the Almighty.

As we reached the midpoint of part two for the second time, it occurred to me that Jim and I, having finished our respective scenes, had a considerable wait before our stint in the wings. There was a cocktail bar right by the stage door. "What about a martini to kill time?" I suggested. Jim jumped at the idea and we wended our way downstairs and into the dimly lit bar.

We had our martinis, glancing dutifully at our watches at intervals, and realized we had time for a couple more. As we trudged back upstairs to the theatre, neither of us was feeling any pain.

The time came for us to join the throng of actors in the wings. Those on stage piled the wood against the stake and the off-stage taunts began. I joined the chorus of, "Burn her! Death to the heathen! Kill the witch!"

Beside me, the inebriated Jim Parks yelled, "SHOW US YOUR TITS!"

By the time Maxwell had finished tinkering with his screenplay, two entire movies had been made about Saint Joan, and his series never left the ground. If it had, I doubt Jim Parks or I would have been asked to participate.

~

Sandra Bates called. She had a new piece by Peter Quilter—*Duets*, four one act plays to be performed by the same two actors. Noeline and I both leapt at the opportunity.

Play one brought two hapless people together on a blind date. Jonathan claims in his personals ad to be forty-seven with olive skin when in fact he's over sixty and whiter than white. I played him overweight, with a really bad toupee and questionable teeth. I had a Hollywood makeup artist construct the teeth to look not so much grotesque, just bad enough to require the services of a good orthodontist. Noel played her blind date character as an ingenuous failure at anything romantic who brings cheese to a first date rather than wine.

The second play depicted a gay American PR executive and his long-time secretary who keeps hoping to convert him. The third, a divorced Australian couple who, having paid for a non-refundable holiday in Spain, get together again. And the fourth, two upper class Brits, she about to marry for the fourth time, he her conservative brother and a harbinger of doom.

For the PR couple, we had our sole chance in the program to look glamorous. The Spanish jaunt had me a mustachioed loser and Noel an inebriated gal looking forward to her freedom. In the fourth we were unrecognizable, Noeline in a wedding dress resembling a parachute, me in fat padding, low-browed grey hair and specs.

The Sydney Morning Herald gave me the highest compliment possible when their critic mentioned that as the lights came up on me in play four, a woman beside him turned to her friend and asked, "Is that the same actor?"

Duets played to full houses and we were rewarded with a terrific response. The pleasure of working with Noel was, as ever, a rare and wonderful treat.

Opening night, she gave me a card that read, "Make a Lunt of yourself tonight!"

FIFTY

BACK HOME IN LA, I was summoned to the office of famed audio producer Yuri Rasovsky. He was known for writing, adapting and directing audio plays which were broadcast and committed to CD for international distribution. He was greatly respected and major stars were eager to be part of his productions.

While his long-time partner Lorna Raver stood by anxiously, he told me unemotionally, and in matter-of-fact tone that he was dying. His cancer was terminal and time was short. He'd heard of my success with *Peace in Our Time*, and asked me point blank if I'd take over his productions.

I said "Yes" at once. It was not a difficult decision.

He'd adapted and directed a highly successful audio CD of *Zorro*, starring Val Kilmer as the masked avenger. It was so popular, the McCulley estate asked for a sequel. Yuri wanted me to write it and direct.

To acquaint me with his method of working, he asked me to play a role in a new audio play he'd written, *Die, Snow White! Die Damn You!* It was due to begin recording in a couple of weeks for Blackstone Audio Productions.

It was a very funny parody of the famous story. The leads were Sandra Oh (of *Killing Eve*) as Snow White and Kate Burton (star of many Broadway productions, daughter of Richard) as the evil duchess. He offered me a choice of roles, and I decided on the idiot duke who is rendered insensible by the sight of the disrobed duchess.

The recording studio on Hollywood Boulevard was state of the art. Six separate booths were established so that individual tracks could be made of all the voices. We spent an entire day recording just the voices. Everything else would be done post production—foley, sound effects, music score.

Recording was greatly enjoyable. I'd known Kate socially since New York, but it was a special pleasure to work opposite her.

The voices recorded, Yuri spent a week booking studios for foley and sound effects. I was to meet him at a foley studio in the Valley the following Sunday. I arrived early, armed with the production script, and met the sound tech and the walkers. At this tiny studio, major movies had recorded foley. We were fortunate to have two experienced foley walkers, two men who could find the necessary items on a wall crammed floor to ceiling with bric-a-brac to create the various sounds required.

Yuri was late which was not like him. After an hour of cooling our heels, Lorna called to say Yuri had been rushed to the hospital and wasn't expected to live.

There was little time even to register shock. Time was the producers' money and we'd spent an idle hour already.

The day was long, but I learnt much as I dispensed direction to walk on wood, tiles, dead leaves, what kind of shoes, tearing paper, cloth, opening creaking doors, shutting and bolting doors, the "twang" of a crossbow, fumbling with door keys of various sizes and so on.

Later I expressed sympathy to Lorna and offered whatever support I might give; she simply requested that I do a good job of the post production and make Yuri proud.

I spent two weeks poring over the hundreds of musical inserts. The production company had access to thousands. I marked my choices into the script, sometimes editing and adjusting them to fit the action with my own computer equipment. For instance, I wanted ominous, threatening music to underscore the act one finale where the duchess vows to kill Snow White. I found a parody of the *Jaws* shark music which was a perfect fit. Then I juggled the hundreds of sound effects Blackstone supplied and marked some for integration.

I flew to Ashland, Oregon where Blackstone's studios were based and spent a week putting the whole together.

My engineer was a great guy, Brian Barney who, as well as a total understanding of the banks of sound equipment, had a terrific sense of humor. We needed crowd voices—"walla", it's called in the US. We corralled a dozen of the sound technicians and secretaries into the studio and I coached them in cheers, boos, laughs and various comments. Then we set about assembling the jigsaw.

My aim was to produce a recording which sounded like a movie without the picture. It struck me as strange that all these multi cast recordings were monaural. I proposed to Brian that we pan for stereo in the final mix—characters with their matching foley footsteps would enter or exit left or right and conversations would be conducted across the breadth of the sound arena. This, I was told, was a first for such audio recordings. Later it was adopted across the industry as essential.

The CD was released to great reviews and this encouraged Blackstone

Audio to engage me to adapt and direct a series of Shakespeare's plays for audio.

Ashland is the home of the annual Oregon Shakespeare Festival, renowned throughout the nation. With three major theatres, and several smaller spaces, they attract top names and perform classic plays and musicals as well as inventive productions of Shakespeare.

I admit I'm a purist when it comes to Shakespeare. I generally find no joy in seeing *Julius Caesar* set in Nazi Germany, or *Taming of the Shew* set on a Coney Island pier. But given that Shakespeare's work is finite, at a venue devoted to his plays, over the years repetition must occur, so variations must be considered.

I adapted and directed three productions for Blackstone. In a little over a year, I did *Romeo*, *The Tempest* and *King Lear*. All were reviewed glowingly. Audiophile Magazine said of *Lear*: "Well-mixed transitions, percussive music, and intense and convincing sword and battle sounds add layers to the production, making it more film-like than stage-like...A solid interpretation of a time-honored classic."

The film-like sound was my aim and it became the new standard for multi-cast audio productions. Hitherto, they'd been little more than actors reading lines into a single microphone.

~

As one thing leads to another, the greatly prestigious LA TheatreWorks company called asking if I'd adapt and direct for them.

LA TheatreWorks is a unique institution. It harks back to the glory days of live radio productions like the Lux Radio Theatre, for which actors read to microphones on a stage, and to a live audience while the play is broadcast.

LA TheatreWorks operates from a large theatre on the UCLA campus with six microphones ranged across the wide stage, foley being performed on the fly in the orchestra pit, and music and effects are played by an engineer at the rear of the auditorium.

Each play is given for five performances, always to packed houses, then working from notes made by the director at each performance, edited to reflect the best takes, assembled, then broadcast internationally and committed to CD.

My first for them was *Cyrano de Bergerac* and my star was Hamish Linklater, a splendid actor movie goers might recognize as Australian Jacki Weaver's son in Woody Allen's *Magic in the Moonlight.*

Starting with the English translation by Anthony Burgess, I scripted in much the same way I had for the Blackstone audio productions—music, effects, foley all stated as well as fades in and out which, due to the live nature of the audio, had to be performed physically by the actors.

I eliminated many of the rhyming couplets of the Burgess text in favor of a more accessible play, and rewrote the balcony scenes for more comedy than in the original.

One of the actors was Morgan Richardson, Kate Burton's son. Kate came to a performance and said to Morgan after, "I never knew the balcony scenes were so funny."

Morgan replied, "There's a great deal of Creyton in there."

~

Now that I was allowed to act, LA TheatreWorks cast me as the benevolent uncle in *Daniel Deronda.* Then they brought the entire cast of the Off Broadway success, *Tribes*, from New York, but lost the leading man to a theatre commitment; I played the lead opposite Mare Winningham.

The next adaptation I directed for them was Shakespeare's *As You Like It.* As well as a perfect cast, I had the legendary Stacy Keach as Jaques.

We first read the entire cast, with foley and sound tech present at my house in the Hills, then after a week's rehearsal, settled into the UCLA theatre for the run which played Thursday, Friday, Saturday matinee and evening, and Sunday matinee.

The actor playing both dukes, the good and the bad, was a star of *Buffy The Vampire Slayer*, James Masters. There were no understudies, obviously for such a short, high profile run, but this somehow slipped the *Buffy* actor's mind. Masters came to me, untroubled on Thursday night after the performance and said, without apology, that he was shooting a scene for a movie on Saturday afternoon and would be unable to do the matinee.

Panic.

Unwilling to cancel a packed house, the producer's eyes turned to me. I performed both dukes at the matinee, overjoyed to be playing many scenes with the great Stacy Keach. After the performance, the producer suggested she'd like to use my recording as the final to be broadcast and cut to CD. But Masters' agent insisted otherwise. When the cavalier Masters reappeared for Saturday night's performance, he offered no apology to anyone in the cast, not to me, nor to the producers. He was never engaged by the company again.

~

Meanwhile, I worked on the Zorro script. I met Val Kilmer at a one-man play he did about Mark Twain and I thought him extremely good. He was also known to be extremely unreliable, as we found out.

I read Yuri's script for the first play, then several of the original Johnston McCully novels from the early 20th century. I noted the use of language in those, and did my homework about the Californian politics of the early 19th century, the period in which the novels are set. I constructed a script which I called *The Vengeance of Zorro*. It met with Blackstone's approval, the McCulley estate's approval and most importantly, with Lorna's approval and her assurance that I'd written a worthy sequel to Yuri's script.

Now came the hard part—trying to pin Mr. Kilmer down to recording dates. He dicked us around for six months during which recording dates were set, and canceled, actors set and then unavailable due to film or TV offers.

Tina Bursill was in town staying at our house when I had an invitation to another performance of Kilmer's *Mark Twain* at the Kirk Douglas theatre in Culver City. Tina came with me and we were met by Kilmer's assistant who said Kilmer would meet us backstage after the performance. We dutifully traveled backstage only to be told that Mr. Kilmer had just remembered he had a film shoot first thing in the morning and had left the theatre.

So it went, until we finally nailed him down to dates. Actors were booked, the studio reserved—and a few days before we were due to begin, the assistant called to cancel, citing Kilmer's ill health.

Blackstone gave up.

Much later, my script reached Bold Venture Press, who publish all the Zorro novels. They loved the script and sent me a contract to write a novel based on it. The novel was published on my birthday in December 2023.

FIFTY-ONE

A FEW YEARS AGO, my friend the splendid Stages podcast presenter, Peter Eyers interviewed me for two solid hours about my life and work. When we reached the year I decided to move to New York he asked the pointed question, "Why?" My mind had been on a one-way street about work and that's the reason I gave. Later, I realized his intention was for me to talk about Vaughan and how we met.

I called Peter and offered to record an insert about our meeting and relationship, but the quality differed and the insert was unusable.

When I broke the news to Vaughan, he paced the house wailing, "I'm an afterthought! My life is on the cutting room floor!" When I'd done laughing, I realized what a significant omission this was, and determined to rectify it in this tome.

Vaughan and I have been together for thirty-six years. When asked how we did it, I usually answer, "Either extraordinary devotion, or a lack of imagination." But gags aside, it's the former. In three decades, the conversation has never ceased; we still have much to talk about, and much to laugh about, all on a daily basis. Moreover he can make me laugh at myself which is a great asset where ego is involved.

Was it luck we happened to be in the same place at the same time thirty-six years ago? My respect for Freud would tell me otherwise. Freud said there are no accidents, so in his view, that rules out luck. Coincidence? When we began to examine each other's life and events, we discovered that on several occasions I was sitting in a London theatre watching the very play that Vaughan was working backstage. For some shows, we had been in the audience on the very same night. We found we had friends and acquaintances in common none of whom ever bothered to introduce us.

Had we met in any earlier year than 1988, we might have said a polite "How do you do?" and gone our separate ways. But on that particular night, in that year, we carried no emotional baggage; we were expecting nothing more than pleasant conversation, so were open to the extra something that seemed to occur to us simultaneously.

Freud aside, whatever led to it, this partnership has provided me with the thirty-five happiest years of my life.

When it became legal in the US, we were married, and that was prompted less by extraordinary devotion, than by the benefits of joint taxes. The ceremony was conducted by a celebrant in the living room of our house in the Hollywood Hills.

The guests numbered about thirty. Present were Vaughan's brother and sister-in-law and several of their sons and their wives, my old friends Jeanie Drynan and her husband Antony Bowman, Jimmy Darren (of all those *Gidget* movies from the 50s) and his wife Evy, and several other close friends including British director Waris Hussein, and our oldest friends in LA, Steve and Rhonda Halbert—Steve, a movie sound engineer, Rhonda Aldrich an actress.

Our silver wedding rings were a gift from George Chakiris who, apart from being the recipient of an Oscar for *West Side Story*, makes silver jewelry. Besides being a legendary movie star, he happens to be one of the nicest people on earth.

While Vaughan and I were perfectly aware of the practical reasons for the nuptials and were unemotional about the ceremony, not so our guests. Steve sniffled throughout while his wife passed him tissues; our chum Bryony Foster's sobs were audible. Vaughan's brother Chris made a moving speech in which he referred to me as family, and Jeanie Drynan made an emotional speech magnanimously on behalf of Australia.

My speech went something like this:

"I'd like to extol the virtues of this person to whom I am now legally joined. He is the soul of equanimity, his spirit is one of generosity and goodwill, the milk of human kindness flows through his every vein. … And he's lucky I came along to knock some of that out of him."

Gags aside, he is indeed composed of all those extraordinary qualities. I remember long ago when a friend asked Noeline, "Did Barry actually leave Australia for this person?"

Noel replied, "Hell, I'd leave Australia for Vaughan."

~

We moved house. We were sad to leave the rambling house in the Hills, but its upkeep was becoming the province of millionaires. In the eighteen years we'd lived there, it had more than tripled in value. It sold at first viewing, and to a millionaire, who offered us more than the asking price to secure it.

The search for another house took us into the San Fernando Valley. Three months, dozens of houses and an exhausted estate agent later, we found the one we wanted. It had formerly belonged to one of the anchors on TV's *Entertainment Tonight*, and overall, was larger than the house we left—and had the bonus of a 40 foot long pool.

Just as we settled on the house, I had a call from Simon Burke. A Lifetime Achievement Award was in the planning for Noeline, and I was asked to be the surprise guest.

I had only four days to spare before signing the deal for the new house and organizing the move, but I certainly wanted to be part of the tribute.

FIFTY-TWO

IN SYDNEY, I was stashed away from public view in Simon's attractive house until the event, which was starry indeed. The ploy for my appearance was cunning: Towards the end of the evening, Chloe Dallimore announced that I had sent a video greeting from Los Angeles. They began to play one I had actually done a few years earlier for Jacki Weaver, minus the sound. Chloe apologized for the technical problem and asked if there was anyone in the house who could repair it. I walked onto the stage proclaiming, "I can fix that."

Noeline was so surprised, she thought at first someone had been hired to impersonate me. I spoke of our meeting, our long friendship and the unrivalled pleasure I had in our working relationship for so many years, adding, of course, that no one deserved an award of this kind more than Noel.

The following day, there was a small cocktail party at Simon's to catch up with old friends and the morning after that, I was on a flight back to LA. Vaughan met me at the airport and we drove directly to the lawyer's office to sign the hundreds of documents for the house.

~

There followed a month or so of renovation, but on the whole the house was intact and welcoming. The open plan led from the lobby, through an area with a fireplace which we designated the library, on to a spacious dining area and down a few steps into the living room. Beyond this was a terrace and the pool. Again we had four bedrooms two of which we kept as such, the third became a den, and the fourth, the gym. We built a staircase to the attic which was vast, covering half the square footage of the house below. This became the office with two desks, shelves of reference books, a lounge area with TV and sound system, and a smaller separate area where Vaughan set up a drafting table.

No sooner had we settled, than the plague descended. And Covid scared the crap out of all of us.

Most of our friends went into hiding, reachable only by phone. Some instigated Zoom conversations, others became paranoid to the degree that they never left the house, not even for a stroll in the garden.

Lockdown provided a couple of benefits—the freeways were deserted, and the LA air was clear of smog. The downside was that theatre, movie and audio production were halted. Many businesses closed never to open again.

Rather than sit it out twiddling the thumbs I use for the space bar, I put the keyboard to good use and wrote a novel. Aside from the *Dogs* books, I'd written only one other, a parody of the Hollywood noir genre called, *Murder is Fatal*. It was reviewed very favorably and sold well.

This one alleviated the boredom of being housebound. It was a serious novel. No comedy this time, but a fairly tragic story which followed the lives of two boyhood friends over three decades. *The View From Olympus Mons* was published by NineStar Press late in 2022 to overwhelmingly positive reviews, healthy worldwide sales, and a nomination for the Annual Goodreads Award. Of all the praise heaped on it in editorial and the often lyrical reader reviews, my favorite compliment came from eighteen year old reader, Nora in Canada who said, simply, "Holy shit! This was good!"

My second novel for NineStar, *Phoenix*, was released in May, 2023 to universal critical praise. The marketing blurb made it sound a little like a Joan Crawford movie of the '40s, but I dare to boast it's of superior stuff:

"A suspenseful jigsaw of lies, deception and murder, in which two damaged people find that rising from the ashes comes with a cost."

The year 2024 temporarily obliged me to shelve a couple of novels in favour of a lucrative contract with Ray Of Light Motion Pictures to write a screenplay about the life of William Haines. Based on the biography by William J. Mann, *Wisecracker* tells the story of Haines' extraordinary life leading to his becoming the number one male box office movie star in the United States.

He was unashamedly gay in a time when no leading male movie star could survive scrutiny. The famously quoted line at his departure from MGM in 1932 was prompted by studio head, Louis B. Mayer who demanded, "Give up your boyfriend, or lose your contract with MGM."

Haines replied, "I'll give up my boyfriend when you give up Mrs Mayer."

He walked away from international stardom to pursue a career as one of the most celebrated interior designers in the world, and hence, a mega-millionaire. When Haines died in 1973, his partner of forty-seven years found life was too unbearable without him, and committed suicide.

Of course, no such tangled drama could play out in the movie business today. Everyone knows there are no gay actors in Hollywood.

FIFTY-THREE

A WORD ABOUT WOKE.

Woke (adj.): A social attitude which promotes the fear of offending those who are actually offended by everything.

While there are the many valid reasons of equality, protection of identity and ideals to be considered, extreme distortions are gaining ground. I remember the days when, if the theme of a novel seemed interesting, you read it hoping to be surprised by the twists and turns of the story. Not so these days. Dire warnings are given before you turn the first page.

I quote some of the trigger warnings deemed necessary by NineStar Press for my latest book *Phoenix*:

Racist and homophobic slurs
Fat shaming and misogynist language
Depiction of graphic violence in a murder scene

Plotting to commit violence
Use of guns
Depiction of arson.
Death of a prominent character
Gay bashing

So much for the element of surprise.

As for sex… I've always maintained that Americans don't like to talk about it, but love doing it; the British love talking about it, but don't like doing it.

Now the British are cautioned from even *thinking* about it. In the London tube, a sign is prominent in every car:

STARING

Intrusive staring of a sexual nature is harassment.

I was tempted to call emergency.

EMERGENCY:	911. What is your emergency?
ME:	Someone is staring at me.
EMERGENCY:	Hard?
ME:	No, just staring.

Then there's diversity. I'm all for it if it doesn't render a play or movie unfathomable.

Was the day when a play was cast based on talent. Now, casting comes with the obligation to include every race, color, and sexual variety, often regardless of talent. Producers have become conditioned to believe that by working this way, they offend no one, when often they're offending the primary essential of theatre, the audience.

One of the first lessons I was ever taught regarding theatre, is: Never confuse your audience—they're the guys who pay you. Well known plays of a perennial nature such as Shakespeare's can be cast across the widest possible spectrum of diversity and not suffer; lesser known plays can be destroyed by it.

And that brings us to pronouns.

We were in London in March, 2022, a respectable theatre advertised a revival of Sondheim's seldom produced *Anyone Can Whistle*. This was one of the few failures of the Sondheim oeuvre. Wow, we thought, at last, an opportunity to see this worthy, if flawed piece.

The first indication that we were in trouble was the program. Everyone from cast through production team to stage hands were listed as: "he him his", "she her hers", "they them theirs."

In a wild effort to be diverse, the opening chorus was performed by actors of not only every color, but every shape and variation of gender. In defense of my criticism, I add that not one of them could sing, and choreography seemed to be left to individual choice.

The leading man entered. This I knew because I'd read the script. But for the life of me, I had no idea for the entire first act if the actor was male or female.

We left at intermission, as did every one we know, though some had the good sense to leave after the first number.

The director, I noted, was listed as a "they". We concluded they were the three worst directors in London.

We left with the sentiments of famed novelist and playwright James Kirkwood in mind. After seeing a bad production, he said:

"Don't even walk past the theatre in case you faint and they carry you inside."

FIFTY-FOUR

I SELDOM THINK OF age, if at all. My aim was always to get as old as possible as slowly as possible. But Ronnie Frazer's words come to mind fairly often these days: "He won't know anybody."

This sentiment was hammered home recently when the producers of *This is Your Life* contacted my brother Trevor with a view to doing my life. They spoke at some length, and as is the rule, he was sworn to secrecy. A couple of weeks later, they called to let him know they'd cancelled their plans. They explained that apart from Noeline Brown, there was no one left alive who could pop up as the surprise guest.

Upon hearing the news, I spent a half hour convulsed with laughter. When I sobered, I thought, *Ronnie Frazer was right!*

~

In spite of advancing years, neither Vaughan nor I have slowed down. Vaughan is currently designing *CSI Vegas* for CBS TV, while I have two new novels and the Haines screenplay in the works.

> Are there any stones I've left unturned in this checkered life?
> Emotionally, I doubt it!
> Professionally? Few.
> Any regrets: Two.
> I never played the Sydney Opera House.
> And I was never asked to do a centerfold for Playgirl.

But seriously folks, at the earliest hint of youthful ambition, I wanted to explore the entire field covered by the broad label "Entertainment"—to be a Jack-of-all-trades, and perhaps, to master a few. So far, I've enjoyed success on three continents as actor, playwright, composer, director and novelist and screenwriter . Not bad, I guess, for a skinny, self-educated kid from the poorer suburbs of Brisbane.

Meanwhile, booze has not passed my lips for about twenty years, and my diet is exemplary. I work out in my fully equipped home gym daily—I don't want to wake one morning and find my tits round my ankles.

I continue to write—but only if the theme is commercially viable and, as is my writing habit, I always pen the "Happily ever after" before I write the "Once upon a time."

While the "Ever After" seems finite at this age, "Happily" is how I end this saga.

~

Most memoirists tend to leave their story with wise advice gleaned from traveling the cobbled path of Life. I resist giving advice to anyone unless my arm is twisted, and certainly not about life. It's an individual's prerogative to screw up his own existence without any help from me.

But recently, I was asked to fill a very serious questionnaire from the Antaeus Theatre's artistic director regarding the reasons I love theatre so much. If any wisdom can be gleaned from my sixty-seven years' association with theatre, I quote my responses here:

1. I LOVE THEATRE BECAUSE........
When it's good, it's nice to be in the audience; when it's bad, it's nice to be in the audience.

2. THE MOST EXCITING THING ABOUT PERFORMING IS........
Knowing there's a practical cake in act two.

3. THEATRE IS MAGIC BECAUSE........
The panto dame is not what she seems.

4. A GREAT ACTOR IS ONE WHO.......
...can prevent a large group of people from coughing.

5. THE POWER OF THEATRE IS........
An agent who has Mafia connections.

6. MY NUMBER ONE ACTING TIP IS........
If not playing the king, wear comfortable shoes.

7. ADVICE TO A YOUNG ACTOR...
Always take your wallet on stage with you.

~

On a recent checkup at my eye doc's, I was obliged to update a questionnaire for my insurance. Considering they already had all the relevant info on file, I replied thus:

AGE: N/A
PREFERRED PRONOUNS: NO
SEX: YES

Certainly, there are a few indications of the advancing years, but due to all that exercise which Gordon Chater thought might kill me, and the regimen of "kelp" he so disparaged, I'm in better shape than many who are thirty years younger than I.

You'll be hearing from me.

AFTERWORD

I LEAVE YOU WITH an irrelevant anecdote which may prompt a smile.

Political animal that I am, I was devastated, as were the majority of sane Americans, when Donald J. Trump became president of the United States in 2016. Thanks to the distorted gerrymander in this country, he lost the popular vote by millions, but won the presidency according to the rules. And there began the reign of terror which has never been relieved, even with his absence from the White House. The lies, the corruption, the fraud go on, and while he's being held legally accountable at last, it's not before he divided the country so decisively, that the rift between left and right will not be healed in my lifetime.

The popular historian Will Durant said, "No great civilization is conquered from without until it has destroyed itself from within."

Somehow Trump's fan base and the majority of the republican party overlook his misdemeanors and felonies—the extra-marital affairs, his political bribes, fueling an insurrection, stealing classified documents—and one incident in particular that would have extinguished the chances of any other legitimate presidential candidate: the infamous *Access Hollywood* tape where he bragged he could grab women by their genitals and get away with it.

During Trump's occupation of the White House, I was at a specialist in Beverly Hills to delve into my sinuses. The offices were posh and the waiting room was a beautifully furnished haven for meditation on one's nasal passages.

As I entered, an overweight woman of at least sixty was standing over two elderly patients who huddled together in abject terror as the woman berated them with much finger-wagging, loudly lauding Trump.

"He's the greatest president this country ever had! Idiots like you need to wake up! Watch Fox News! They tell you the truth! The rest are all liars!"

The woman's weed of a husband tried to get her to quieten down. She told him, "Shut up!" and went on. "Trump is the only man who can save this country from the bleeding hearts who want to rob you! People like you should realize Trump is your saviour!"

When she drew breath, I piped up. "I take it you voted for Mr. Trump."

"You bet your life I did!"

"And you accept his every edict as a rule of law?"

"Of course!"

"In that case," I asked politely, "may I grab you by the pussy?"

In the stunned silence that followed, I went to the reception desk where the receptionist was stuffing tissues into her mouth to stifle the giggles. "I'll wait outside until someone gets the hook to that woman."

As this goes to publicaton, Donald J. Trump has been elected president once again and is proceeding to grab the United States by the pussy.

ACKNOWLEDGEMENTS

I acknowledge two people of the many who have contributed information, knowledge, learning, love and wit to my life...

With warmth and immeasurable affection for Noeline Brown who suffered my psychotic bid for perfectionism through every production we shared, and who, in return, gave me as much and more.

And Vaughan Edwards, who deserves a medal for being part of this LIFE for the past 37 years.

www.ingramcontent.com/pod-product-compliance
Lightning Source LLC
LaVergne TN
LVHW050926080826
845145LV00001B/230

* 9 7 8 1 7 6 3 6 9 0 9 0 5 *